Culture and Mass Schooling

Education is central to politics, economic growth, and human well-being. Yet large gaps in levels of education persist across groups, often for generations. Why? This book argues that culture – specifically, community norms about schooling – plays a central role in explaining the persistence of educational inequality across groups. Melina R. Platas uses the case of the Muslim–Christian education gap in Africa, where Muslims have on average three fewer years of education than Christians, to examine the origins and persistence of educational inequality. She documents the colonial origins of this gap and develops a cultural theory of its persistence, focusing on the case studies of Malawi, Nigeria, and Uganda. Platas uses census and survey data from over 30 African countries, archival documents, interviews, focus groups, and coordination games to explore this ubiquitous yet underappreciated gap in educational attainment, and to measure divergent schooling norms across religious communities in Africa today.

Melina R. Platas is Associate Professor in the Division of Social Science at New York University Abu Dhabi. Her research explores the social and political determinants of human development, with a focus on sub-Saharan Africa. She holds a BA in Human Biology and a PhD in political science from Stanford University.

CAMBRIDGE STUDIES IN THE COMPARATIVE POLITICS
OF EDUCATION

Culture and Mass Schooling: The Colonial Roots of Educational Inequality in Africa

Editor

Terry M. Moe, Stanford University

Education and its reform are matters of great political salience throughout the world. Yet as Gift and Wibbels observed, "It is hard to identify a community of political scientists who are dedicated to the comparative study of education." This series is an effort to change that. The goal is to encourage a vigorous line of scholarship that focuses squarely on the politics of education across nations, advances theoretical thinking, includes a broad swath of educational terrain – from elementary and secondary education to vocational education to higher education – and explores the impacts of education on key aspects of society. The series welcomes books of very different types. Some may be grounded in sophisticated quantitative analysis, but qualitative work is welcome as well, as are big-think extended essays that develop agenda-setting ideas. Work is encouraged that takes on big, important, inherently messy topics, however difficult they may be to study. Work is also encouraged that shows how the politics of education is shaped by power, special interests, parties, bureaucracies, and other fundamentals of the political system. And finally, this series is not just about the developed nations, but encourages new work on developing nations and the special challenges that education faces in those contexts.

Books in the series

Mobilizing Teachers: Education Politics and the New Labor Movement in Latin America
Christopher Chambers-Ju

A Liberal Education: The Social and Political Impact of the Modern University
Brendan Apfeld, Emanuel Coman, John Gerring, and Stephen Jessee

Education for All? Literature, Culture and Education Development in Britain and Denmark
Cathie Jo Martin

Making Bureaucracy Work: Norms, Education and Public Service Delivery in Rural India
Akshay Mangla

The Politics of Comprehensive School Reforms: Cleavages and Coalitions
Katharina Sass

A Loud but Noisy Signal? Public Opinion and Education Reform in Western Europe
Marius R. Busemeyer, Julian L. Garritzmann and Erik Neimanns

The Comparative Politics of Education: Teachers Unions and Education Systems around the World
Edited by Terry M. Moe and Susanne Wiborg

Culture and Mass Schooling

The Colonial Roots of Educational Inequality in Africa

MELINA R. PLATAS
New York University Abu Dhabi

CAMBRIDGE UNIVERSITY PRESS

Shaftesbury Road, Cambridge CB2 8EA, United Kingdom

One Liberty Plaza, 20th Floor, New York, NY 10006, USA

477 Williamstown Road, Port Melbourne, VIC 3207, Australia

314–321, 3rd Floor, Plot 3, Splendor Forum, Jasola District Centre, New Delhi – 110025, India

103 Penang Road, #05–06/07, Visioncrest Commercial, Singapore 238467

Cambridge University Press is part of Cambridge University Press & Assessment, a department of the University of Cambridge.

We share the University's mission to contribute to society through the pursuit of education, learning and research at the highest international levels of excellence.

www.cambridge.org
Information on this title: www.cambridge.org/9781009640350

DOI: 10.1017/9781009640398

© Melina R. Platas 2026

This publication is in copyright. Subject to statutory exception and to the provisions of relevant collective licensing agreements, no reproduction of any part may take place without the written permission of Cambridge University Press & Assessment.

When citing this work, please include a reference to the DOI 10.1017/9781009640398

First published 2026

Cover image: Photograph by missionary Dr. A. T. Schofield, probably 1930s. The image was intended to illustrate a school cookbook developed by Mrs. Schofield. Courtesy Myfanwy Frost-Jones & History in Progress Uganda.

A catalogue record for this publication is available from the British Library

A Cataloging-in-Publication data record for this book is available from the Library of Congress

ISBN 978-1-009-64035-0 Hardback
ISBN 978-1-009-64036-7 Paperback

Cambridge University Press & Assessment has no responsibility for the persistence or accuracy of URLs for external or third-party internet websites referred to in this publication and does not guarantee that any content on such websites is, or will remain, accurate or appropriate.

For EU product safety concerns, contact us at Calle de José Abascal, 56, 1°, 28003 Madrid, Spain, or email eugpsr@cambridge.org.

For my parents.

Pride, they say, always has a fall; I hope it mayn't be so, but I cannot help a strong feeling of pride in seeing the influence I have attained over these people, so that in the face of these damaging reports they laughed at them, and trusted me, though the reports were in exact accordance with their own repeated suspicions.
Frederick Lugard's diary, January 26, 1891. Buganda.

Contents

List of Figures		*page* ix
List of Tables		xiii
Preface		xv
Acknowledgments		xxi
1	The Puzzle of Persistent Inequality	1
2	Schooling as a Norm	30
3	The Colonial Origins of Inequality	57
4	The Limits of Existing Explanations for Persistence	81
5	Education as Seen from the Ground	105
6	Empirical Evidence of Schooling Norms in Malawi	129
7	Generalizing the Argument	164
8	Matters of Culture	185
Appendix		203
	A.1 Religious Affiliation and Schooling Outcomes	203
	A.2 Muslim Majority Status and Educational Attainment	205
	A.3 Bivariate Relationships between Democracy, Income per Capita, and the Country-Level Muslim–Christian Gap	207
	A.4 Educational Attainment in Colonial Buganda	208
	A.5 Religious Demographics and Wealth	209
	A.6 Historic Islamic Rule	211
	A.7 Malawi Surveys and Coordination Games	213
	A.8 Colonial Administrators in Uganda and Northern Nigeria	227
References		229
Index		245

Figures

1.1	Years of schooling (age 25+) by religion and cohort. *Source*: DHS, various years.	*page* 3
1.2	Average years of schooling by religion and country. *Source*: Pew Research Center (2016).	3
1.3	Muslim–Christian schooling gap by country, three models. *Source*: DHS, various years.	16
1.4	Muslim–Christian gap in years of schooling within ethnic groups. *Source*: DHS, various years.	18
1.5	Likelihood of school attendance by religion, as the percentage of Muslims in administrative units increases. *Source*: IPUMS.	20
1.6	Percentage of cohort with any schooling in Nigeria, Malawi, and Uganda by religion. *Source*: DHS, various years.	26
3.1	Literacy by religion in (a) the Nigerian Emirates and (b) Buganda. *Source*: DHS and Uganda 2001 Census.	59
3.2	Islamic states 1000–1900 AD. *Source*: Sluglett and Currie (2015).	60
3.3	Native Administration and population in Nigeria in the mid colonial period. (a) Nigerian population, 1952 Census. Modifies from an original map by A. T. Grove with permission from his estate. (b) Native Administration, 1946–1947. *Source*: Buchanan and Pugh (1955).	67
4.1	Distribution of Muslim population in Malawi, by administrative area. *Source*: Malawi 2008 Census.	84

4.2	Cumulative number of primary schools, by proprietor, Malawi. *Source*: Malawi Education Management Information System.	90
4.3	Occupation by religion and gender in Malawi and 28 African countries. *Source*: DHS.	95
4.4	Mean expected income across levels of schooling, by religion and village type. *Source*: Malawi 2018 Survey.	97
4.5	Availability of school infrastructure by subnational religious demographics. (a) Subnational regions across 32 African countries. (b) Enumeration areas within Malawi. *Source*: Afrobarometer Round 6, World Religions Database Malawi National Statistics Office.	98
4.6	Informal schooling by administrative area percent Muslim. *Source*: Afrobarometer Rounds 2–6, census samples from IPUMS International.	100
6.1	Sampled enumeration areas. *Source*: Malawi 2008 Census.	134
6.2	Distribution of responses to the question, "Who is more likely to complete primary school?" by religion and village type. *Source*: Malawi 2018 Survey.	138
6.3	Level of schooling considered appropriate among ingroup, by religion and village type. *Source*: Malawi 2018 Survey.	141
6.4	Gap in expected years of schooling between Christians and Muslims. *Source*: Malawi 2018 Survey.	142
6.5	Timeline tool.	143
6.6	Expected level of schooling, normative beliefs. *Source*: Malawi 2018 Survey.	144
6.7	Social appropriateness response sheet.	145
6.8	Percentage of Muslim respondents who believe other Muslims think it is appropriate to leave school, by area type. *Source*: Malawi 2018 Survey.	146
6.9	Sampled districts, Traditional Authority Survey.	148
6.10	Traditional Authority (TA) empirical expectations about completion of primary school, by child's religion. *Source*: Malawi 2019 TA Survey.	151
6.11	Percentage of Muslims by State in Nigeria. *Source*: Nigeria 1952 Census.	155
6.12	Predicted probability of agreeing that schooling is more important for boys than girls. *Source*: Nigeria EdData II, 2004.	157

List of Figures

6.13 Predicted probability of engaging with children's school and teachers. *Source*: Nigeria EdData II, 2004. ... 159

6.14 Reasons why it is important to send children to school. *Source*: Uganda Household Survey, 2013. ... 162

7.1 School attendance rates in (a) Nigeria, (b) Malawi, and (c) Uganda by religion. *Source*: DHS, various years. ... 165

7.2 Average years of schooling by cohort and religion, British and French cases. *Source*: IPUMS census data. ... 171

7.3 Schooling rates by religion and gender in Senegal: (a) any school, age 13+; (b) years of school, age 25+. *Source*: IPUMS census samples. ... 174

7.4 Schooling rates by religion and gender in Rwanda: (a) any school, age 13+; (b) years of school, age 25+. *Source*: IPUMS census samples. ... 178

7.5 Mean schooling rate by exposure to Islamic states and religious affiliation. *Source*: DHS and Sluglett and Currie (2015). ... 182

7.6 Predicted years of education by province-level religious demographics. *Source*: DHS, World Religions Database, Sluglett and Currie (2015). ... 183

8.1 Voter turnout by religion and highest level of education completed. *Source*: Afrobarometer Round 7. ... 193

8.2 Differences in political participation between Christians and Muslims. *Source*: Afrobarometer Round 7. ... 194

A.1 Literacy rate (age 14+) by religion and cohort. *Source*: DHS, various years. ... 203

A.2 Gap in school attendance for Muslims compared to Christians, ages 6–12. *Source*: DHS. ... 205

A.3 Bivariate relationship between regime type and the Muslim–Christian education gap. *Source:* DHS and Polity IV project. ... 207

A.4 Bivariate relationship between logged GDP per capita in 1990 and the Muslim–Christian education gap. *Source:* DHS and World Bank DataBank. ... 208

A.5 Missionary schools by county in the Uganda Protectorate, 1915–1928. *Source*: Uganda Protectorate Blue Books 1915–1928. ... 209

A.6 Household wealth quintile and region percent Muslim. *Source*: DHS. ... 210

A.7	Predicted margins for educational attainment by exposure to Islamic trade routes and religious affiliation. *Source:* DHS and Sluglett and Currie (2015).	211
A.8	Predicted margins for educational attainment by exposure to Islamic influence and religious affiliation. *Source:* DHS and Sluglett and Currie (2015).	212
A.9	The Muslim–Christian schooling gap by enumeration area in Malawi. *Source*: Malawi 2008 Census.	213
A.10	Images shown in discrimination experiment. (a) Treatment A: no religious cue. (b) Treatment B: religious cue.	220
A.11	Mean expected income across levels of schooling, by religion and Christian and Muslim majority areas. *Source:* Malawi 2014 Survey.	221
A.12	Percentage of respondents who believe others think it is appropriate to leave school (Muslim majority villages), by religion. *Source:* Malawi 2018 Survey.	226

Tables

6.1	Summary statistics of respondents' children.	*page* 135
7.1	Religious and educational demographics by country in sub-Saharan Africa.	168
A.1	Religious affiliation and schooling outcomes.	204
A.2	Educational attainment and Muslim majority status, by country.	206
A.3	Missionary schools by county and Muslim educational attainment.	210
A.4	Balance across cluster-level covariates by exposure to Islam.	212
A.5	Interviews in Malawi.	213
A.6	Mfano education committee members.	217
A.7	Ethnic and religious cultural explanations.	222
A.8	Summary statistics of villages.	224
A.9	Summary statistics of Traditional Authorities.	225
A.10	Characteristics of Traditional Authorities by project type.	226
A.11	Predictors of Traditional Authority education project proposals.	227
A.12	Colonial administrators in Uganda and Northern Nigeria.	228

Preface

One day in a year I'd rather not disclose I sat at a wooden desk in Kyambogo, a leafy Kampala suburb, staring at household survey data on my laptop. I was casting about for a dissertation topic, ideally on health and politics, which was my initial interest and how I had found myself doing a PhD in political science in the first place. But in poking through the survey data, I stumbled across something I found both surprising and puzzling: a pervasive gap in educational attainment between Muslims and Christians in Africa. Across African countries, Muslims have on average about three fewer years of education than Christians, and while educational attainment has risen for everyone over time, this gap has persisted, mostly unchanged, from the colonial period to the present. Piecing together the puzzle of both the origins and persistence of this gap would come to dominate, dare I say it, a decade of my academic career, culminating in this book.

For a long time I have wanted the space to elaborate on the journey that began at that desk and has resulted in the pages that follow. Earlier versions of the manuscript weaved more of the intellectual and research journey throughout the text, but more experienced hands suggested prioritizing clarity of argument and evidence rather than documenting the way there. They were right, but I still think there is value in conveying how crooked the path has been. At times I doubted there was even a path at all.

Uganda was an accidental entry point for me, and has remained the source of many of the insights I have since gleaned, including on the relationship between religion and mass schooling that I examine here. A stint as a youthful-if-not-so-useful intern at an HIV/AIDS clinic served as the inflection point that rerouted me toward political science instead of public health and also centered my attention (permanently I suspect) on this piece of land straddling the equator. The combination of seeing first-hand the contrast between the well- (and donor-) funded HIV clinic and the dilapidated government health facilities, and a still rebel-ridden north of the country described at the time as the "biggest forgotten, neglected humanitarian emergency in the world,"[1] made me realize that public health is every bit as much about politics and governance as it is about, say, the clinical aspects of medicine.

By the time I started a PhD in political science, the sorts of explanatory variables in the rather limited literature on health and politics were things like regime type and ethnic diversity. Neither of those captured what was at the heart of my vague intuition about the relationship between politics and health. So it was that I found myself at said desk, combing through survey data, squinting at distributions of outcomes like rates of immunization and delivering in a health facility, mostly in African countries where child and maternal mortality rates tend to be the highest. I had just finished running some cross-tabs on religious affiliation and health-seeking behavior after hearing an anecdote about Muslim women avoiding public health facilities due to privacy concerns. Although this story sounded plausible, empirically there was not much there that I could see in the data at hand. And while I can't now recall why, next I looked at the relationship between religious affiliation and educational attainment.

Here it became quickly and strikingly apparent that Muslims across nearly all the countries I looked at had lower levels of education than Christians, and substantially so – a gap of up to four or five years in some cases. The majority of Muslim adults in countries like Nigeria and Kenya had never been to school at all. Religious affiliation seemed to be a key predictor of educational attainment, and I had never heard anyone mention education gaps across religious groups in Africa, nor had I come across the topic in anything I had read in popular media or academic work. Ethnic favoritism, yes, but inequalities across religious groups? Not so much. The pattern was also surprising given my experience in Uganda up to that point, where at first glance there is no obvious difference in levels of education between Christians and Muslims, where families are often religiously mixed, and where you can and will be awakened by loudspeakers from both a mosque and a church that are within a stone's throw.

---

[1] Jan Egeland, United Nations Undersecretary-General for Humanitarian Affairs and Emergency Relief, 2004.

Looking back, I now realize I was conducting these initial analyses while sitting just a few hundred meters away from the former palace of a king who would come to play a central role in helping me make sense of how this gap emerged in the first place. One hundred and fifty years earlier, on the hill overlooking my flat, Kabaka Muteesa I had received (and sometimes detained) visitors to Buganda. It was under his rule that these multiple foreign religious influences began to take root. As I discuss at greater length in Chapter 3, it was an accident of history that the timing of the arrival of Islam in Buganda only slightly preceded colonial rule and the arrival of Christian missionaries, which for a time led to violent religious conflict, but ultimately produced high levels of education for both Christians and Muslims. Missionaries built hundreds of schools, creating new pathways to political power and generating new norms about school attendance. The competition induced Muslim communities to establish similar schools of their own.

In the upcoming chapters, I argue that Uganda is an important case for understanding how colonizers treated newly and only partially Islamized societies in Africa – it was one of the few countries where Muslims had, if anything, higher levels of education than Christians on average. But the features that made it unique, including having a sizable and prominent Muslim population that was nonetheless a minority almost everywhere, meant that it wasn't well suited for explaining a second part of the broader puzzle. This was that within countries, the gap tended to be largest where Muslims were a local majority.

To try to explain this pattern – which was central to understanding the overall puzzle of lower educational attainment among Muslims today – I ended up focusing on Malawi, where I had never set foot. In Malawi the Muslim population was distributed in such a way that I could study and compare minority and majority Muslim areas while holding constant ethnicity and geography. Motivated by elite interviews and existing literature on educational investments, I proceeded to conduct a survey with parents to test hypotheses about relative poverty, discrimination, and beliefs about returns to education. This approach made sense if one assumes, as I did, that education is a good that everyone wants more of if they can possibly get it – I wanted to find out what the barriers were. The survey was not a bad place to start, but I didn't find much support for any of these explanations.

At the point at which I finished the dissertation, I had done a decent job of documenting the unappreciated education gap, and I felt that I had a reasonable understanding of its origins. In broad strokes that I discuss at length in the chapters that follow, the gap is a colonial legacy, due in large part to the outsize role of Christian missionaries in introducing this new form of education, which also served as a means of conversion. But I still didn't have a clear or convincing answer to the question of why it had persisted in spite of many institutional and policy changes since independence, and in particular why it seemed to be largest in Muslim majority areas. The numerous dead ends I encountered while pursuing potential explanations in my dissertation work were frustrating, and I felt I was missing something.

I was fortunate to have more road and resources before me as an assistant professor. I used them to return to Malawi and start afresh. Having crossed off the answers I had come up with so far, I wanted to simply listen to the families whose lives and decisions I was trying to understand and set aside any preconceived explanations of my own or others. The conversations I had with parents and teachers, sitting on doorsteps, porches, and classroom chairs, sometimes going back several times over the next few years, changed the way I thought about the decision to go to school, and what education meant in a setting like rural Malawi. Here I found that, in a context where almost no one finished secondary school and opportunities in the formal sector were extremely limited, the puzzle was not so much why children dropped out of school but rather why they stayed at all.

Throughout these discussions I found that community-level norms played an important role in the daily decision of children and parents about whether the kids would go to school or not. Norms about school attendance in this context are in part a function of historical exposure to mass schooling and also what mass schooling had meant historically across religious communities.

Among Christians and in predominantly Christian communities, to stay in school as long as possible was simply expected, regardless of the economic returns, while among Muslim communities, these expectations were much weaker. I document these discussions in Chapter 5 and the results of my efforts to demonstrate and test more systematically the role of community-level norms in shaping schooling behavior in Chapter 6.

In parallel, a closer reading of the historical literature and colonial-era accounts changed the way I thought about what education had meant during the colonial period, and what it must have been like for communities that were bombarded with strangers who sought to convert them and reshape their societies, sometimes violently. As I endeavor to articulate throughout the book, it is a mistake to think of education – as I confess I did at the start of this project – as a universally desired, politically neutral public good. Education is almost never neutral, and certainly was not at the time of its introduction in colonial Africa. It was not conceived as a human right, and it was not intended to promote individual freedom. On the contrary, it was designed to support the colonial apparatus, and when provided by missionaries, which it usually was, to convert Africans to Christianity. For these reasons, this new form of education was not universally desired, and not infrequently avoided by those wishing to maintain their existing beliefs and practices. Much has changed in the intervening years, but even today there remains great contestation both across and within countries over what constitutes appropriate education, and not only in Africa. And religious communities in particular continue to differ markedly in preferences over educational content.

This insight, the existence of variation in preferences over not just the amount but also the nature of public goods, extends beyond education. Even healthcare and medicine – my first passion and to which I hope to return – are not universally desired in their contemporary (some would say "Western") form. This is made painfully, even deadly clear by growing skepticism around vaccines and other health innovations that for a time seemed self-evidently beneficial. The content of goods and services like education and health can be contested, and can certainly be politicized. Much of the work in the political science literature that concerns public goods provision implicitly assumes universal demand for these goods, so that explanations for their variation tend to focus on the distribution of supply. But the politics of public goods like health or education is not just a competition over who can get more, it is also a debate over what constitutes the good in the first place.

At multiple points along the journey I have questioned whether it did in fact make sense to pivot toward political science, given that my underlying interest has always been outcomes related to human development, such as health and education, rather than political processes or institutions per se. I have also been asked what makes this work political science. In my case I'm certain there was not a single "right" path, but the past few years have also underscored to me the importance of research that explores the social and political factors shaping behavior and producing such divergent outcomes in human well-being. I continue to believe that the social sciences – and I believe we benefit greatly by reading across and not only within them – have much to offer in helping us to understand and improve the world around us, which we need perhaps now more than ever.

This book covers a lot of ground, both geographically and temporally, and also crosses and applies insights from numerous disciplines. Even so, the end result is certainly not a definitive account of all that is to be said about the Muslim–Christian education gap, much less the persistence of inequality across groups. Parts of the book will undoubtedly remain unsatisfying to those with expertise in particular domains touched upon, or to those looking for a single tight and causally identified effect of an X on a Y. I opted to pull together many strands of evidence at multiple levels, in order to discover and share what I hope is a compelling account of the origins and persistence of this understudied educational inequality. Questions remain, of course, and some pieces of evidence are stronger than others. What I hope is that what I have been able to show in these pages – first, the religious and colonial roots of the modern education system in Africa generated initial inequalities in levels of schooling across religious groups, and second, that social influence and beliefs about schooling can perpetuate initial inequalities – will spur further interest and research on education, culture, and inequality in Africa and elsewhere.

Acknowledgments

I have had what is truly an embarrassment of riches when it comes to support along the journey of writing this book. Indeed, the question "How is the book going?" came to be one I dreaded because I always felt there was so much more that I could do, especially given all the helping hands. But I'll be glad to be able to – finally! – say that it is done, very much thanks to many of you. Any and all shortcomings that remain are certainly my own.

In graduate school I was lucky to have the best advisors anyone could ask for, and many faculty who were not on my committee provided feedback and support along the way. My committee, including Pascaline Dupas, Jim Fearon, David Laitin, and Jeremy Weinstein, each provided guidance, feedback, and support at every stage of the dissertation process, and were unfailingly generous with their time. I learned so much from each of them, not just about the research process, but also about the place of social science in understanding and, ideally, improving the world around us, as well as how to support and mentor others. Each of them is, without exaggeration, among the most accomplished and brilliant scholars of our time, while at the same time helping others up the ladder. I am so grateful to have the opportunity to learn from them. I am also grateful for the conversations and feedback I received from others at Stanford during my graduate studies and beyond, including David Abernethy, Stephen Krasner, Larry Diamond, Kate Casey, Lisa Blaydes, Jonathan Rodden, Vicky Fouka, Grant Miller, Anna Grzymala-Busse, and Sean Hanretta, as well as dear friends I made in graduate school, especially Mackenzie Israel-Trummel, Ken Opalo, and Lauren Prather. The Center for African Studies was second family during the dissertation years, and I am grateful to Laura Hubbard for building community and to Jess

Auerbach, Kathryn Takabvirwa, Mata Seck, Sarah Quesada, Vivian Lu, Vanessa Watters, Chad and Nancy McClymonds, George China, Landry Signé, and David Tswamuno for their support and laughter during that time.

The initial fieldwork for this project was supported through the O'Bie Shultz Research Travel Grant, the Center for African Studies, the Abbasi Program in Islamic Studies, the Stanford Institute for Innovation in Developing Economies, the Europe Center, the Graduate Public Service Fellowship, the Lieberman Fellowship, the Enhancing Diversity in Graduate Education Doctoral Fellowship Program, the Freeman Spogli Institute for International Studies, and from the generous support of Pascaline Dupas, Tino Cuéllar, Grant Miller, and Eran Bendavid. Later fieldwork was made possible through support at NYU Abu Dhabi, and a team of dedicated administrators, especially Diana Pangan and Emily Del Monte.

In Uganda, I am grateful for the time and support of many individuals who made this work possible and provided valuable feedback and research assistance. These include Waswa Balunywa and his family, Abdu Katuntu, Kirunda Kivejinja, Amama Mbabazi, Yusuf Serunkuma, Felix Warom, Dennis Kimera, Shaban Nkutu, Frederick Golooba-Mutebi, Isa Matovu and his colleagues at the Uganda Muslim Teachers' Association, the Uganda Muslim Education Association, the Uganda Muslim Supreme Council, Uganda Catholic Secretariat, staff at the national archives in Entebbe, and the Jinja, Iganga, and Arua local government staff. Habib Kagimu very kindly granted me access to his Rolodex that spanned across the continent, as well as provided valuable insights on the history of Islam in Uganda.

Earlier on in my dissertation I conducted fieldwork in Ghana that, while informative, did not make it into the manuscript. I want to thank Elias Kogo Dery, who helped me navigate Tamale and took me under his wing throughout my stay in northern Ghana. In Nigeria I am thankful to Olawale Maiyegun and Abdulrahman Balogun for introducing me to their networks and contacts in southwestern Nigeria, and to Ashley and Sam Immanuel who hosted and helped me navigate – and yes, enjoy!– Lagos.

In Malawi, Kim Dionne, Amanda Robinson, Jason Kerwin, Anna West, Rebecca Dizon-Ross, and Synab Njerenga all helped me prepare for my initial field work, and James Mkandawire and his staff at IKI made my work possible and provided a fantastic team of enumerators and colleagues for my first survey there. Starting in late 2016 I began working with Shem Yuda, who was a wonderful companion and interlocutor. We did many interviews together, and he continued this work in my absence. He was truly my eyes and ears when I could not be there, and helped me to follow several communities over time, as well as to test survey protocols. I could not have done the postdissertation work without him, and without this time together and what I learned from it, there would be no book to write. I am also grateful to Boniface Dulani, Happy Kayuni, and John Tengatenga, who helped me conduct the second survey and coordination games in 2019, together with a fantastic team of enumerators from the Institute of Public Opinion and Research (IPOR) in Zomba.

I received excellent feedback and questions at various stages of the project from participants at WGAPE, AALIMS, APSA, the APSA Africa workshop in Ouagadougou, and presentations at the London School of Economics, University of Oxford, Duke University, Columbia University, Cornell University, the University of Wisconsin–Madison, Emory University, the University of Southern California, and Stanford University. At NYU and NYU Abu Dhabi I am grateful to my colleagues and friends for their support, especially Peter van der Windt, Andy Harris, Christopher Paik, Leonid Peisakhin, Erin Pettigrew, Rahul Sagar, Giuliana Pardelli, Gabe Kohler-Derrick, Elisabeth Anderson, Maria Grigoryeva, Blaine Robbins, Rachel Brulé, Bob Kubenic, Kanchan Chandra, Rebecca Morton, Chris Dawes, Dana Burde, Elisabeth King, Kinga Makovi, Jeff Jensen, John O'Brien, Morgan Hardy, Cyrus Samii, and my deans Hervé Crès and Paula England. Thank you to the Hoover Institution for providing the time and space to cross the final ts and dot the final is.

In 2019 I was fortunate to have a book conference (coplotted with Leonid, which helped tremendously for motivation) at NYU, generously chaired by Gwyneth McClendon and with the thoughtful and constructive comments and feedback from David Stasavage, Rebecca Littman, Daniel Posner, Melani Cammett, Evan Lieberman, and Eric Dickson, with notes documented by Shana Warren. As anyone who has had a book conference can tell you, this was an incredibly humbling and invaluable experience. The book is so much improved from their careful reading and generous feedback. I am also grateful to two anonymous reviewers who provided excellent feedback and helped me further sharpen the argument and organization of the book, and to the editorial and production team at Cambridge University Press. Marissa Mika, a friend whose work on health in Uganda and elsewhere I have admired over the years, provided editorial assistance that helped me get the manuscript over the finish line. I have also benefited from research assistance over the years from an outstanding team including Sarah Stein, Clara Bicalho,

Frederic Cochinard, Imelda Wellington, Julien Esposito, Karolina Wilczynska, Koki Ajiri, Keshar Shahi, and Roberta Danieliūtė.

A number of friends have read versions and pieces of the manuscript, helped me keep putting one foot in front of the other, and generally cheered me on. Leah Rosenzweig and Kelly Zhang provided a much-needed hand to hold in the aftermath of COVID and a new baby, when I struggled to get things moving again. Pia Raffler and Guy Grossman have been tremendous friends and coauthors from whom I have learned so much. Jon Pevehouse has been a generous advocate and supporter of my work and career; I am so grateful. Tom Pepinsky read the manuscript from start to finish, and provided not only very helpful feedback but also encouragement, and has become a dear friend along the way. Evan Lieberman has been a great source of support over the years, provided generous feedback on multiple occasions, and tempered my doubts whenever motivation began to wane. Lauren Davenport has been a wonderful friend on whom I can count for laughter or a steady hand. Friends outside of academia have kept me sane and are a source of joy and comfort, only gently and occasionally asking over my book progress, including Aaron Kheifets, Yair Tygiel, Laura Reed, Kathleen Fehrenbach, Elizabeth Kosobucki, Jenny Coyne, Lauren Banks, and Dontae Rayford.

Thank you to members of "The Clan" – especially Eshban Kwesiga, Begumya Rushongoza, Joel Mukisa, Nnanda Kizito Sseruwagi, Kwezi Tabaro, Ivan Rugambwa, and Raymond Qatahar, several of whom participated in a second mini book conference – and to wonderful friends and family in Uganda over the many years, including Benjamin Rukwengye, Timothy Muhereza, and Joseph Were, Agather Atuhaire, and Lisa Komuhendo. Thank you to Andrew Mwenda, a travel companion extraordinaire, long-winded reciter of facts and fables, and friend with whom I don't always agree but with whom I can question any idea without judgment, to Kalundi Serumaga, whose initial skepticism was warranted and who helped me rethink what education means, to Alan Kasujja with whom I shared meals at every opportunity in both London and Kampala and who has been a buoy of spirits, to Apollo Makubuya, a coconspirator in finding and sharing all material Buganda-related, to Haggai Matsiko, a constant support on whom I know I can always count, including for a chat over a Nile or three as soon as I reach my favorite city, to Jacky Kemigisa, who has a clarity of thought and purpose I aspire to, and to Daniel Kalinaki, who lent his editorial prowess to the manuscript toward the final stages and has endured all manner of rabbit holes I have tripped and dragged him into.

I owe a great debt to the hundreds of individuals who participated in the surveys and interviews with me over the years in Uganda, Malawi, Nigeria, Ghana, and Rwanda. I cannot name them here, but this work would have been impossible had it not been for the time and insights they shared with me. There is much work left outstanding on the topic of education, culture, and inequality, and I hope the end product and any work that follows will do justice to their time, generosity, and the experiences and knowledge they shared with me.

Finally, I am deeply grateful to my family, who have supported me throughout. My parents, Linda and Oscar Platas, have provided me with every possible opportunity to pursue each of my dreams, and have always supported my decisions, even when they took me thousands of miles from home. Angelo Izama has been a sounding board for my many musings over the years, and has been a source of ideas, guidance, and support. Thank you to Brenda Caracuel for helping raise our children and for the care given to all of us, and to Nice Kateeba, sister and friend who took loving care of my eldest as I raced to finish my dissertation. My two (big) babies, Gwiza (Amandla) and Amani, are a source of never-ending joy and purpose, providers of perspective on the things that really matter. I have learned so much from watching them grow, and they inspire me every day.

1

The Puzzle of Persistent Inequality

We live in a time of tremendous and growing inequality. Some of this inequality reflects the "escape"[1] of large swaths of humanity from conditions of impoverishment, insecurity, and premature death that have characterized much of human existence to date, and which still feature in the lives of too many people. Reams of paper have been dedicated to making sense of the wealth – or poverty – of nations,[2] and innumerable projects, programs, and policies have been deployed to promote economic development in the poorest parts of the world. However, inequality is not only found across countries, but also within them. Within countries, far from being randomly distributed, opportunity is often correlated with characteristics like skin color, language, ethnicity, or religion. The group-level differences that emerge in outcomes like income, life expectancy, and education can persist for generations.[3] Why? The answer to this question is key to understanding the persistence of inequality generally.

In this book I add a piece to the puzzle by examining a particular type of group-level inequality in a particular place: the Muslim–Christian

---

[1] Deaton (2013)
[2] In recent decades, for example, see the enormous literature spawned by 2024 Nobel Laureates in economics James Robinson, Daron Acemoglu, and Simon Johnson on the role of institutions in shaping variation in the long-term economic growth of countries.
[3] Cross-nationally, Stevens and Dworkin (2019) document racial and ethnic gaps in education across such varied contexts as Israel, Argentina, Russia, Turkey, Canada, and South Africa. In the United States, there are persistent Black–white gaps in income (Chetty et al. 2020), mortality (Boustan and Margo 2015), and education (Collins and Margo 2006, Gamoran 2001, and Hanushek and Rivkin 2009).

schooling gap in Africa.[4] Despite nearly universal free primary education, close to 250 million children are out of school globally.[5] More than half of these children live in sub-Saharan Africa, the only region where their numbers are growing in absolute terms.[6] However, these striking figures mask the considerable inequality in educational attainment within African countries. While scholars and policymakers have long recognized gender[7] and ethnic[8] gaps in education, few have turned their attention to the widespread gap in schooling rates across religious groups in Africa.

Compared to Christians, Muslims across Africa have fewer years of education, are less likely to be literate, and their children are less likely to be in school. This gap has persisted from the colonial period to the present. Nearly two-thirds of Muslim adults in Africa born between 1965 and 1995 are illiterate, compared to about one-quarter of Christians.[9] Three in five Muslim adults have never attended school, compared to about one in five Christians.

Figure 1.1 shows the average years of school among Christians and Muslims across three cohorts: those born in the two decades before independence (1945–1964), those born in the two decades after independence (1965–1984), and those born in the most recent cohort for which complete data on educational attainment are available (1985–1997). Figure 1.1 shows that while average years of schooling are increasing for both Christians and Muslims, a gap of about three years has persisted throughout the postcolonial period.[10] Literacy rates show similar trends; there is a 30 percentage point difference in literacy rates between Christians and Muslims in the most recent cohort.[11]

Figure 1.2 shows the gap in average years of schooling by country.[12] Clearly, the magnitude of the gap varies across countries, as do levels of

---

[4] For ease of exposition, going forward I will refer to sub-Saharan Africa as "Africa." Unless otherwise noted, I do not include North Africa in the analyses or theoretical discussion.
[5] UNESCO (2019b)
[6] UNESCO (2022)
[7] Baten et al. (2021), Grant and Behrman (2010)
[8] Alesina, Michalopoulos, and Papaioannou (2016)
[9] Figures from Demographic and Health Surveys (DHS) among 1.3 million respondents across 37 African countries and also documented in Pew Research Center (2016) The DHS are conducted in over 80 countries worldwide and focuses on health outcomes of women and children. They were funded by the United States Agency for International Development until February 2025 and were conducted approximately every five years in the countries where the surveys take place.
[10] Figure 1.1 includes the population weights provided by IPUMS DHS.
[11] See Figure A.1.
[12] Figure 1.2 uses religion and country level average years of schooling as reported in Pew Research Center (2016).

1 The Puzzle of Persistent Inequality

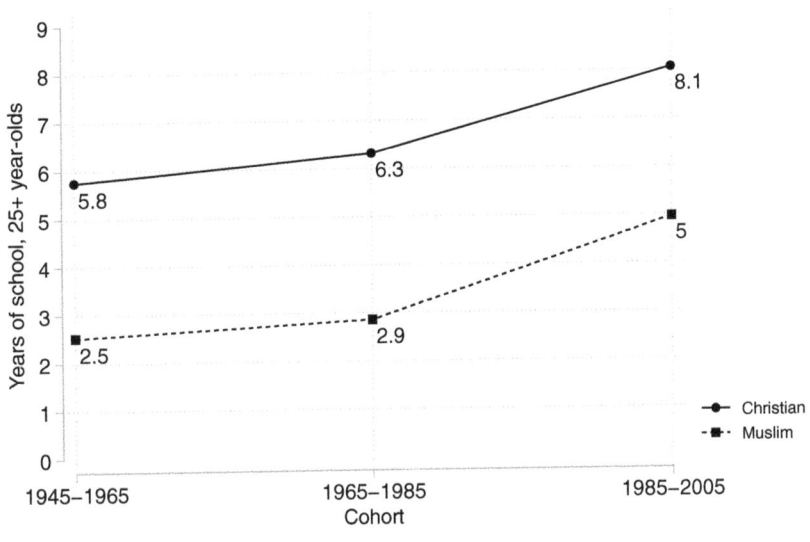

FIGURE 1.1 Years of schooling (age 25+) by religion and cohort.
Source: DHS, various years.

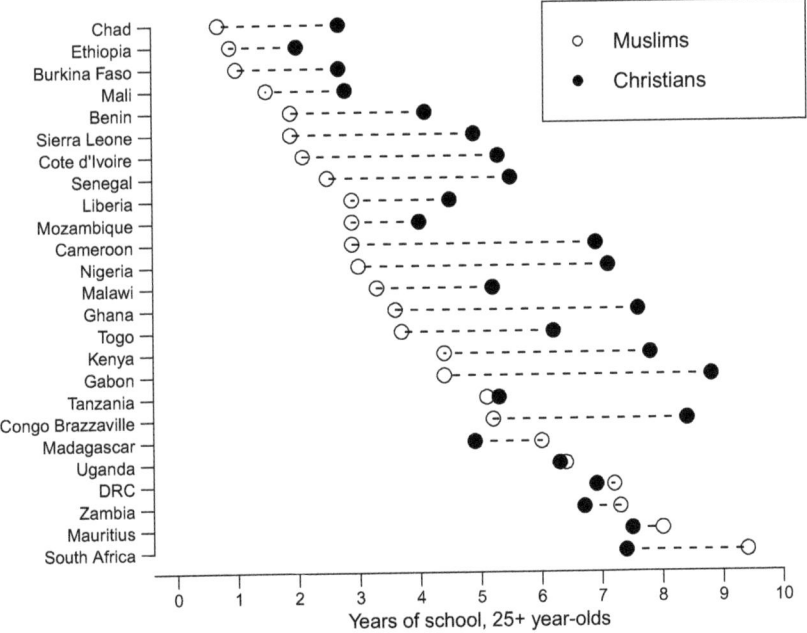

FIGURE 1.2 Average years of schooling by religion and country.
Source: Pew Research Center (2016).

schooling generally. For example, although the gap in years of education between Christians and Muslims in Nigeria is nearly twice that in Chad, Christians in Chad have on average as many years of education as Muslims in Nigeria. It is also the case that while the gap is quite large in the majority of countries shown here, there are several that deviate from the overall pattern, exhibiting either little to no gap (e.g. Tanzania, Uganda) or a positive gap (e.g. South Africa), where Muslims have more years of education than Christians, on average. Places where the gap is very small or even reversed tend to have very small Muslim populations, and often these are populations that have migrated to Africa in the relatively recent past. In this book I will focus primarily on African communities that converted to Islam or Christianity rather than those that migrated from elsewhere.

Unraveling the puzzle of persistent inequality involves understanding variation in the gap at both the national and subnational levels. For this gap is observed not just at the national level, but also within ethnic groups and subnational regions. These subnational patterns suggest that religion is not merely a proxy for ethnicity and this gap does not only reflect regional inequality. And while Muslims are in some cases poorer than Christians, this schooling gap persists after taking into account household wealth and urbanization. Within countries, one of the strongest predictors of Muslim educational attainment is the size of the Muslim population at the subnational level – the gap increases, and Muslim levels of education decline, with the relative size of the local Muslim population. Why?

Over the course of this book I will argue that, while there are numerous factors that produce and perpetuate inequality, culture plays an important role in explaining schooling behavior and the persistence of education gaps across groups. In particular, I argue that schooling norms – empirical and normative expectations of others' beliefs and behavior regarding school attendance and achievement – comprise a form of social pressure to attend, persist, and perform in school, and that these norms can vary in strength across groups. While the origin of schooling norms will differ across contexts, I suggest that the strength of these norms varies with the extent of exposure to mass schooling historically, and with the extent to which mass schooling is associated with a particular identity. In the case of the Muslim–Christian schooling gap, I argue that African communities that converted to Christianity developed stronger schooling norms than Muslim communities because of the historical association between mass schooling and Christianity in colonial Africa, and the relatively lower exposure to mass schooling in Muslim communities during the colonial period.

Colonial rule is central to understanding the emergence and persistence of this education gap, and there are two channels through which colonial rule mattered for long-term schooling patterns and schooling norms. The first is a bricks-and-mortar channel: Those living in predominantly Muslim areas had lower exposure to colonial-era schooling; there were simply fewer schools built in Muslim areas. The second channel is one of *ideas* about schooling. Christian missionaries' outsize role in the provision of schooling, and the role schools played in conversion to and consolidation of Christian beliefs, meant that norms about attendance of mass schooling were stronger (on average) among Christians than among Muslims. However, where Muslims lived as a minority and faced competition with Christians, they developed their own mass schooling system as well as norms about attendance of these schools.

At the time of its introduction in Africa, mass schooling was a cornerstone of the colonial and proselytizing project. Mass schooling was provided overwhelmingly by Christian missionaries and their followers, and its primary objective was to convert Africans to Christianity.[13] Missionaries tended to avoid, and were in some cases prohibited by colonial authorities from operating in, Muslim areas. Colonial governments established a limited number of schools, but in no context did government schooling – schools established by colonial governments, without missionary influence – approximate mass schooling. Government schools were not designed to educate the masses but rather to train a limited number of Africans to work in the colonial bureaucracy and governance structures.

The distribution of the early investments in schools and the association between Christianity and schooling during the colonial period served as a critical juncture,[14] establishing the Muslim–Christian schooling gap and setting in motion several factors that led to its persistence. First, since few schools were located in Muslim areas, few children attended these schools, a fact which produced the initial gap in schooling. Second, few inhabitants of Muslim areas were qualified to serve in colonial bureaucracies or to be employed as teachers or medical workers, which disadvantaged them in the emerging colonial economy, often though not always leaving them less well-off economically than those who obtained colonial education. Third, alongside the institutional and infrastructural differences that emerged between Muslim communities and those that converted to Christianity

---

[13] Mackenzie (1993)
[14] Capoccia (2016)

were differences in *norms* about school attendance. These norms affected attendance – demand – but also the supply of schools by Muslim elites.

In the postindependence period, access to school has become much more even and Muslim areas are, for the most part, no longer left behind in terms of educational resources. Moreover, nearly universal policies of free primary education mean that financial constraints to schooling are lower. However, in contexts where school attendance is not enforced, and where the returns to basic schooling are low or uncertain, norms can continue to affect schooling behavior and allow initial differences in levels of schooling across communities to persist.

These norms have evolved over time, and access to school has expanded dramatically, but differences in the strength of schooling norms across religious communities can persist. Schooling norms may be especially important in explaining behavior where the economic returns to education are low or uncertain, and when state capacity to enforce attendance is low. Although the vast majority of children globally attend school for at least some period of time, the quality of education is often very poor in low income countries. It has long been recognized that "schooling ain't learning,"[15] but recent work suggests the quality of schooling is particularly low in sub-Saharan Africa and appears to be getting *worse*. Nearly 95 percent of students in Africa do not reach basic skill levels in math and science,[16] and in most countries, the likelihood of being literate, conditional on schooling, has declined.[17] In a context where quality is declining, returns are uncertain, and enforcement is weak, it is unlikely that expected economic returns are the only, or even primary driver of school attendance.

Making an argument about culture does not imply that this is the only factor that matters, nor do I wish to downplay the economic or structural factors that also perpetuate inequality. In this book, I focus on culture because existing models of educational attainment – those that treat education as universally desired, and educational investment decisions as primarily economic, and made independently by individuals – simply could

---

[15] Pritchett (2013)
[16] Gust, Hanushek, and Woessmann (2024)
[17] For example, of women that have completed grade five, the fraction that are literate has declined by 13 percentage points on average across Africa. Countries like Uganda, Mozambique, and the Republic of Congo have experienced much larger than average declines – between a 30 and 50 percentage point drop in literacy, conditional on school attendance (Pritchett 2024).

not help me make sense of the pervasive education gap between Christians and Muslims that I observed in the data and in real life.

This cultural argument is a complement – not a substitute – for a set of important economic and structural explanations for inequality in education. It is certainly the case that poverty is correlated with educational outcomes, and that structural inequality – for, example the uneven distribution of educational resources, sometimes intentionally – perpetuate differences in educational attainment across communities. Nevertheless, gaps in educational attainment often persist after taking into account these factors, suggesting they do not fully account for persistent differences across groups. Cultural, economic, and structural factors can also interact, producing feedback loops that reinforce differences in educational attainment across groups, and the relative importance of each of these factors will vary across contexts. The point is not that culture matters most, but rather that we will not be able to fully explain inequality or design policy interventions to equalize opportunity without understanding how and when culture – particularly expectations and beliefs about what others will do and think – matters for behavior.

Education As We Know It

Thus far I have been using the term education and mass schooling interchangeably, without much definition, because education is something everyone is familiar with, particularly if you are reading this book and have, in all likelihood, close to two decades of education under your belt. But while education has always been present in human societies, the particular form in which we know it today – mass schooling – is a very recent entrant. The transformation of the global educational landscape has been so swift and the paradigm shift to mass schooling so widespread that it is easy to overlook the journey that has led us here. Two hundred years ago, very few people could read or write. Today, literacy rates are at 90 percent, an all-time high. This dramatic reversal is the product of mass schooling, which in a span of only two centuries has overtaken all other previous forms of knowledge transmission.

Today, whether you are in China or Chad, you will find children in walled classrooms organized by grade. In each classroom, a teacher instructs the students using a standardized curriculum that includes language, arts, and mathematics. Students and schools are assessed using examinations, and schools are managed by a centralized state authority, such as a Ministry of Education, which has become a fixture of the modern state.[18] Global spending on education is estimated at US$4.7 trillion annually, with governments spending approximately 15 percent of their budgets on this sector.[19]

Two decades into the twenty-first century nearly 90 percent of all children attend school of this type, even if only for a few years. The extraordinary effort and expense to structure the lives of nearly all children in a particular fashion is unprecedented in human history. It is an effort that has been undertaken because education as we understand it today – mass schooling – has been codified as a universal human right[20] and is viewed as central to economic growth. Some go further, suggesting that education is not merely the cause of economic growth, it *is* growth.[21] To have high levels of education is part and parcel of "what it means to be prosperous" and, according to the World Bank, is a "key dimension of human progress."[22]

But although we measure educational outcomes today through standardized tests and often refer to education as producing "human capital," education is not a mere technical or bureaucratic process, and it never has been. Education is about the transmission of knowledge; not only skills, but also values, beliefs, and ways of understanding the world. Education is therefore a vehicle of cultural transmission, and the particular form that education takes is itself an expression of culture.

Much existing work on education in political science and economics has operated under the implicit assumption that decisions about school attendance are nonsocial – that all parents have an independent preference for more schooling for their children, regardless of the schooling decisions of others. This assumption leads us to focus on individual and family-level barriers to school attendance, such as economic constraints, but also unable to make sense of many parents' behavior, such as the failure to make education a political priority. For example, Gift and Wibbels (2014, p. 301) write, "… it seems axiomatic that all parents want a better life for their children. This makes it hard to fathom why everyone does not make education a political priority."

---

[18] Benavot et al. (1991), Anderson-Levitt (2003)
[19] UNESCO (2019a), Chapter 19.
[20] Article 26 of the Universal Declaration of Human Rights states that education is a right and should be free at the "elementary and fundamental stages." It also states that elementary education should be compulsory (UNGA 1948).
[21] North and Thomas (1973)
[22] Narayan et al. (2008)

By contrast, I argue that both social beliefs about whether and how much schooling is appropriate, and whether education of this type is likely to produce a "better life," has varied historically across religious communities, and that these beliefs are sensitive to the local political and social context. The social benefits of school attendance, and the social costs of dropping out, are an important – but often overlooked – determinant of schooling decisions, and these social benefits can differ across communities. More broadly, I argue that schooling is a behavior that is subject to social pressure, and is in part a function of empirical and normative expectations about what is considered "appropriate" behavior in a given social group.

Parents play a central role in setting these expectations, but they are also reinforced, or sometimes, counteracted, by other members of the social group, including children's peers, parents of peers, and community leaders. While schooling decisions are frequently considered family-level decisions involving primarily economic factors, I suggest that group-level norms, both normative and empirical, also play an important role in shaping schooling behavior.

Defining Culture

To make a cultural argument, it is important to be clear about what culture is and is not. There is no universally accepted definition of culture either within or across disciplines.[23] However, most definitions used in empirical studies of culture in the social sciences have several features in common: First, they include both group-level norms and individual attitudes, preferences, or values; second, culture is conceptualized as something that is transmitted across generations; and third, cultural groups are conceived as the set of individuals holding a common set of norms and individual preferences or beliefs. Together, these definitions provide analytical traction because they explain behavior as a function of beliefs that can be measured, and there are predictions for behavior arising from beliefs. They also describe the process through which cultural beliefs

---

[23] On the contrary, the definition of culture has been a source of contestation, and social science disciplines have quite different intellectual histories with the concept. For a recent discussion of conceptualizations of culture within sociology, see Patterson (2014). By 1950 there were more than 150 definitions of culture, Kroeber and Kluckhohn (1952), cited in Fernández and Fogli (2009, p. 147).

are maintained, namely, through ritual and high levels of interaction.[24] Building on existing work,[25] I define culture as a set of norms – both empirical and normative expectations – and individual-level beliefs held by members of a cultural group.

Norms are fundamentally about our perceptions of others' beliefs, and our expectations about how others will behave. Scholars across disciplines typically note a distinction between beliefs about what people actually do, often called descriptive norms or empirical expectations, and beliefs about what others think *should* be done, often called injunctive or prescriptive norms, or normative expectations.[26] Both types of norms can play a role in shaping our behavior. While norms are comprised of second-order beliefs – beliefs about others' beliefs – we also hold first-order beliefs, which are our personal beliefs and preferences, including rules of thumb or moral values. Although these personal beliefs are not strictly dependent on our expectations of others' beliefs and behavior, social groups are relevant for the formation of these beliefs because the learning and transmission of individual-level beliefs typically takes place within social groups. A cultural group, therefore, is the set of individuals among which there exists common knowledge about beliefs and expectations for behavior, and within which individual-level beliefs are transmitted. I conceive of cultural groups as overlapping, with any given individual at the intersection of several cultural groups. Thus, an individual will likely belong to numerous cultural groups, just as an individual holds many different identities (e.g. gender, race, religion).

This definition draws particularly closely on Laitin and Weingast (2006) who propose an "equilibrium approach" to culture, in which culture is defined by "an equilibrium in a well-defined set of circumstances in which members of a cultural group, through shared symbols, ritual practices, and high levels of interaction, are able to condition their behavior on common knowledge beliefs about the behavior of all members of the group."[27] They define cultural beliefs as "common knowledge beliefs shared by members of a cultural group about what a member of the group would do under a range of conditions …" I draw and build upon this equilibrium approach to culture, incorporating and differentiating between types of beliefs. I include first-order beliefs in

---

[24] Chwe (2001), Laitin and Weingast (2006)
[25] Valentino and Vaisey (2022)
[26] Gelfand, Gavrilets, and Nunn (2024)
[27] Laitin and Weingast (2006, p. 16)

addition to second-order beliefs (norms), and within norms, differentiate between empirical and normative beliefs.[28]

A number of other definitions of culture also delineate between types of cultural beliefs. For example, Greif (1994) defines cultural beliefs as "the ideas and thoughts common to several individuals that govern interaction – between these people, and between them, their gods, and other groups ... cultural beliefs become identical and commonly known through the socialization process by which culture is unified, maintained, and communicated,"[29] Nunn (2012) defines culture as "... decision-making heuristics, which typically manifest themselves as values, beliefs, or social norms,"[30] and Mokyr (2016) defines culture as "... the set of beliefs, values, and preferences, capable of affecting behavior, that are socially (not genetically) transmitted and that are shared by some subset of society."[31]

In what follows, I will argue that different cultural groups developed distinct norms about schooling during the colonial period in Africa. Because Christianity was strongly associated with this new form of education in much of colonial Africa, norms about schooling were initially stronger in communities that converted to Christianity, and were weaker or even antagonistic in many Muslim communities, who often rightfully feared children would be converted. However, it was not the case that the entire religious group – say, all Muslims, or all Christians – constituted the relevant cultural group for schooling. Variation in the intensity of missionary investments in education, and the overall religious composition of the community, also shaped the strength of schooling norms among both Christians and Muslims. In particular, schooling norms were more likely to spill over where Muslims were exposed to substantial missionary investments and larger Christian communities.

Given the contested nature of the term, it is also useful to say something about what culture is *not*, at least for the purposes of this book. Some conceptions of culture, such as Weber's *The Protestant Ethic and the Spirit of*

---

[28] Bicchieri (2016)
[29] Greif (1994, p. 915)
[30] Nunn (2012, S109)
[31] Mokyr (2016, p. 8). Mokyr's (2016) definition is also similar to the one I propose in that individuals can have traits from multiple cultural groups, that cultures are more like Venn diagrams than nonoverlapping, mutual exclusive sets of beliefs: "... a single individual cannot have a cultural trait that is not shared by others, but each individual is unique in that it is highly unlikely that two people share precisely the same combination of cultural elements" (Mokyr 2016, p. 9).

Capitalism (1958) or Huntington's "The Clash of Civilizations?" (1993), attribute particular values or beliefs to all members of a particular group and consider values and beliefs relatively immutable. In these accounts, although not always stated explicitly, individuals are typically conceptualized to belong to a single cultural group, rather than belonging to many. For example, Huntington (1993, p. 23) posits that while individuals hold many identities, they are members of broad civilizations whose differences "are not only real; they are basic."

Another influential set of ideas stems from work by Lewis (1966, p. 21), who argued that a "culture of poverty" explained persistent suboptimal conditions among some poor communities. In his account, culture is not limited to a particular identity group, and not all people who are poor experience a culture of poverty. But while arguably less essentialist or reductionist than Huntington's approach, many view this model as akin to victim-blaming, ascribing poverty to the values held within poor communities. The implication of such a model is that if only these communities could adopt better or different values, they would be able to pull themselves out of the so-called pathologies of the culture of poverty.[32] Given the many structural barriers communities in poverty face, many are put off by the idea of placing on these communities so much responsibility for the situation they find themselves in. From a policy perspective, such arguments can be (mis)used to discount the importance of investments or changes at the institutional level and instead task the poor with bringing themselves out of poverty.[33]

Why continue to grapple with the concept of culture, given the historical baggage and debates over definition? First, we know that there are evolutionary reasons for why humans care about the beliefs and opinions of others, that children learn, practice, and police norms from a young age, that these norms vary considerably across groups, and that they are transmitted within groups and across generations.[34] Second, there are limits to the explanatory power of economic factors in explaining all kinds of behavioral patterns, including the roles and expectations of different groups within and across societies. Modeling behavior – and most relevantly for the purposes of this book, the decision to "invest" in education – as a purely economic calculation misses

---

[32] Small, Harding, and Lamont (2010, p. 7)
[33] Within sociology, which was the main audience for Lewis' work, fear of victim-blaming put the brakes on the entire study of culture and poverty for several decades.
[34] Henrich (2016)

important aspects of human motivation, without which understanding patterns of human behavior becomes an impossible task.

I build on the intuitions underlying many conceptions of culture – that group-level beliefs matter for behavior, and that these beliefs can at some times supersede and at other times reinforce economic factors driving behavior. However, I do not treat cultural beliefs as fundamental to particular social groups or fixed in time. I define culture as *context-specific beliefs* about how members of a social group will behave in a given situation, an empirical concern, and how they *should* behave, a normative concern. I examine how and why normative expectations – say, about the appropriate level and type of school to complete – vary across and within groups, the conditions under which these beliefs change, and why, out of many social groups to which one can belong, particular social groups become relevant for some behaviors at some times and not others.

THE MUSLIM–CHRISTIAN SCHOOLING GAP

Having defined culture and presented an overview of theoretical argument, I turn now to a richer description of the particular schooling gap under investigation. While there is no such thing as a person who is representative of African Muslims or the Muslim experience in Africa, I start by introducing a Muslim woman named Margaret, whose experience dispels some assumptions and stereotypes, and begins to cast doubt on economic explanations for the gap.

Margaret lives with several of her children in a village called Kutambua, in southern Malawi. While nearly 90 percent of Malawians are Christian, about 13 percent are Muslim, and most, like Margaret, live in this southeastern corner of Malawi, near the border with Mozambique. When I met her in 2016, Margaret was thirty-two years old, just one year older than me, and a mother of nine.

Kutambua village lies at the foot of a mountain range along Malawi's southeastern border with Mozambique. The village is two hours down a winding, bumpy dirt road from Mangochi town, the headquarters of one of Malawi's largest districts and home to one-third of the country's Muslim population. Children play in the patches of packed earth flanking the road, chasing one another. The younger ones sit cozily in their mothers' laps, or strapped securely to their backs. Young men ride overloaded bicycles, ferrying goods to and from villages. When the rain falls, suddenly and heavily in pea-sized droplets, the mountains seem to catch the water and hurl it down to the villages in the valley below, creating in moments small rivers that can swallow the road entirely.

The homesteads of Kutambua are small mud houses, connected by well-trod footpaths running through fields of cow peas and maize. I find Margaret sitting on the step just outside her one-room house, a toddler burying his face in her skirt. His six-year-old sister Mariam has just started her first year of primary school, while his teenage sister Aisha slips out of sight on my arrival. Aisha left school after a few years, as did her older siblings, some of whom have married already. Margaret herself never went to school, and works as an agricultural day-laborer (sometimes called "piecework") to support her children. When I ask how much she makes in a year, she pauses to think, and suggests around 36,000 Malawian Kwacha, equivalent to about 50 US dollars. If accurate, this would put her well below Malawi's income per capita, which was around 300 dollars in 2016.

Although Margaret is Muslim, her religion is not obvious. She does not wear a hijab or any other attire that would identify her as Muslim, does not speak or read Arabic, and neither she nor her children have ever attended Qur'anic school.[35] Even her name does not suggest a particular religious affiliation. There is one mosque but no Qur'anic school in Kutambua. When I ask why, I'm told the villagers cannot afford to pay a Sheik to teach their children.

As in much of Africa, Islam in Malawi initially spread through trade, and reached what is now Mangochi shortly before the arrival of European missionaries and colonizers in the late nineteenth century. In Malawi today, religion is not typically thought of as a salient political cleavage, and there has never been religious conflict – or any significant conflict for that matter – in the country.

The public primary school serving the village, like many in the country, was established by the Roman Catholic Church in the early 1960s. While Muslims in Malawi, as in other parts of Africa, used to fear conversion to Christianity in mission-founded schools, today few parents report concerns with the religious affiliation of schools or teachers. Still, while most children in Kutambua start primary school, very few finish, dropping out after a couple of years to get on with their lives in the village.

A day in the life of the average person in Kutambua is spent on subsistence farming, fishing in the nearby lake, running a small kiosk, or

---

[35] Throughout the text I use the term Qur'anic to describe schools providing Islamic religious education only. These schools are also commonly referred to as madrasa.

working for a meager wage in fields owned by large landholders or foreign corporations. Most people will spend the entirety of their lives in Kutambua and nearby villages, living off the land and lakes. Whether a child attends school for two, four, or even the full eight years of primary school, the trajectory of her life course will look very similar. Almost no one has attended secondary school, and many adults, like Margaret, have never attended school at all. Teaching and work in healthcare are the only formal sector jobs in this rural area, and most people filling these positions are from elsewhere.

Malawi has been a leader in promoting access to education, especially among the poor. The country held its first-ever multiparty elections in 1994, and is one of the region's longest standing democracies. It was among the first countries to implement free primary education, leading to a massive increase in school attendance and the construction of thousands of new schools in the mid 1990s to serve the growing student population.

But nearly three decades later, children like Margaret's leave school after only a few years, and some never go at all. Malawi's Muslim population has two fewer years of school than Christians, on average, and are less likely to be literate. According to the 2008 Malawi census, Muslim children are 50 percent more likely to be out of school than Christian children and nearly twice as likely to have never attended school at all. Nearly one-third of Muslim children between the ages of 8 and 12 were not in school at the time of the census, and close to one in five had never set foot in a classroom.

Malawi is not unique in this regard. The schooling gap between religious groups has persisted and sometimes grown even in Africa's most vibrant economies and those countries considered stable democracies, often decades after the removal of school fees. In Kenya, home to the Silicon Savannah and among the "African Lion" economies, nearly 60 percent of Muslim adults have never attended school, compared to only 11 percent of Christians. In Nigeria, Africa's most populous country and the region's largest economy, with the fifth-largest Muslim population in the world, Christians have five more years of schooling than Muslims.

Despite more than a half-century of independent rule, increasing democratization, and after two decades of free primary education, more than four in ten Muslim children aged 6 to 12 are out of school, compared to less than one in five Christian children.[36] While there is

---

[36] For county-level estimates, see Figure A.2.

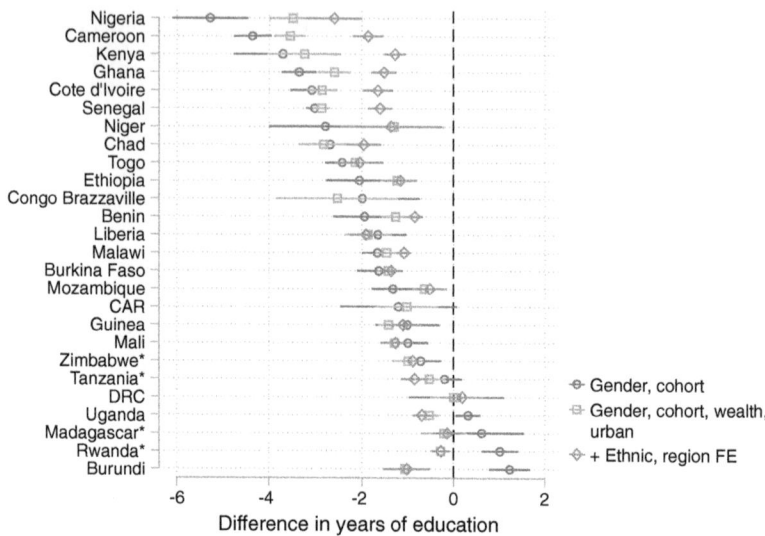

FIGURE 1.3 Muslim–Christian schooling gap by country, three models.
Source: DHS, various years.

considerable variation across countries in the Muslim–Christian gap in the out-of-school population, the gap exists in almost all countries with substantial Muslim populations. Across countries, the gap is smallest and Muslim schooling highest where Muslims comprise a tiny minority of the population, for example in Rwanda (1.8 percent Muslim) or the Democratic Republic of Congo (1.5 percent Muslim).

The Muslim–Christian schooling gap persists after controlling for household assets and living in a rural area. As shown in Figure 1.3, which presents the coefficient on Muslim in a set of country-level estimates, where years of education are regressed on religious affiliation, the addition of covariates for wealth and urban residence does not substantially alter the overall pattern. While in countries like Nigeria or Cameroon, which have the largest gaps, the addition of these covariates reduces the coefficient on Muslim by a full year or more, in most other countries, the estimates across models are quite similar. In some cases, such as Uganda or Rwanda, the (negative) gap *emerges* with the addition of wealth as a covariate.

Figure 1.3 also shows that the Muslim–Christian gap exists within regions and ethnic groups. Including region and ethnic group fixed effects reduces the magnitude of the gap substantially in countries where it is largest, but even then, a gap of one to two full years of schooling exists. As with the inclusion of covariates for wealth, including region and ethnic group fixed effects in some cases even increases the magnitude of the coefficient on Muslim. These results demonstrate that religion is not merely a proxy for wealth or region; Muslims do not have fewer years of schooling only because they are relatively poorer or live in less advantaged areas. These factors matter, but they are not sufficient to explain the persistent gap. Moreover, even though there were major differences in educational policies across colonizers, particularly between the British and the French, the gap is found across all.[37]

To provide further evidence that these patterns do not merely reflect ethnic differences – the Muslim–Christian education gap also exists within ethnic groups. Figure 1.4 shows the Muslim–Christian schooling gap within ethnic groups for over 80 groups from 18 countries. While the magnitude of the gap varies, it is present in nearly all ethnic groups.[38] There are gaps of two or more years of schooling among nearly a dozen groups from nearly as many countries, even after taking into account urban residence and wealth. Groups with Muslim majorities (shown in darker shades of gray) tend to have larger gaps than those where Muslims are a minority. These intra-ethnic gaps also suggest that the gap is not being driven by the fact that Muslim groups in Africa were more dependent on pastoralism historically,[39] a typically nomadic practice which could have made school attendance more difficult. In fact, Figure 1.4 shows that religiously diverse ethnic groups are quite common in Africa. A large number of groups have both Christian and Muslim subpopulations within them.

The country-level Muslim–Christian schooling gap is not well-predicted by either regime type or income per capita, two factors associated with inequality in economic development.[40] According to common measures of regime type, democratization has been on the rise in Africa and elsewhere since the mid twentieth century. While the period from

---

[37] The exception is Belgian territories, namely the Democratic Republic of Congo, Rwanda, and Burundi, which all have Muslim populations of less than 2 percent. Even these have a gap once covariates are added.
[38] Data come from the Demographic and Health Surveys. To be included in the analysis, there must be at least 100 Muslim and 100 Christian respondents in the group. Alternative cutoff points for inclusion yield similar patterns. In each regression, covariates for gender, birth cohort, urban, and wealth, with fixed effects for region.
[39] Michalopoulos, Naghavi, and Prarolo (2018)
[40] See Appendix A.3.

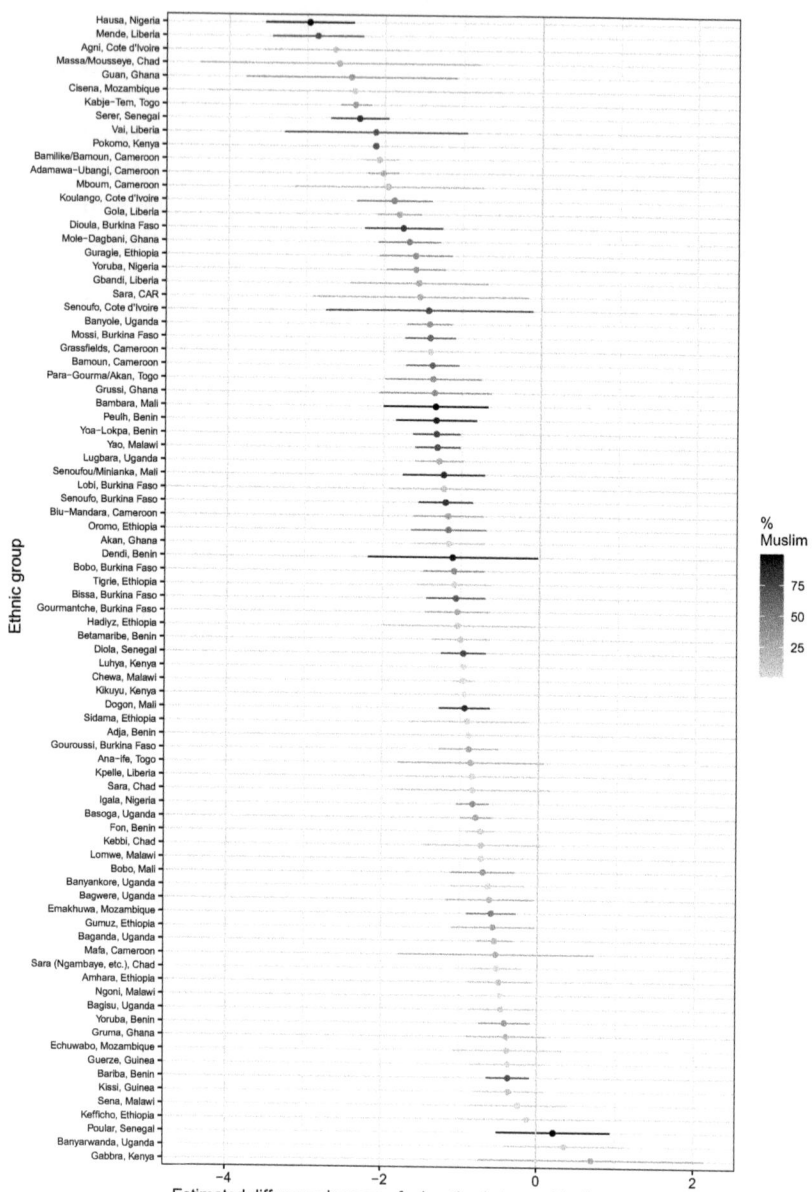

FIGURE 1.4 Muslim–Christian gap in years of schooling within ethnic groups. *Source*: DHS, various years.

the 1960s to late 1980s marked a period of steadily increasing autocratic rule, the number of countries in sub-Saharan Africa considered autocracies plummeted following the end of the Cold War. Since then, the number of democracies has been increasing, as have the number of hybrid regimes, or "anocracies."[41] Democracy has been associated with increased spending on public goods, and the stock of democracy associated with improvements in measures of health, such as infant mortality.[42] Political competition in the form of multiparty elections has led to the removal of school fees and thus increases in school attendance.[43] For these reasons we might expect democratization to be associated with declines in historical schooling gaps. Empirically, however, there is no clear relationship between regime type and the postindependence Muslim–Christian schooling gap.

We might also expect that resources matter, and that a country with a higher income per capita would experience lower gaps in schooling, having more resources to fund the education of minorities or marginalized groups. African countries are among the poorest in the world, as measured by income per capita, and fared especially poorly in the decades after independence. Nevertheless, if anything there is a positive relationship between income per capita and the postindependence Muslim–Christian schooling gap, though this too becomes weaker over time.

Within countries, the Muslim–Christian schooling gap is driven by areas with a substantial Muslim population. Where Muslims comprise a small minority, there is no such gap. Using census data from eleven African countries,[44] which allows me to calculate the percentage Muslim of the administrative district in which a person lives, Figure 1.5 shows the predicted values for school attendance among Christian and Muslim children as the percentage of Muslims of the area increases. The likelihood that a Muslim child attends school falls 15 percentage points as the area in which they live increases from less than 10 percent Muslim to greater than 90 percent Muslim. Among Christians, school attendance remains

---

[41] Trends in regime type come from Polity IV; see Marshall and Gurr (2020).
[42] Gerring et al. (2011)
[43] Stasavage (2005)
[44] The sample includes eleven countries where data on religious affiliation and administrative units of comparable size were available as of 2017: Burkina Faso, Cameroon, Ethiopia, Ghana, Malawi, Mali, Mozambique, Nigeria, Senegal, Sierra Leone, and Uganda. Data are compiled by Minnesota Population Center. Integrated Public Use Microdata Series, International: Version 6.3 [Machine-readable database]. Minneapolis: University of Minnesota, 2014. Census data are used for all countries except Nigeria, where only survey data is available on the IPUMS website, and to the public.

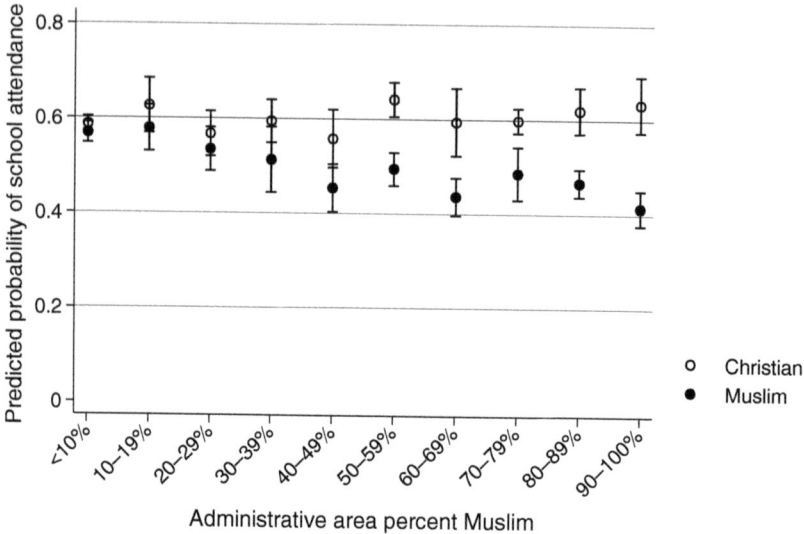

FIGURE 1.5 Likelihood of school attendance by religion, as the percentage of Muslims in administrative units increases.
Source: IPUMS.

constant at about 60 percent regardless of the religious demographics of the area in which they live.

Among adults, there is a similar pattern. Where Muslims are a very small minority – around 5 percent or less of the district or province – the average literacy gap is about zero, or even negative. However, once Muslims comprise a fifth or more of the population of the district, the Muslim–Christian literacy gap is almost always positive – Christians are almost always more literate, on average, than Muslims. In sum, schooling outcomes are significantly worse for Muslims living in majority Muslim areas.

The population of sub-Saharan Africa today is approximately 1.2 billion,[45] and of these, about two-thirds are Christian and about one-third Muslim.[46] Because of rapid population growth in many African countries, the continent is home to the fastest growing Christian and Muslim populations globally. By 2050 it is estimated that the region will be home to nearly 40 percent of the global Christian population – the center of Christendom with respect to the sheer number of the faithful. While Islam

---

[45] World Bank estimate as of 2022.
[46] A small minority, less than 10 percent, report practicing traditional religions to the exclusion of Christianity or Islam.

is often associated with the Middle East and North Africa (MENA), in the next few decades there will be more Muslims living in sub-Saharan Africa than in the Middle East, North Africa, Europe, and North and South America combined.[47] Thus, the Muslim–Christian schooling gap is consequential both in magnitude but also with respect to the number of individuals affected.

WHO SHOULD READ THIS BOOK?

At first glance, the subject of the Muslim–Christian schooling gap in Africa may feel rather niche, and the topics of religion, Islam, education, and culture are also somewhat at the periphery of the related work on which they draw. For example, among those who study African politics, ethnicity is a far more common identity cleavage to investigate than is religion. Among scholars who do study religion in Africa, the vast majority of the work is on Christianity and Christian missionaries rather than Islam. Among those who study Islam, politics, and development, most work concerns the Middle East and North Africa,[48] and to a lesser extent, South Asia[49] and Europe,[50] despite the fact that there will likely be more Muslims living in sub-Saharan Africa than in the MENA region by 2050. More generally, in comparative politics, both religion and education have been understudied relative to their place in other social science disciplines.[51] And while there have been lively debates about culture in sociology for decades,[52] and increasing attempts to incorporate culture in economics,[53] in political science the study of culture, following earlier work by Almond and Verba (1963) and Huntington (1993), has – with a few important exceptions[54] – either been sidestepped or studied

---

[47] Pew Research Center (2015)
[48] For example, Kuran (2011), Cammett and Issar (2010), Lust (2011), Blaydes (2014), Rubin (2017), Nielsen (2017).
[49] For example, Pepinsky, Liddle, and Mujani (2012).
[50] Adida, Laitin, and Valfort (2016), Dancygier (2018)
[51] For example, see Grzymala-Busse (2012) on the study of religion and Gift and Wibbels (2014) on the study of education in comparative politics.
[52] See reviews over the years by Peterson (1979), Patterson (2014), and Valentino and Vaisey (2022).
[53] Including most recently an article by Acemoglu and Robinson (2021), which presents a new framework for understanding how culture and institutions interact. Their answer to the question of whether culture matters for development in earlier work was "mostly no." (Robinson and Acemoglu 2012, p.57)
[54] For example, Laitin (1986).

under a variety of different banners,[55] the latter of which has made the accumulation of knowledge and progress on theory difficult.

Perhaps as a consequence of being at the periphery rather than at the center of current debates in comparative or even specifically African politics, part of the beauty (and challenge) of this project, which I did not appreciate at the outset, was that it allowed – even forced – me to look beyond research in political science to understand what I was observing on the ground. By reaching across disciplinary boundaries, I hope this book will contribute to and open up new avenues for research on culture, religion, politics, development, and inequality. What are some of these avenues?

First, we are missing much of the social environment in Africa if we do not examine religion, particularly given that the region exhibits some of the highest levels of religiosity in the world.[56] Although this book is primarily concerned with education as the outcome of interest, I hope it will also be useful for helping others think through how and when religious organizations and the beliefs held within religious groups (which may not even be religious beliefs per se) matter for other economic, political, and social outcomes.[57] This study of religion also complicates our understanding of ethnicity in Africa. Some commonly used data sources implicitly suggest the homogeneity of beliefs and behavior within ethnic groups. For example, Murdock's 1967 data have been used as a measure of a variety of ethnic group-level attributes, which leaves little to no room for heterogeneity within ethnic groups. But if ethnic group members belong to different religious groups, as I show they frequently do, there is necessarily variation in beliefs and behavior along several dimensions that may be quite consequential.

Why hasn't religion featured more centrally in the study of African politics? One reason, perhaps, is that religion does not seem as frequently politicized as ethnicity, and there has been significant evidence collected on the phenomenon of ethnic favoritism.[58] Laitin's 1986 seminal work on religion, culture, and politics in Nigeria grappled with this puzzle – why doesn't religion matter more for political behavior, given the large

---

[55] Wedeen (2002)
[56] Pew Global Religious Futures Project, 2022.
[57] Although this body of work is relatively small, some recent work on religion and politics in Africa includes McClendon and Riedl (2019), McCauley (2017), Sperber and Hern (2018), as well as earlier work on Islam in West Africa by Villalón (1995).
[58] Franck and Rainer (2012), Kramon and Posner (2016)

socioeconomic disparities across religious groups? His answer had to do with the relative prioritization or importance of social cleavages as a result of colonial rule, namely that colonialism tended to emphasize, reify or even create ethnic identity, which continued to be useful for political mobilization in the postcolonial period. Posner's (2005) later work on the broader question of why some identities are politicized sometimes and not others points to the role of relative group size, and the identity-group configurations that would allow minimum winning coalitions to emerge – perhaps the demographics are such that ethnicity tends to win out over religion in this calculation. It is also possible that part of the emphasis on ethnicity has been due to the fact that in many of the most studied cases in contemporary political science,[59] racial and ethnic identity do seem to matter more for politics than religious identity, at least at the national level.

Apart from political mobilization, ethnicity – and specifically ethnic diversity – has been studied extensively in Africa, particularly in relation to public goods provision. Easterly and Levine's 1997 foundational paper on ethnic diversity in Africa, which helped spawn an enormous literature in both economics and political science on ethnic diversity as a key independent variable for understanding Africa's (under)development, did not mention religion a single time. As Miguel (2004) noted in another of the seminal pieces on ethnic diversity and public goods provision, religious diversity was not included as part of the analysis because it wasn't plausibly exogenous, but rather a function of missionary activity. Indeed, religious makeup at both the local and national level is a function of complex historical processes, some of which I document in this book, which makes causal relationships difficult to identify.

But even if religion does not seem to feature centrally for explaining electoral behavior for national-level offices, and even though religious composition is not randomly assigned and it is thus relatively difficult to study its causal effects, religion almost certainly matters for local politics in Africa, and particularly public goods provision, given the central role that religious organizations continue to play in the provision of social services, particularly though not exclusively education. It's also quite likely that if we look more closely, we will find evidence of religious organizations continuing to exert influence on national-level politicians and laws

---

[59] In both political science and economics, these countries include South Africa, Nigeria, Ghana, and Kenya (Briggs 2017, Das et al. 2013).

in Africa, much in the same way Grzymala-Busse (2015) has documented in Europe and North America. Certainly, the apparent role of the church, American missionaries, and religious beliefs in shaping policy concerning sexual minorities provides prima facie evidence that this is the case.[60] Journalistic accounts also suggest that religious organizations frequently weigh in on legislation pertaining to the family, such as marriage, divorce, and abortion.

More broadly, it is impossible to make sense of patterns of economic development in Africa today without understanding how and when religious organizations worked with colonial states, again particularly but not only in the area of education. For all of these reasons and more, religion deserves a closer look among those who study African politics and development, and I hope this book will encourage some scholars to pursue this vein of inquiry further.

Second, this book complements recent work on the relationship between education and politics, and particularly *why* governments and nongovernmental organizations have provided education historically.[61] As noted earlier in the chapter, the human rights/public goods lens through which we so often view education today simply does not align with the origins of its widespread provision. Although we think of basic education today as a right and its (ideally high-quality) provision as a central goal of the modern state, the origins of the earlier spread of mass schooling were not as beneficent as we might imagine, and its effects are not always benign.[62] Mass schooling was a tool for states, and an important component of nation building. Understanding its original role and content, the earlier costs and benefits of attendance, and *who* provided education historically are all critical for understanding patterns of educational attainment today.

Third and finally, this book provides insights on how we might think of the role of culture in economic development, and in the persistence of inequality. The idea of linking culture and inequality is not new, but it is one that has been developed at much greater length in sociology and economics, although even then primarily in high-income contexts. This book brings together ideas about culture from multiple disciplines

---

[60] Grossman et al. (2015)
[61] Particularly Paglayan's (2022, 2024) work on the spread of mass schooling around the world, as well as work by Ansell (2010) and Ansell and Lindvall (2013).
[62] For example, King (2013) shows how education fostered conflict in Rwanda, leading up the 1994 genocide.

to a new context and a new inequality puzzle. I hope this book lends further credibility to the idea that culture does matter for education, economic development, and inequality, while acknowledging the central role of other important economic, structural, and institutional factors whose paths have been more well-trodden in the literature. While there is far more work to do, I believe the conceptual development, multimethod approach, and measurement innovation presented here can be useful to scholars who seek to investigate culture and inequality going forward. I hope this book will inspire others to lean into culture as a concept with which we can better understand the social, political, and economic world around us.

ORGANIZATION OF THE BOOK

In this book I use three cases to demonstrate how the colonial encounter produced the initial gap in schooling between Christians and Muslims, and how differences both in educational investments and in ideas about new forms of education varied across religious communities. These cases are Malawi, Nigeria, and Uganda, focusing in particular on three societies: the Yao (southeastern Malawi), the Emirates of northern Nigeria, and the Kindgom of Buganda in Uganda.

All three cases are former British territories, often with overlap in colonial administrators. These cases vary in the distribution and size of the Muslim population at the time of colonization. In both Malawi and Nigeria, the majority of the Muslim population is concentrated in a particular region of the country, and among particular ethnic groups, whereas in Uganda, Muslims are a minority everywhere and in all major ethnic groups. While Muslims constitute approximately 12–13 percent of the population in both Malawi and Uganda, they are much more concentrated geographically in Malawi.

Figure 1.6 shows rates of schooling by cohort for Christians and Muslims across these three cases. While rates of schooling among Christians in recent decades are similar across all three countries, there is significant variation in schooling rates among the Muslim population across contexts, both in the level differences during the colonial period and in the rate of change over time. Muslim schooling rates are much higher in Uganda than Nigeria and Malawi during the colonial period, and today rates of schooling among Muslims in Nigeria remain quite low, with nearly one-third of the 1995 cohort having never attended school.

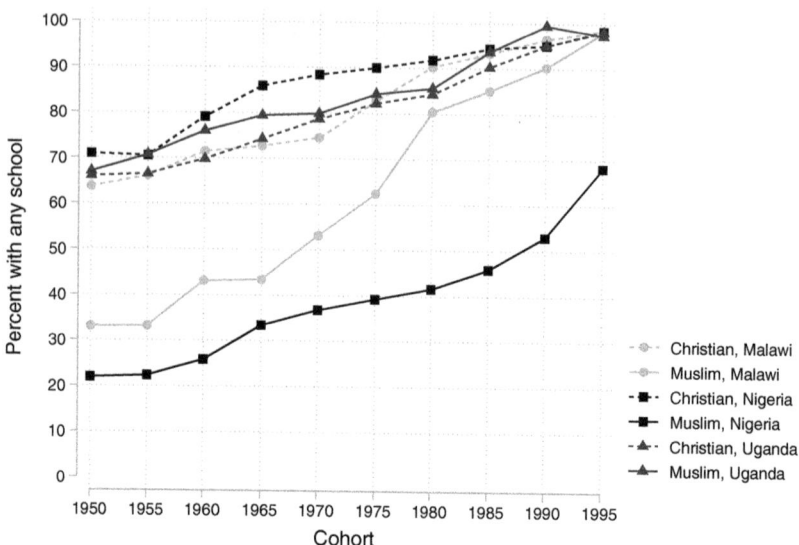

FIGURE 1.6 Percentage of cohort with any schooling in Nigeria, Malawi, and Uganda by religion.
Source: DHS, various years.

The variation in Muslim schooling rates suggests that it is not Islam per se that explains the Muslim–Christian schooling gap. Rather, these patterns are explained by a set of contextual factors that vary across these three cases – particularly, the distribution of the Muslim population at the time of colonization, the distribution of educational investments during the colonial period, and the variation in schooling norms that emerged as a result.

In Uganda today, Muslims actually have higher levels of schooling than Christians at the national level. This is because the majority of Muslims in Uganda reside in the central region, where Buganda is located, which is the economic and political heart of the country. As described in Chapter 3, this was the site of heavy investments in mass schooling in the colonial period. By contrast, the majority of Muslims in Nigeria today live in the north of the country, and the majority of Muslims in Malawi live in the southeastern corner, neither of which experienced significant investments in education during the colonial period.

There are benefits and drawbacks to focusing on former British territories instead of comparing across colonial powers. On the one hand, colonial strategies, engagement with missionaries, and educational policy differed in important ways across colonial powers. In this sense,

1 The Puzzle of Persistent Inequality

examining only British cases provides an incomplete picture of colonial rule and how it impacted long-term outcomes. On the other hand, some of the greatest variation in the Muslim–Christian schooling gap is observed *within* former British colonies, with Nigeria and Uganda being important cases in point. This is due in large part to the fact that it is within British territories that investments in mass schooling were highest – by Christian missionaries – and thus the upper bound for Christian levels of schooling was significantly higher than in French cases, on average. Access to school was simply much greater in British colonial than French colonial territories, and was particularly low in French West Africa, which was home to the largest Muslim populations in colonial Africa south of the Sahara. Although I focus primarily on former British territories in developing and testing the argument, I discuss cases from elsewhere in Africa in Chapter 7.

In Chapter 2, I develop the theoretical argument about the role of norms in allowing differences in schooling rates across communities to persist. I draw on work in education, psychology, sociology, political science, and economics to explain how and when social influence matters for educational outcomes, and why religious groups and organizations may be particularly important for explaining variation in provision of and norms about schooling.

Chapter 3 then examines the colonial origins of schooling norms in Africa, and particularly how precolonial religious demographics shaped colonial-era institutions and investments in mass schooling. I conduct a comparative historical analysis of the Kingdom of Buganda and the Nigerian Emirates to show how Europeans treated areas governed by Islamic political institutions compared to those that were not, with long-term implications for Muslim schooling, as well as how religious demographics affected schooling investments and the emergence of schooling norms in Malawi.

In Chapter 4 I then select a case – Malawi – that allows me to more cleanly identify causal mechanisms of persistence. Within Malawi, as in the broader set of African countries, the Muslim–Christian schooling gap is largest and Muslim schooling lowest where Muslims comprise a majority. I discuss a set of economic, institutional, and religious explanations that have been proposed to explain divergence in schooling, and use evidence from administrative and survey data to show that these explanations are insufficient to explain the persistent gap in Malawi and elsewhere in Africa. Contemporary interviews with Muslims who grew up during the colonial period also show widespread concern that attending mission schools would lead to conversion, and the active discouragement of school attendance by parents and religious leaders.

Chapter 5 follows the case of Malawi to develop the argument that the strength of social norms about the appropriateness of school attendance differs across religious communities, and that social norms play a central role in reproducing the Muslim–Christian schooling gap. This chapter presents findings from interviews and participant observation with over a hundred parents, teachers, and village and religious leaders. These interviews point to the important role of beliefs and expectations in shaping both children's and parents' decisions about whether and how long to attend school. They demonstrate that in Muslim areas, although fear of conversion is now rare, persistence in school is not expected, and that instead young adults tend to aspire to start families and begin life as an adult member of their communities. The benefits either socially or economically of completing primary school are not clear, and completion of secondary school is almost never observed. Importantly, norms in Muslim areas are not oppositional to school in the way that they were during the colonial period, but they are not as strong as norms about schooling in Christian communities. In this chapter I also use evidence from the case of Mfano, a village I followed over several years, to show how school quality in Muslim areas is hampered by weak oversight by local institutions such as school management committees and parent–teacher associations.

To examine beliefs about school attendance empirically, I conduct a survey and a set of coordination games in twenty villages in Malawi, half majority Muslim and half majority Christian. The findings, presented in Chapter 6, show that there are indeed differences in beliefs about what constitutes an appropriate level of schooling between Christians and Muslims, and that expectations about the imperative of attending and completing primary and especially secondary school are lowest among Muslims who live in predominantly Muslim areas. I use survey data from Nigeria and Uganda to provide suggestive evidence that cultural beliefs about schooling also vary across religious communities beyond Malawi.

Chapter 7 examines the argument and implications beyond the three main cases presented in the book. I show that, despite some differences in colonial policy, patterns of schooling in British and French territories look quite similar, and short case studies of Senegal and Rwanda show that in both French and Belgian colonies, with large and small Muslim populations, respectively, the dynamics outlined with respect to precolonial religious demographics shaping colonial investments and long-term outcomes holds beyond the British cases of Malawi, Nigeria, and Uganda.

Chapter 8 concludes by reflecting on the implications of the findings and argument presented in the book. I discuss strategies for norm change, including the potential roles played by policy, media campaigns, and local leaders, while also raising the possibility that efforts like these do not always change norms in the expected directions. I also examine the implications of the Muslim–Christian schooling gap on other outcomes of interest, namely income and political participation. I show that while the relationship between education and these outcomes is not clear-cut, there are several avenues for future research that would be fruitful to pursue. Finally, I conclude with a reflection on how we might strengthen education systems and content going forward in a way that will better suit the needs of those growing up in a fast-changing world.

2

Schooling as a Norm

Humans are highly social creatures, and we are acutely attuned to how we are perceived by others. When we consider what to wear, what to say, and how to behave, we consciously and unconsciously[1] incorporate into our decision-making beliefs about what others will do and what they will think. These two types of beliefs, about what people do *in practice* and what they think *should* be done, comprise norms.[2] Norms matter for such varied behaviors as intimate partner violence,[3] proenvironmental behaviors like recycling and energy consumption,[4] voting,[5] and health behaviors like masking or alcohol consumption.[6] In this chapter, I argue that norms also matter for schooling behavior, and explain why norms about schooling might vary across groups and contribute to the persistence of attainment and achievement gaps. In doing so, I develop a cultural explanation for the persistence of educational inequality.

SOCIAL BASES OF SCHOOLING DECISIONS

I begin by examining the social bases of schooling decisions and schooling as a behavior for which culture might matter. For some readers, such a connection will feel intuitive. Others may remain skeptical or

---

[1] Sherif (1936)
[2] Gelfand, Gavrilets, and Nunn (2024)
[3] Boyer et al. (2022)
[4] Farrow, Grolleau, and Ibanez (2017), Allcott (2011)
[5] Gerber and Rogers (2009), Gerber, Green, and Larimer (2008), Hansen and Tyner (2021), Rosenzweig (2019)
[6] Carey et al. (2023)

even suspicious about the idea that culture matters for schooling. This suspicion is entirely warranted given the way cultural arguments can and have been deployed to create the illusion of fundamental difference where none exists, or to downplay or ignore factors far outside the control of any given individual (race-based segregation in schools, for instance). I too am afraid of a cultural argument being wielded in such a fashion. However, this does not mean we should ignore social influences on schooling behavior.[7] I will attempt to thread the needle in a way that demonstrates how culture matters for schooling, but also show how culture interacts with other structural, institutional, or economic factors which may, in many instances, be first-order considerations for rectifying inequality.

What are the social bases of schooling decisions, which groups or communities matter for schooling decisions, and what are the origins of differences in schooling norms across groups? These are the questions I take up next. I begin with a discussion of two of the most widely studied forms of social influence: peer and neighborhood effects. Existing research provides substantial evidence of peer and neighborhood effects on educational outcomes, but these effects are often heterogeneous. Although much work on this topic has been conducted in the United States, a common finding is that peer effects are stronger among members of minority or marginalized groups.

Peer Effects in Education
Perhaps the most obvious influence on the behavior of youth is other youth. Peer influence, or peer effects, are probably the most common type of social influence that has been studied to explain educational attainment and achievement. Evidence from both high and low income settings suggests peers can have a substantial effect on educational attainment and achievement. However, peer effects may be stronger in some subgroups than others, for example by race, gender, or level of ability.[8]

The 1966 Coleman Report[9] was among the most influential early studies on peer effects and the role they might have in perpetuating educational inequality. The goal was to determine whether – despite the US Supreme Court's ruling in *Brown vs. the Board of Education* that *de jure*

---

[7] Indeed, there has been increasing interest in understanding how social interactions matter for economic outcomes of interest, see for example, Manski (2000).
[8] Sacerdote (2014)
[9] So named for its author, sociologist James Coleman.

racial segregation in schools was unconstitutional – *de facto* segregation was preventing public schools from offering equal educational opportunities, and to determine the relationship between the school environment and student achievement. Coleman and his team found that racial and ethnic segregation in public schools remained high even after *Brown vs. the Board of Education*.

The Coleman Report also suggested that the composition of the student body was particularly consequential for the achievement of minority students. In particular, the performance of minority students was affected to a greater extent by the quality of schools and teachers than was that of white students. Further, they noted that achievement was "strongly related to the educational backgrounds and aspirations of other students in the school," but that these peer effects were stronger – for better or for worse – among minority students than white students.[10]

Scholars have critiqued the methods used in the Coleman Report, but the underlying ideas have remained highly influential in the study of racial inequality in the United States. These insights are that: Peers matter for schooling outcomes, the effect of peers may matter for some students and in some environments than others, and peer effects combined with segregation may in part explain the persistence of inequality of educational attainment and achievement across groups. An enormous body of work has since developed to examine the extent to which peers matter for educational attainment and achievement, among other behaviors.[11]

Although the idea that peers influence one another's behavior is intuitive, peer effects are difficult to measure because of the problem of sorting.[12] In the case of peer effects in education, children are usually not randomly assigned to schools or classrooms, and classmates may have similar achievement levels for reasons other than peer effects.[13]

---

[10] Coleman et al. (1966, p. 22)
[11] For a review of peer effects in education, see Sacerdote (2011). Other examples of behaviors for which peer effects are studied include risky behaviors like alcohol consumption (Kremer and Levy 2008) and smoking (Nakajima 2007), energy consumption (Wolske, Gillingham, and Schultz 2020), and eating and activity habits (Salvy et al. 2012).
[12] For reviews discussing methodological concerns in estimating peer effects, see Sacerdote (2014), Bramoullé, Djebbari, and Fortin (2020), and Angrist (2014).
[13] For example, low income families will likely live in low income neighborhoods, and find it difficult to move into rich neighborhoods. Similarly, wealthy families will rarely elect to live in a low income neighborhood or in an area with low quality schools. If school quality drops or there is an influx of low income children, wealthier families often move or send their children to private schools that are inaccessible to poorer families. Within neighborhoods there are likely to be a number of outcomes that are correlated

Nevertheless, recent work which attempts to address the empirical challenges in estimating peer effects validates several of the original findings in the Coleman Report. Peers matter, but not equally for everyone. For example, Imberman, Kugler, and Sacerdote (2012) find that the influx of evacuees into Louisiana and Texas following Hurricane Katrina did not affect incumbent students (children who already attended schools in these places) on average, but find evidence of nonlinear and monotonic peer effects – an influx of high achieving evacuees increased incumbent test scores while an influx of low achieving evacuees decreased scores. They also find negative effects of peers on attendance were especially large for Black students.

Using data on student achievement from Texas, Hoxby (2000) finds that the percentage of a classroom that is Black is more strongly correlated with the performance of Black than white (or Hispanic) students. Hanushek and Rivkin (2009) further find that the proportion of Black students in a school is predictive of larger Black–white achievement gaps, and that Black students with initially high levels of achievement seem to be most disadvantaged. These findings underscore the idea that peers do not necessarily affect one another equally, and that peer effects may be stronger among the minority group (which, in these examples, is also a marginalized group).

Neighborhood Effects and Persistent Inequality

Peer effects are also thought to matter within neighborhoods, and are often a central component of the study of neighborhood effects. Neighborhoods have been linked to socioeconomic outcomes such as poverty and educational achievement,[14] and an underlying goal of many studies is to understand why poverty and inequality across neighborhoods tend to persist. Neighborhood effects can include, but need not only operate through, peer effects among residents within neighborhoods. Neighborhood effects can also operate through differences in resources across neighborhoods, which can be a result of local financing of public goods and social services.[15]

– household income, parental education, student achievement – in a way that makes it difficult to assess what is the independent effect of high (low) performing peers on student performance.

[14] Sampson, Morenoff, and Gannon-Rowley (2002), Jencks et al. (1990), Sharkey and Faber (2014)

[15] Durlauf (2004)

Neighborhood factors have long been thought to affect or perpetuate inequality, with a central idea being that intergenerational mobility varies across neighborhoods, and in particular that concentrated poverty tends to reproduce itself.[16] Recent empirical evidence from the United States has indeed found that there are a set of neighborhood-level correlates of intergenerational mobility, including residential racial and income segregation, income inequality, the quality of primary schools, social capital, and family stability.[17] These suggest that intergenerational mobility is not merely a function of the behavior of individuals or families but rather a product of communities or local environments, and that these place-based factors operate primarily through their impact on children who grow up on these environments rather than on labor market opportunities for adults.[18]

Like peer effects, neighborhood effects have been difficult to nail down empirically due to selection bias, the challenge of nonrandom assignment of individuals and families to neighborhoods. Nevertheless, the small but growing number of studies with convincing causal identification of neighborhood effects – conducted almost exclusively in North America and Europe – collectively suggest that neighborhoods have a particularly large influence on the long-term outcomes of children rather than adults.[19]

Like the study of peer effects, these studies sometimes find that the effect of neighborhoods varies across subgroups, and in particular – at least in the case of the United States – by race, and sometimes gender. For example, in the USA, Black men experience lower levels of intergenerational mobility than Black women or than white men, even when they grow up in the same neighborhoods, and even after controlling for parental income.[20] Further, the childhood exposure effects of neighborhoods also seem to be race specific. Chetty et al. (2020) find that Black boys who move to better neighborhoods have higher incomes and lower rates of incarceration, but that the outcomes of Black boys are predicted by the performance of Black rather than white residents of their neighborhoods.

While the majority of research on peer effects in education has been conducted in high income countries, both experimental and observational work from low and middle income countries suggest that peers, and the

---

[16] For early descriptive work on this idea, see Wilson (2012) and Jencks et al. (1990).
[17] Chetty et al. (2014)
[18] Chetty and Hendren (2018)
[19] Chetty and Hendren (2018), Chetty, Hendren, and Katz (2016), Chyn and Katz (2021)
[20] Chetty et al. (2020)

social environment more broadly, also matter for schooling decisions in these contexts.[21] For example, a large educational subsidy program in Mexico which provided cash grants to mothers in poor households, PROGRESA, led not only to an increase in school attendance of those who received the cash transfer but also to an increase in the attendance of their peers. The overall effect of the program on schooling in the villages in which it was introduced – to those who received cash and to those who did not – was not only directly, through the transfers, but also indirectly through social interactions. In fact, Lalive and Cattaneo (2009) find that the effect of social interactions on school attendance is almost as large as the direct effect of the cash transfer. Bobonis and Finan (2009) further find the peer effects on children ineligible for the program were largest among relatively poorer households, once again underscoring the idea that peer effects matter differentially across subgroups.

Together, this body of work provides strong evidence that children and adolescents have a causal effect on the schooling decisions and outcomes of their peers, and that these effects are often concentrated or accentuated among marginalized groups. The cultural theory of persistence in educational inequality I develop here builds on this existing body of work on social influence and peer effects, research which has primarily been conducted within the domains of economics and education, and ties it to work in sociology, psychology, and political science that examines the role of norms, which are one of the hypothesized channels through which social influence operates.

Because peer effects can be broadly defined as any type of externality that arises as a function of peers' background, outcomes, or behavior, there is a large list of potential mechanisms through which they might operate.[22] These mechanisms include quality of the school or teacher, which is a function of monitoring, effort, or student abilities; direct learning from or competition with peers; and perceptions (norms) about what constitute acceptable behavior. For example, Bursztyn and Jensen (2015) find that students' performance is responsive to perceived norms, which are group or class specific. They find that signup rates for free SAT preparatory classes increased in honors classes when students knew the signup would be made public, while it decreased in nonhonors courses. The differential signup rates are explained by differences in norms about effort and performance in honors and nonhonors classes.

[21] Kremer and Holla (2009), Hoff and Stiglitz (2016)
[22] Sacerdote (2011, p. 250)

The goal here is not to suggest that one mechanism will always matter the most, nor that social influence generally matters more than other factors in explaining schooling outcomes, or differences therein across groups. Rather, building on existing work, as well as extensive fieldwork in the context of southeastern Malawi, I argue that perceptions of schooling behavior and expectations about persistence in school – schooling norms – can vary across groups, and can play a role in explaining group-level differences in schooling outcomes. Specifically, I suggest that norms can develop and persist within groups about the level of school that is considered appropriate for group members to attain.

Feedback Loops Reinforce Inequality

Norms and individual-level beliefs do not operate in isolation but rather in tandem with economic and institutional factors which we know also matter for educational attainment.[23] To understand how, consider two communities, one in which most children attend school through the end of primary school, and one where most children do not. In the first community, a parent will observe that most children are in school (an empirical belief) and likely infer that most parents think that children *should* be sent to school (a normative belief). She will be motivated to keep her child in school at least in part by social considerations – she will want to fit in, not be one of the few parents whose children are out of school.[24] In this community she is also likely to personally know children who have completed school and gone on to have successful careers in formal employment. The child's behavior is also guided by social considerations. If most of his playmates are in school during the day, school becomes a more attractive place to spend time than home.

In the second community, the parent observes that most children stop school after a few years and will likely infer that other parents aren't too bothered about this outcome. Though she may think attending school is a good thing to do, it will not be unusual if her child stops attending, and she will not feel out of place if this occurs. The child too will be less motivated to go to class if many or even most of his friends have stopped attending. There will be few examples of those who have completed school and have used this education to secure a well-paying job.

---

[23] Glewwe and Muralidharan (2016)
[24] Cialdini and Goldstein (2004)

Parents in the first community will want to see their child's school thrive and invest resources in contributing to its success. They are also likely to have attended school themselves and be familiar with how schools are managed. Since they expect the child to be in school for up to seven years, investing time and energy in the school and teachers will seem like a good use of resources. Parents may talk to the teachers to see how the child is doing, or volunteer for school projects and committees. If a teacher is routinely absent, parents may seek out the head teacher or talk to a local leader to figure out how to solve the problem of absenteeism. All of these actions will improve the quality of the school as well as make it more likely that the child finishes each year successfully. As a group, parents in this community may work together to contribute and raise funds to continue supporting and developing the school. The teachers will feel valued and supported, and may therefore put in more effort, increasing the probability of student success.

Parents in the second community are less likely to do any of these things. First, these schools are institutions with which parents have little if any experience, as many will have never been to school themselves. Second, if parents do not expect their children to stay in the school for long, the benefits to their own family of investing time and resources in the school are few. Investments in the school are a classic collective action problem that is made more difficult by the expectation that any benefits from contributions are likely to be short-lived, useful only until a child stops attending. These parents will thus have few incentives to participate in activities that contribute to school quality, such as serving on a school committee or contributing labor or resources to school construction projects.

Parents in the second community may be less able or willing to help children with homework, both because they are less likely to have had this kind of education themselves, but also because they do not expect the child will stay in school. A lack of parental support will also make it less likely that the child successfully completes each grade, which further discourage both the child and parents. Teachers may become frustrated with the apparent disinterest of parents, and face few repercussions for coming late or not at all.

These two communities demonstrate feedback loops in which norms play an important role. In the first community there is a positive feedback loop, where high empirical and normative expectations about school attendance combined with higher levels of parental education drive children's school attendance, parental involvement, and the quality of schools and school management. These all make schools more likely to function well, which makes school more attractive for children and parents, which makes children more likely to perform well, which makes them more likely to persist in school.

In the second community, low empirical and normative expectations about school attendance combined with low parental education lead to lower levels of investment in children's schooling and in schools themselves, which leads to poor management and worse quality schools. Low school quality further discourages attendance, and children's poor performance is frustrating for children, parents, and teachers.

Norms are an important factor in this feedback loop because they influence parental enforcement of children's schooling, children's own incentives to attend, and community participation in school management and development. Norms about schooling are likely to matter more for behavior when top-down enforcement, for example by a government, is not present or not credible. While schooling is compulsory on paper in many countries, governments' ability to enforce schooling is often weak, particularly in low income settings. In cases where enforcement of school attendance is high at the primary level, norms may kick in at higher levels, for example the completion of secondary (high) school or the pursuit of tertiary education.

This argument does not imply that communities with relatively weak schooling norms necessarily have norms that are oppositional to this form of education. Neither does it imply that these communities are low in social capital or generally dysfunctional. Rather, communities with weak norms about mass schooling are likely to have strong norms about other behaviors and expectations in childhood and adolescence. These include other forms of education, or other behaviors from which community members derive social status.

When Do Norms Matter for Schooling?

Where and under what conditions are norms likely to matter for schooling behavior? First, for norms to matter, opportunities for basic schooling must be available. As administrative and survey evidence suggest, primary school is generally physically accessible[25] and policies of free primary education are in place almost everywhere in Africa today. In the few

---

[25] For example, in recent Afrobarometer surveys, around 90 percent of survey clusters had a school in the enumeration area.

contexts where access is still lacking – if there are no schools nearby or if school is prohibitively expensive – norms are unlikely to matter for schooling behavior.[26]

Second, norms are likely to matter more when the ability of the state to enforce school attendance is weak. Top-down enforcement of rules often renders norms less useful, and the introduction of external enforcement can even crowd out norms.[27] Norms do not necessarily substitute for external enforcement, and vice versa, but they are more likely to matter in its absence.

Norms may also matter more where there are competing demands for children's time, particularly providing income or food for the family, and where the material or economic benefits of school attendance are less visible or more uncertain. These conditions tend to be more common in rural areas. Families living in rural areas, and especially the poor, are likely to experience higher opportunity costs to children's school attendance as their labor is frequently needed in food production.[28] In rural areas, there will also be few opportunities to see high levels of schooling put to use.

By contrast, inhabitants of urban settings will have regular opportunities to observe those with high levels of education, as well as the lifestyles that income from high-paying occupations affords. Not everyone who attains secondary, or even university, education will access high-paying jobs, and there will be steep competition for the few formal sector jobs available in relatively small economies. Still, the link between education and income will be more tangible for those residing in urban rather than rural areas, where jobs requiring high levels of education are scarce. The importance of social influence on schooling outcomes is likely to matter more in the absence of a visible link between schooling and income.

Religion and Schooling Norms

Which groups matter in the development and persistence of schooling norms? Recall that cultural groups are those sets of individuals within

---

[26] For example, in the context of Afghanistan, where a large percentage of families live more than 5 kilometers from a school, building new schools dramatically increased enrollment, particularly for girls (Burde and Linden 2013). Norms may still matter in this context, but if there are no schools nearby, building them is obviously the first-order priority for increasing schooling rates and reducing educational inequalities.
[27] Ostrom (2000)
[28] Basu (1999)

which there is a set of common expectations about behavior. The cultural groups that are relevant in the sphere of education are going to vary from place to place. In the USA, while not the focus of this book, race and ethnicity seem to be important groups within which peer effects operate, for historical reasons having to do with slavery and race-based discrimination in education and beyond. Geographically-based cultural groups are also probably going to matter (e.g. a village or neighborhood as being a cultural unit) inasmuch as there are shared educational resources within their boundaries.

However, while the cultural groups that matter for schooling behavior will vary across contexts, religious groups are particularly relevant for schooling behavior for three reasons: their stake in the content of education, their role in the provision of education, and their influence over families' schooling choices.

First, religious groups are important for understanding schooling behavior because of how important the *content* of education is to religious organizations. While religious organizations have been involved in a variety of forms of service delivery, including health (for better and for worse),[29] education is unique. Religious organizations – and the state[30] – care particularly about education because the content shapes what we know and believe. Schools are a place to instill and inculcate ideas and norms, and have historically been where conversion, religious teaching, and the production of religious leaders take place. They are the institution with which individuals have the most regular and sustained interaction, with the possible exception of the workplace. Education has been and continues to be a site of contestation between the state and religious organizations precisely due to differences in preferences over the content, with debates over the teaching of evolution and creationism in the USA being a contemporary case in point.[31]

Second, in part because the content of education is so important to the transmission of religious ideas, religious organizations have played a central role in the *provision* of education historically and in the present, and especially in the particular formulation of education that is mass schooling. Contemporary mass schooling has its roots in the education systems

---

[29] For example, while Calvi and Mantovanelli (2018) find a positive association between Protestant health missions and contemporary health outcomes in India, Cagé and Rueda (2020) find that proximity to Christian missionary settlements is positively associated with testing positive for HIV.
[30] Paglayan (2022, 2024).
[31] Berkman and Plutzer (2010).

of Christian churches in Europe, both Catholic and Protestant. Churches had the benefit of a hierarchical organizational structure that often covered the entire territory of a state, sometimes with greater moral authority and even administrative capacity than the state itself.[32] Although church–state relations varied (e.g. whether there was a state church),[33] churches nevertheless played a central role in the provision of education across Europe. Islam also played an important role in the provision of education, though often in a more decentralized fashion than Christian churches.[34]

Third, religious organizations shape the educational *choices* of their congregants, encouraging or even requiring them to attend particular types of schools or prohibiting them from attending others. For example, in the late nineteenth century, Catholic bishops in the United States, concerned with the content of state schooling, ordered every parish in the country to open their own Catholic school and encourage Catholic children to attend those and not state schools.[35] Some ultra-orthodox Jewish communities circumscribe the educational options of their members, reducing the amount of time on secular education and increasing the hours and years devoted to religious studies, particularly for men.[36]

Religious organizations and communities thus matter for schooling decisions, and can provide incentives or impose penalties for making choices at odds with their interests and preferences. This influence can range from mild (dis)encouragement on the one hand to excommunication from the religious community on the other. Forms of influence can include norms within a given religious community and formal rules about what constitutes acceptable behavior for group members.

---

[32] Grzymala-Busse (2015)
[33] Ansell (2010)
[34] As Quinn and Quinn (2003, p. 7) note, Islam in Africa is local: "There is no Islamic pope or curia, no ordained clergy, and no international body to regulate doctrine. Since there are no specific educational or doctrinal standards beyond adherence to the five basic tenants of Islam, there is considerable variety within the preaching and practices of individual mosques throughout the continent."
[35] West and Woessmann (2010)
[36] Berman (2000)

Religion and Education in Africa

> To all intents and purposes the school is the church... An appreciation of this fact is cardinal in all considerations of African education.
>
> A. Victor Murray, *The School in the Bush*, 1929

Religious groups may be especially important for understanding schooling behavior in Africa. While education policy varied in consequential ways across and within empire,[37] and changed over time, there was in no instance a colonial government in Africa that provided mass schooling – that is, schooling designed to be available to all inhabitants.[38] Colonial governments had neither the resources nor interest in providing mass schooling to all children residing in their territories. Mass schooling is an extraordinarily expensive undertaking, and one that can – and did – produce independent thinkers. To the extent that mass schooling existed in colonial Africa, it was entirely as a result of the interests of religious organizations. As a result, the roots of mass schooling today, both infrastructurally and conceptually, have their foundations in the schools established by Christian missionaries in the very recent past.[39]

A look at the numbers demonstrates the overwhelming dominance of missionaries in the education sector. By 1945, 96 percent of African students in British territories were attending mission schools.[40] This amounted to over three million children enrolled in African primary schools across 14 territories.[41] In the Belgian Congo, by 1938 there were more than 15,000 mission schools, about one-third of whom received government subsidies, compared to only seven state schools for African students (*écoles officieles pour noirs*). In Ruanda Urundi (Rwanda and Burundi), there were nearly 470,000 students in mission schools and just 1140 in state schools. Portuguese Africa looked similar, with over 900 Catholic schools and only 36 state schools in Mozambique by the 1950s.[42]

French West Africa departs from the trend in that there were more state schools than mission schools, and the work of missionaries far more limited than in other colonial territories, in part a function of postrevolutionary anticlericalism in France that restricted the work of the church both at home and abroad.[43] Still, by the late 1930s, nearly 20 percent of

---

[37] White (1996)
[38] Frankema (2012)
[39] Garnier and Schafer (2006, p. 154)
[40] Hastings (1994, p. 542)
[41] Hailey (1957, p. 1258)
[42] Cross (1987)
[43] Daughton (2006)

pupils in French West Africa were enrolled in mission schools.[44] In some territories, the ratio was significantly higher. In Togo, for example, about half of primary school pupils were enrolled in predominantly missionary "private" schools, and six out of the nine secondary schools were run by missions.[45] In the French Cameroons, by 1953 there were more than 113,000 pupils enrolled in mission schools compared to just under 43,000 in government schools.[46]

Moreover, the relatively greater reliance on state schools in French West Africa obscures the fact the overall level of schooling provided was low, especially compared to areas under British influence. Among the French territories, limited missionary schools meant there was nothing resembling mass schooling. By 1952, there were fewer pupils in all of French West Africa (108,788) than in Nyasaland (224,600), Kenya (363,288), Uganda (272,766), the Gold Coast (418,924), or Tanganyika (227,766). A 1947 survey found school attendance rates of only 5 percent in Soudan (Mali), 12.4 percent in Senegal, 3.4 percent in Niger, 1.3 percent in Guinea, 10 percent in Dahomey (Benin), and 3.7 in the Ivory Coast.[47] Government schools, whether British or French, were clearly not designed to provide mass schooling but were rather reserved to train the children of the elite or those being trained for positions in the colonial administration.

As the aforementioned figures make clear, for all intents and purposes, Christian missionaries were *the* providers of mass schooling in colonial Africa. As the epitaph of this section suggests, the school was the church, and vice versa. Of course, these broad-brush statements sweep across and pile together diverse colonial contexts and missionary efforts. How consequential were these differences? On the one hand, missionaries varied in their interests, doctrine, and strategy, and their schools varied in quality and content. Colonial policy with respect to both education and missionaries varied across empire, and differences were most notable in comparing British to French policy. On the other, the long-term effects of missionaries look relatively similar regardless of denomination, and, with a few exceptions, across colonial empires.[48]

The two channels of long-term missionary influence on education that I will highlight – investments (infrastructure) and ideas (culture) – are

---

[44] Hailey (1957, p. 1197)
[45] Hailey (1957, p. 1202)
[46] Hailey (1957, p. 1204)
[47] Thompson and Adloff (1957)
[48] An edited volume on missionaries in Africa similarly concluded, "In the long run, underlying similarities [across missions] outweighed eye-catching differences," Etherington (2012, p. 280).

relatively similar regardless of denomination or empire. While differences in policy and doctrine may have affected average levels of education among those who converted to Christianity as well as the number who converted, the Muslim–Christian gap emerged regardless of whether the mean years of schooling for Christians was one or six years. In fact, as Cogneau and Moradi (2014) find, differences across colonial territories – particularly French and British – are largest where missionaries were allowed to operate. Where missionaries were restricted, namely in Islamized areas, there were no differences in schooling levels across colonial powers. For these reasons, although it is useful to understand the sources of heterogeneity across colonial powers, which I discuss in brief shortly, the argument concerning how Christian missionaries shaped educational outcomes is a general one, and can be applied broadly across empire and denomination.

How did policies toward missionaries differ by colonizer? Compared to the French, the British allowed many more missionaries to operate in their territories, had less rigid policies with respect to education (for example, the language of instruction), and allowed both Catholic and Protestant missionaries, which led to competition between denominations. Catholic missionaries had a monopoly in colonies of the Belgians, Portuguese, and Spanish, limiting Protestant activity there. The French restricted both Catholics and Protestant missionaries, so their numbers tended to be fewer than in other colonial territories.[49] Missionaries also tended to expand their educational efforts most effectively where they held the same national identity as the colonial power in question.[50] For these reasons, Protestants were particularly successful in British colonial Africa. Conditional on access to a colonial territory, Protestants also spread relatively faster than Catholics. Their advantage may be due in part to the fact that training of Protestant missionaries often took significantly less time than for Catholics, whose clergy underwent many years of training and required an oath of celibacy. Protestants also had a numerical advantage due to differences in gender roles; Protestant women could generally play a more active role in missionary work than was the case for Catholics.[51]

A number of studies have investigated whether doctrinal differences between Christian denominations – particularly between Catholics and

[49] White (1996)
[50] Becker and Schmitt (2023)
[51] Hastings (1994)

Protestants–mattered for the content of education or target populations. Some argue that Protestants placed greater emphasis than Catholics on literacy of the masses, as this allowed congregants to read the Bible, and that Protestants had a greater focus on female education as a result of Martin Luther's emphasis on girls' (religious) schooling.[52] Indeed, in support of this idea, some evidence suggests Protestant missions in Africa had a greater effect on women's education than Catholic.[53] Moreover, Catholic missions seem to have had a larger impact on long-term educational outcomes in parts of Africa where they were in direct competition with Protestants.[54]

At the same time, records from within countries – sometimes down to colonial-era marriage records in Catholic and Anglican churches – suggest that the differences between Catholics and Protestants are not so clear-cut. In Uganda, there were actually larger gender gaps in the Protestant than Catholic Church.[55] Baten et al. (2021) find that the presence of missions in Africa is associated with lower gender inequality in education in the postcolonial period, but do not observe significant differences across missions. Wietzke (2023) argues, in a similar vein to my own, that external influences, namely local religious competition, rather than doctrinal positions, better explain variation in investments in education.

Moreover, regardless of the empire within which they operated, missionaries of all denominations were similar in that they infused much of the curriculum in their schools with Christian and proselytizing content, and implemented policies that were designed to convert children to Christianity, such as mandatory baptism, prayer, church attendance, and using a Christian name. The fusion between Christianity and mass schooling, and specifically proselytizing, is reflected in historical accounts, literature, and even African languages. For example, in Luganda, a language spoken in central Uganda, an early version of the verb "to read" – *kusoma* – could also mean "to pray," indicating the intimate relationship between the two activities.[56]

Understanding the goals and interests of missionaries is important to interpreting their long-term effects, but also in understanding how African populations responded to them. Christian missionaries in colonial Africa

---

[52] Becker and Woessmann (2008)
[53] Nunn (2014)
[54] Gallego (2010)
[55] De Haas and Frankema (2018)
[56] Hastings (1994)

and elsewhere have been viewed in recent academic literature as having positive effects on long-term development.[57] Their presence has even been presented as "a crucial catalyst initiating the development and spread of religious liberty ..."[58] despite the fact that their explicit goal was to rid indigenous peoples of their own beliefs and practices, a rather far cry from religious liberty.

The school was among the primary places where conversion, cultural rupture, and transmission of beliefs was achieved. While missionaries may have operated with what they considered the best of intentions, in all cases the goal was – through means ranging from cajoling to caning – to replace indigenous beliefs with Christian ones.[59] As Mackenzie (1993, p. 56) writes, "... the missionary educator was himself or herself a coloniser in the ontological sense of the term. He or she sought to usurp the spiritual beliefs of the non-believer, and to replace them with an alien (and alienating) religious value system."

Like the colonial replacement or reconfiguration of political institutions, cultural change was sometimes achieved, or at least attempted, violently. This phenomenon was not limited to Africa. The so-called "residential schools" in North America, many run by the Catholic Church, physically removed native children from their parents with the explicit goal of breaking ties with their communities.[60] These schools have recently come under increased scrutiny after mass graves were found at multiple sites.

In the words of Ako Adjeii, Ghana's first Minister of Foreign Affairs, "The establishment of Christian missions in Africa has been an act of spiritual aggression; they operated on the principle that everything African and indigenous is contrary, while everything European and foreign is acceptable, to the Will of God."[61] It should not be surprising then, that those wishing to keep their own religion refused to attend these schools.

The Emergence of Schooling Norms in Colonial Africa

Among those who did convert to Christianity, school attendance became an important part of religious life, and areas that converted to Christianity

---

[57] Cagé and Rueda (2013)
[58] Woodberry (2012)
[59] Etherington (2005)
[60] NCTR (2015)
[61] Adjei (1944, p. 189)

tended to develop strong norms about attending these schools. School attendance was seen as desirable, appropriate, and even imperative. In predominantly Muslim areas, there were fewer such schools, and Muslims specifically avoided attending schools associated with Christianity. In Muslim areas, therefore, norms about attending mass schooling were relatively weak or even oppositional to this new form of education. Where Muslims lived as a minority among Christians, there was greater competition with Christian missionaries, both to win over converts or maintain existing members, and to hold influence politically and economically. Where Christians operated and provided mass schooling, literacy and numeracy rates increased, and these skills became important to political and economic success in the colonial apparatus. Muslims responded with efforts to establish their own, parallel, schooling system, and developed relatively stronger norms about this new type of education than Muslims living as a majority.

Christians developed norms about the attendance of this type of school regardless of whether they lived as a majority or minority because of the central role these schools played in the process of conversion, and school attendance was an important part of what it meant to be a Christian. While not an exclusively or essentially "Christian" norm, once established through the early linkage of schooling and evangelism, Christians could maintain schooling norms even in contexts where they were a minority.

Recent empirical research has documented the persistence of many types of norms, and how individuals can carry norms with them. For example, Fisman and Miguel (2007) document the persistence of "corruption norms" among United Nations diplomats in New York City, demonstrating that diplomats from countries with high levels of corruption commit more parking violations. Nunn and Wantchekon (2011), in their examination of the long-term effects of the slave trade on interpersonal trust, find that "internal factors," such as norms, beliefs, and values, are at least if not more important as institutions for explaining this relationship. One of the ways they demonstrate the persistence of norms is to show that individuals from an ethnic group that was heavily impacted by the slave trade report lower levels of trust even when they have moved away from the affected ethnic homeland.

Similarly, schooling as a norm can spread within a community, persist across time, and, once inculcated, survive among a minority even when surrounded by those who have weaker or oppositional schooling norms. For example, Wantchekon, Klasnja, and Novta (2015) find that in Benin, descendants of those who were exposed to, but did not attend, missionary and colonial schools have higher levels of education than descendants of those who were not exposed to these schools. These spillovers are likely the result of peer effects driven by aspirations about school attendance, where those without schooling "emulate the educated." For example, one man reported that his father, who had never been to school but was exposed in his village to those who had, "insisted he make friends only with children who were attending school and stay away from the uneducated children."[62]

Indeed, accounts from Christian communities across Africa suggest that norms about school attendance, specifically, attendance of mission schools, were widespread by the 1940s in many African countries. This did not mean that all children went to school, but there was an expectation that one *should* go to school, if at all possible. Berman (1974) documents seven first-hand accounts of those who attended mission schools across Africa during the colonial period, all of which make clear that mission education was inextricably linked to proselytizing, and highlight the widespread norm of schooling among Christian communities. Bible studies were often the first subject of the day, existing traditional beliefs were denigrated, and every effort was made – sometimes violently – to turn African children into *Christian* African children. Efforts by missionaries to reweave the social fabric, of which norms are the binding thread, were intentional and widespread.

F. Yao Boateng, who grew up in Ashanti in the Gold Coast (Ghana) in the 1940s, noted that, "Attending a Christian institution and going to church on Sundays were considered very 'normal' things to do ... By this time attendance at school had become something everyone expected."[63] Boateng described schooling as the "four Rs" with the fourth being religion. Primary school included recitation of Biblical quotations, subjects such as Bible storytelling, prayers at the end of every school day, and children's church services on weekends.

In southeastern Nigeria, Vine Chukudi Izeogu also described a norm of schooling within the Christian – in this case, a Seventh Day Adventist (SDA) – community. "By the time I was born it was usual to send children to school ... All SDA children were expected to attend that school or another SDA school somewhere, no matter how far away it was and irrespective of the number and size of the other schools around."[64] Both

---

[62] Wantchekon, Klasnja, and Novta (2015, p. 743)
[63] Boateng (1974, p. 80)
[64] Izeogu (1974, p. 168)

Boateng and Izeogu use the language of expectations to describe mission schooling – for example, children were "expected to attend." Izeogu's account also demonstrates how competition between churches affected schooling behavior. When there were multiple Christian missions operating in the same geographic area, members of a particular denomination were expected to attend the school affiliated with their specific church.

An account by Aiah Abu in Sierra Leone demonstrates the social tensions, but also incentives, to send children to mission schools when there was significant missionary presence. Abu's uncle, a paramount chief, began to send some of his sons to mission schools out of fear that without this type of education the family would lose their political position. Abu was sent to a mission school, and recalls that Bible study was the first subject taught every morning. "It was soon obvious that the primary function of the school was to make Christians out of the boys, whatever their backgrounds or previous beliefs."[65] When his father asked him if Muslim prayers were allowed in the school, he recalled, "I told him this was impossible, that all students, even those from Muslim backgrounds, were to be trained in Christianity, and that this meant giving up all former beliefs, of whatever nature."[66]

The relationship between the missionary, the colonial state, and African communities is at the center of numerous works of African literature. Perhaps the most well-known English language work is *Things Fall Apart*, in which Chinua Achebe notes, "from the very beginning religion and education went hand in hand." Across the continent, Ngũgĩ wa Thiong'o writes of Njoroge, a young boy who is the first in his family to attend school in colonial Kenya: "… with his vision of an educated life in the future was blended a belief in the righteousness of God."[67] In fact, Achebe opens his own memoir describing his father as an early convert to Christianity and a man of books, who drank the "irresistible tonic of evangelism and education." The father of Wole Soyinka, another of the most famous African authors was an Anglican minister and headed a school in southwestern Nigeria.

But the tonic of evangelism and education was not in fact irresistible to all. In particular, the historical record is replete with accounts of Muslims avoiding these very same schools. For example, Malawi, Bone (1982) writes that Muslim parents feared "they would lose their children to

---

[65] Abu (1974, p. 105)
[66] Abu (1974, p. 109)
[67] *Weep Not, Child*, chapter 5.

Christianity and discouraged them from attending."⁶⁸ Lamba (1984, p. 185) adds, "... the insistence of missions on conversion to Christianity of pupils in their schools threatened the whole religious and social order of Muslims, something impossible for them to accept... Muslims for a long time saw western schools as brainwashing and deculturizing centers designed to estrange their children."

In Nigeria, Nasiru describes a series of discussions between colonial authorities and Muslim leaders in southern Nigeria in the late 1800s, suggesting that Muslims were not opposed to "Western" education but "they were opposed to its being delivered by non-Muslim teachers, who allegedly could not detach education from Christianity."⁶⁹ In Uganda, Kasozi notes that "Muslim parents were afraid of this kind of education because it exposed their children to Christian ideas and values and had the potential to lead to Christian conversion."⁷⁰

Similar concerns emerged among Muslim communities in French territories, even though the French relied less heavily on Christian missionaries. Thompson and Adloff (1957, p. 519) write of French West Africa:

> ... among the Muslim and tradition-bound elements, the chiefs feared the effect of an alien education upon the tribe's children, especially the girls. This was particularly true of the sahel and desert regions, where, even after the local administrator and his gourmiers had rounded up the children of school age, it was found almost impossible to keep them in school, and the education facilities available in those areas were never fully utilized.

Faced with mass schooling that amounted to religious conversion, Muslims had several options. One option was to continue the way of life and traditional forms of education that had existed prior to colonialism, which often included attendance of Qur'anic school. Why didn't these schools become part of the mass schooling project, and why aren't they considered mass schooling? First, Qur'anic schools in precolonial Africa were not universal. Rather, attendance was structured by factors such as class and gender.⁷¹ Boys were more likely to attend than girls, and those who progressed the farthest, becoming religious scholars and teachers, were almost exclusively men.

Second, while Islamic education varied across space and time, in most cases the content differed from that which we consider comprising

---

⁶⁸ Bone (1982, p. 136)
⁶⁹ Nasiru (1977, p. 96)
⁷⁰ Kasozi (1996, p. 102)
⁷¹ Launay (2016)

mass schooling. This is not just because Qur'anic schools were religious schools, that is, concerned with transmitting religious knowledge, values, and beliefs; so too were missionary schools. Rather, the form of mass schooling – the structuring of time in particular ways to mark progress across days, weeks, and years, a curriculum for which mastery is tested through examinations, and literacy as a means to manipulate rather than memorize words – all differed from classical Islamic education, at least in precolonial Africa.[72]

Part of the difference in the meaning and content of Qur'anic versus missionary (and, by extension, mass) education can be considered a doctrinal one. In Islam, the Qur'an – in Arabic – is considered the literal word of God. Memorization of the Qur'an is therefore important because any form of translation is at least partly a function of the interpretation of humans. For this reason, in classical pedagogy, at least in Africa, memorization sometimes took precedence over the meaning of words.[73] By contrast, missionaries, and particularly Protestants, went to great lengths to translate their religious text, the Bible, into local languages, and the exact organization and pronunciation of words was not important. Memorization was rarely the main emphasis of education, and certainly not memorization of the Bible in its entirety. Literacy, however, was a common goal. A focus on literacy over memorization was more similar to contemporary pedagogical approaches in that there is a greater flexibility in the teaching and use of language. The goal is not usually to reproduce a particular text, but rather discuss and interpret it.

Certainly Islamic education produced highly skilled individuals, and in fact in the early days of colonialism, before widespread missionary education, both explorers and colonial authorities relied on Muslims precisely because this was the population in which they found those who were literate and numerate.[74] Colonial administrators like Frederick Lugard viewed Islam and Muslim states as particularly advanced (and ripe for indirect rule) because of their systems of taxation and administrative capacity. Moreover, there is a very long history of Islamic scholarship in Africa, and particularly in West Africa and on the East African coast.[75] Nevertheless, the jobs available for those who attended Qur'anic schooling were few, both in the precolonial and colonial period. The goal of Qur'anic education was not to produce human capital to fuel colonial

---

[72] Launay (2016)
[73] Launay and Ware (2016, p. 256)
[74] Loimeier (2013, p. 268)
[75] Reichmuth (2000)

and postcolonial economies, and it was not competitive with missionary schooling in doing so.

A second option for Muslims was to attend missionary schools and try to resist conversion. It is impossible to assess the extent of this phenomenon, in part because attendance probably resulted in conversion to Christianity in many instances. We do know of isolated cases of conversion, often when these individuals rose to positions of prominence. For example, one of Uganda's former presidents, Yusuf Lule, was born into a Muslim family but converted to Christianity after attending Uganda's elite, and missionary-founded, education institutions.[76]

A third option for Muslims was to attend or establish a hybrid or parallel school system that mirrored the mass schooling of missionaries, but without the proselytizing content. Hybrid systems incorporated Islamic education into mass schooling, sometimes in government schools and sometimes in schools established and managed by Muslim organizations. Hybrid systems may have been more enticing than entirely secular government schools, and certainly more so than missionary schools, but came with their own challenges. As Launay (2016, p. 16) notes, "this hybridization was never on equal terms. The incorporation of religious instruction, indeed of Qur'anic instructors, came at the price of wholesale adoption of the *habitus* of the colonial school: schedules, curricula, textbooks, examinations, and of course the substitution of the blackboard for the writing board." Nevertheless, where these parallel schooling systems existed, including Yorubaland in southwestern Nigeria and in Uganda, Muslims acquired far higher levels of schooling than in places that relied on purely Qur'anic schooling.

What explains the strategies chosen by Muslim communities with respect to engagement in mass schooling? Although colonial rule took on many flavors both across and within empires, colonialism was a continent-wide shock,[77] one whose effects were heterogeneous, at least in part as a function of precolonial religious demographics. Those areas with less Muslim presence received relatively greater physical investments, a bricks-and-mortar channel, but also an influx of new cultural ideas, one of which was the imperative of a new form of education. These two inputs – investments and ideas – were mutually reinforcing, leading to positive feedback cycles that allowed those places with early stage inputs to take off with respect to levels of schooling.

---

[76] Mubangizi (2012)
[77] With the exception of Liberia and Ethiopia.

A large and growing literature has documented the effects of missionaries and colonial investments on long-term educational attainment, among other outcomes.[78] Thus, the contribution here is not so much to say that missionaries mattered for long-term trends in education, which is already well-documented, but rather to go beyond the bricks-and-mortar mechanism and even the handful of doctrinal mechanisms, and argue that missionaries also influenced long-term outcomes by inculcating new *ideas* about schooling. These new forms of schooling were, in the short-term, primarily a means to mass conversion, which explains why Muslims did not partake. The imperative of schooling among Christian communities generated new norms, a habitus in the parlance of Bourdieu (1977), of school attendance. These norms about schooling behavior would survive after the (at least partial) decoupling of religion and mass schooling in the postcolonial period.

Where Muslims were a majority, mass schooling was largely unavailable during the colonial period – government schools were few and designed only to train the elite and a small civil service, and mission schools were few or were banned altogether. In such an environment, norms about attending mass schooling did not develop, because school attendance was not a typical behavior; very few people attended colonial schools. The alternative to mass schooling, Qur'anic schooling, may have been available but was not universal, again prohibiting the development of a schooling norm that applied to the whole population. To the extent Muslims living as a majority were exposed to missionaries, they frowned upon their members attending these schools, whose obvious purpose was conversion. In such cases, it was possible for norms *against* this new form of schooling to emerge.

Where Muslims were a minority and surrounded by Christians, they feared conversion in mission schools, but social, economic, and political pressure to acquire the skills that were being taught in these schools, including literacy and, in some cases, fluency in colonial languages, led them to risk conversion or to establish their own schools. Further, the widespread availability of mission education allowed colonial authorities to set higher educational prerequisites for holding political power, and offered a way into power that was not based on one's lineage. Thus, political and religious competition with missions led Muslims to invest in their own mass schooling system. Where there were intensive investments

---

[78] For recent reviews see Rueda (2023) and Selhausen (2019).

in schooling by Christian missionaries, norms about schooling "spilled over" into Muslim households. As a result of both competition and norm spillover, norms about mass schooling among minority Muslim populations were more similar to those of the Christian communities that surrounded them than they were to norms in majority Muslim communities.

As the above discussion makes clear, the schooling norms that developed were not strictly along religious lines – in particular, it is not the case that Muslims *in general* exhibited norms against education of the type being provided by mission or government authorities. Rather, religious demographics, the degree of exposure to mass schooling, and the extent to which mass schooling was associated with Christianity explain the emergence of distinct norms across communities, and variation in norms among Muslims. Muslim political and religious leaders also played important roles in shaping the type of educational investments that communities made and encouraging or discouraging attendance of mass schooling, particularly as compared to Qur'anic schooling.

It is also important to note that it was not only Muslim communities that expressed reservations about mission schools, and even rejected them outright. The Masai of East Africa are an example of a group that rejected, and were also shielded from, mission schooling during the colonial period, though not on religious grounds, with similar long-term implications on educational attainment as many Muslim communities. Masai society was relatively ascriptive, with power transferred on a hereditary basis, and thus attending mission schools was unlikely to bring much additional prestige or political power. In an explicit contrast with Buganda, Tyler (1969, p. 151) writes:

> Even where missionary contact was permitted its influence was slight. Masai were able to translate little of what the missionaries had to offer into the values of their society. The achievement opportunities offered by schooling could only be accepted by contracting out of the Masai society. Few Masai were prepared to do this, or needed to.

Missionaries were not very successful in setting up schools among the Masai, in part because there were no obvious political or economic benefits to the Masai of attending these schools, and in part the result of colonial policy that stymied missionary efforts. The British wanted to relocate the Masai in order to construct the Uganda railway, among other colonial projects. As a result, they did not attempt to interfere greatly in Masai social or political organization,[79] which included sparing them missionary interference. Colonial authorities also did not provide financial support to missionaries in Masai areas, which further hampered missionaries' already floundering efforts.[80]

Thus, in the case of the Masai, there were few social benefits, and apparently considerable social costs, to attending missionary schools. Additionally, colonial authorities, as in the case of areas with Islamic political institutions, explicitly limited missionary work in Masai areas. For these reasons, which mirror the dynamics of Muslim majority areas, schooling norms were similarly weak. This may be one reason why the Masai today have significantly fewer years of education than the average Kenyan, even though many later did convert to Christianity.

This example serves to underscore the point that schooling beliefs are not inherently Christian, or inherently un-Islamic; neither is school attendance necessarily related to Christian or Muslim values. Rather, the production of distinct normative beliefs about this type of education is part of a historical process that shaped the distribution of investments and ideas about a new form of education – mass schooling.

As further support to the idea that schooling norms are not inherently tied to religion – if and when schooling was separated from Christianity, positive schooling norms – could be established among Muslims early on. In fact, it seems this did occur in some settings, for example German East Africa, where in Tanganyika (Tanzania) during the early colonial period the majority of schools were government schools, the product of a short-term stint of German colonial rule, which developed a system more closely resembling government sponsored, rather than missionary sponsored, mass schooling. In 1921, for example, there were 48 government schools and only one private (presumably, missionary) school in Tanganyika.[81]

The relatively weaker association between Christianity and mass schooling in colonial Tanganyika probably explains at least in part why Tanzania today is an outlier with respect to the Muslim–Christian schooling gap. Among African countries where at least 20 percent of the population is Muslim, Tanzania has by far the smallest Muslim–Christian gap in years of schooling, around a quarter of a year in the three postindependence cohorts. Cote d'Ivoire has similar sized Muslim population but an education gap of around three years. In countries like

---

[79] Mungeam (1970)
[80] Berman (1974, p. 27)
[81] Blue Book for Tanganyika, 1921, p. 54.

Cameroon (around 20 percent Muslim) and Nigeria (around 50 percent Muslim) the gap is greater than four years.

In the next chapter, I examine the historical origins of the Muslim–Christian schooling gap using two cases, the Kingdom of Buganda in Uganda and the Emirates of Northern Nigeria. I show how the extent of Islamization at the time of colonization affected the implementation of colonial rule and the distribution of investments in education, particularly by missionaries, with long-term implications for Muslim schooling.

3

The Colonial Origins of Inequality

When conjuring up images of colonial rule in Africa, it is tempting to resort to the conventional vision that imperial historian John Darwin has described as one "in which mustachioed titans in shorts impose their authority on resentful populations by sheer assertion of will ..."[1] Indeed, in photos of some of the most (in)famous British administrators in Africa, these mustaches, appended on visages sporting a look of confident defiance, are ubiquitous. Reading diary entries of some of these same individuals renders a similar imagination: white men in colonial outfit seated in tents, writing up their impressions of the chiefs, kings, sultans, and emirs whom they do or do not consider intelligent, conniving, or cooperative, until their hands begin to cramp or fever sets in, whichever comes first.

Caricatures of colonial rule, however, belie consequential differences in how Europeans imagined and treated African people and societies. In fact, it is in these diaries, and in correspondence with those seated at their desks back in London or Paris, that the diversity and happenstance of colonial strategy becomes apparent, as well as the role of administrators' personalities, worldviews, and experience, or lack thereof. Although colonial rule was a continent-wide shock, colonizers' perceptions of the peoples and lands they sought to dominate shaped the implementation of colonial rule, with long-term implications for political and economic development.

This chapter homes in on one such perception – that of the legitimacy of Islam and Islamic institutions as compared to indigenous religions and

---

[1] Darwin (2012, p. 189)

political institutions. This belief shaped the implementation of colonial rule, and the demand and supply of colonial education in particular. Practices and beliefs related to colonial and mission schooling would have long-term implications for patterns of schooling across the continent. I use the cases of the Kingdom of Buganda in Uganda and the Emirates of Northern Nigeria to show how the extent of Islamization in the precolonial period affected the implementation of colonial rule and the distribution of investments in education, setting Muslim communities on divergent paths with respect to long-term schooling norms and outcomes.

These cases show that Europeans treated areas in Africa with large Muslim populations, and particularly areas with Islamic political institutions, differently from those without. Europeans made fewer administrative and infrastructural investments in Muslim areas, particularly in education, and these areas were less exposed to, and faced little competition with, new religious ideas and new forms of education from Christian missionaries. Both the supply of colonial schools – whether government or missionary – and the demand for mass schooling were lower in areas with larger Muslim populations, and especially those with Islamic political institutions.

The Emirates are a case of consolidated precolonial Islamization, governed under a Caliphate employing Islamic law, and with a large Muslim population. Buganda is a case of partial conversion to Islam and incomplete Islamization of political institutions in the precolonial period. Conceptually, these serve as model-building cases[2] and can be thought of as standing in for a broader set of cases that vary with respect to the extent of Islamization by the start of the colonial period. Islamization refers both to the formal incorporation of Islam in political institutions and observance of Islam among the population. Colonial investments, missionary presence and schooling rates among Muslims were high in Buganda and low in the Emirates. Over time, the Muslim–Christian schooling gap closed in Buganda, but has persisted largely unchanged in the Emirates.

To help motivate the comparison, Figure 3.1 shows literacy rates over time across the two cases.[3] Among Baganda, literacy rates converge completely, such that the most recent cohorts show literacy rates of

---

[2] Lieberman (2005)
[3] Data for the Emirates come from the Demographic and Health Surveys, as the Nigerian census has not included data on religion since the early 1960s, and further, microdata is not available for the Nigerian census. The graphs show data for all individuals living within the current administrative boundaries of the following Nigerian states, lying within the boundaries of the historical Emirates: Sokoto, Kebbi, Zamfara, Niger, Katsina, Kaduna,

3 The Colonial Origins of Inequality 59

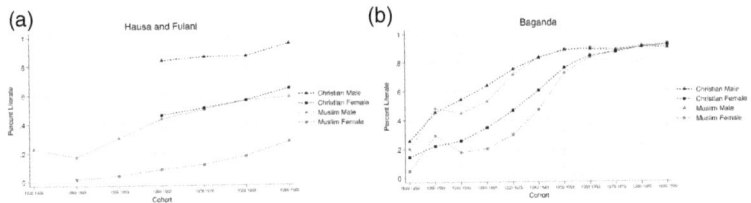

FIGURE 3.1 Literacy by religion in (a) the Nigerian Emirates and (b) Buganda.
Source: DHS and Uganda 2001 Census.

about 90 percent regardless of religion or gender. In Nigeria, there is a large gap that is essentially unchanged from 1960 onward. Among the cohort born in the 1990s, only one quarter of Muslim women and less than 60 percent of Muslim men are literate.

Overview of the Argument

I begin by presenting an overview of the historical processes linking precolonial religious demographics to schooling norms and behavior, starting with the initial spread of Islam on the continent. Islam arrived in sub-Saharan Africa as early as the eighth century, and spread relatively slowly in the millennium preceding colonial rule. Converting to Islam facilitated participation in the trans-Saharan trade, and trading opportunities were often greater among nascent states than among nomadic or less hierarchical societies. Local leaders were typically among the first to convert, at least in part because Islam was useful in terms of trade and skills, such as literacy and numeracy.[4] Muslim clerics were also useful in strengthening and legitimizing leaders' political power.[5]

For these reasons, Islam tended to be found in centralized states, and Islam itself was a centralizing force. The centuries prior to colonialism featured dozens of Islamic states, particularly in the Sahelian region of West Africa and coastal region of East Africa. Figure 3.2 is a map showing the set of Islamic states that existed in Africa between 1000 and 1900 CE, many of which were still in existence by the start of the colonial period.[6]

Kano, Jigawa, Gombe, and Bauchi. Sample is limited to Hausa/Fulani respondents in Nigeria, and Baganda respondents in Uganda.

[4] Austen (2010)
[5] Levtzion and Pouwels (2000, p. 4)
[6] These maps were constructed based on those provided in Sluglett and Currie (2015), maps 15, 33, 40, and 41.

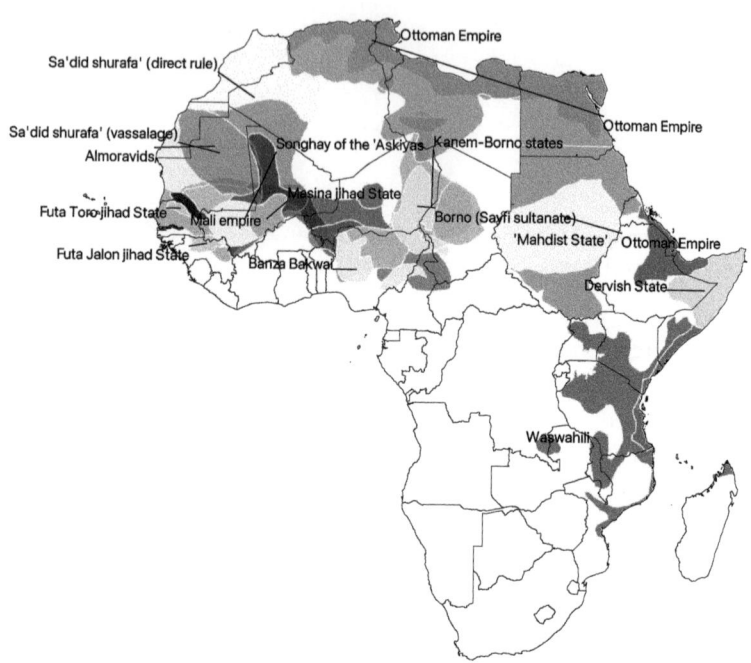

FIGURE 3.2 Islamic states 1000–1900 CE.
Source: Sluglett and Currie (2015).

Thus, when European colonizers began occupation in earnest towards the end of the nineteenth century, they faced a diverse religious landscape. By 1885, when the Berlin Conference carved up the African continent into its colonial pieces, the majority of Africans practiced indigenous religions and lived under indigenous institutions. A substantial minority, concentrated most heavily in North and West Africa and the East African coast, had converted to and adopted Islamic political and legal institutions. Only a very small minority, mostly surrounding coastal port cities and early missionary outposts, as well as the Horn of Africa, practiced some form of Christianity.[7]

These religions – Christianity, Islam, and indigenous religions – were not created equal in the mind of the European. While most colonial

---

[7] It is estimated that in 1900 three-quarters of the African population practiced indigenous religions, about 15 percent practiced Islam, and less than 10 percent practiced Christianity. Today, around 60 percent of the population of sub-Saharan Africa is Christian, and about 30 percent are Muslim, with only around 10 percent practicing indigenous religions (Pew Research Center 2010).

administrators would probably have preferred their subjects to be Christian than Muslim, the latter was considered a significant intellectual and spiritual step above indigenous religions. Loimeier (2013, p. 268) writes, for example: "In European evolutionist worldviews, Islam was seen as a religion almost as developed as Christianity ...", while Triaud (2000, p. 171) writes of French colonial thinking: "... on the scale of civilizations, Islam, because it had a written culture, was considered midway between barbarism and progress." Maps and correspondence from the colonial period documenting religious affiliation at the start of colonial rule typically describe everyone living outside Muslim regions of Africa as "heathens" or "pagans."[8]

As documented in their writings, many colonial administrators also believed political leaders endowed with Islamic religious authority held greater legitimacy in the eyes of their constituents. Louis Faidherbe, governor of Senegal from 1854 to 1861 and from 1863 to 1865, and responsible for much of the French expansion in West Africa, wrote: "... it is universally recognized that, with respect to social organization, the Muslim peoples of these regions are superior to the populations that have remained fetishistic."[9] Decades later, Frederick Lugard, with appointments in Uganda, Nigeria, and Hong Kong, wrote that the more "progressive communities" in Africa "adopted, and owed their advance to the adoption of, an alien monotheistic religion [Islam], which brought with it a written language and a foreign culture."[10]

The presence of Islam in the structures of political power colonizers found upon their arrival thus played a central role in how they conceived of local governance – they believed governance was better organized and control stronger in places where Islam had been established and became part of the political structure as compared to those places with indigenous African religions. Europeans were hesitant to uproot political institutions that they believed were legitimized by Islamic religious authority, both because they feared unrest but also because they perceived these institutions as particularly strong and therefore in need of little interference. Often, areas under Islamic governance also had well-established systems of Islamic education.

Europeans' beliefs and expectations about Islam and Islamic political institutions also played a role in determining where missionaries were

---

[8] See, for example, Bartholomew (1911).
[9] As quoted in Triaud (2000, p. 171)
[10] Lugard (1922, p. 76)

allowed to work, and thus where they set up schools. Although numerous factors affected the initial location and spread of missionaries, they tended to avoid, or were prohibited from working in, Muslim areas.[11] Missionary placement, and in particular the location of missionary schools, affected long-term education outcomes in Africa and elsewhere.[12] These long-term effects operated through several channels: access to educational infrastructure, schooling norms, religious competition, and access to political power. Most obviously, missionaries provided a supply of schools in the tens of thousands. No other entity provided mass schooling of this kind, and so areas with missionary investment had a huge head start, and one that would prove difficult for those with later access to surmount.

There were substantial economic and political benefits to the attendance of colonial schools, particularly for first-movers, who were able to access new kinds of employment in the colonial apparatus, and this new form of schooling became an increasingly desired good. The availability of this new form of education also allowed colonial authorities to require skills such as literacy as prerequisites for holding political power, and broadened the base of those who could enter the civil service and positions of political leadership, undermining hereditary succession and promoting meritocracy. Because this form of schooling was designed first and foremost to convert Africans to Christianity, attending missionary school was not only considered useful in a technical sense, but was also seen as a normatively good thing to do in communities that converted to Christianity. In newly Christian communities, this social expectation provided an additional rationale for school attendance beyond the economic and political benefits. For Muslims, however, missionary schools posed a threat that they either avoided or sought to emulate, depending on the extent of religious, economic, and political competition they faced from Christians.

Where religious groups were in competition with one another, providing services like education became important to the survival and growth of their communities, including their representation in positions of political power. Additionally, those who were able to enter positions of political power by virtue of the skills they had acquired through these new forms of schooling were able to determine who would have access to this education going forward. For all of these reasons, early

---

[11] Jedwab, Selhausen, and Moradi (2022)
[12] In Africa, see Cogneau and Moradi (2014), Nunn (2014), Gallego (2010), Selhausen (2019); in Turkey, see Amasyali (2022); in Latin America, see Valencia Caicedo (2019).

exposure to missionary schools provided a significant advantage in terms of educational attainment, and one that compounded over time.

While existing work has produced copious evidence of the long-term effects of missionaries on education, this work has tended to implicitly or explicitly focus on those who converted to Christianity. However, missionary work, or the lack thereof, also affected communities that did not convert to Christianity, including Muslims. Where they were exposed to competition with Christians – typically, where they were a minority – Muslim elites copied this new form of education, and built education systems that went beyond traditional Qur'anic schooling.

That mission and colonial schools came to be the dominant form of education does not imply that one form of education is necessarily superior or inferior to another. Rather, different forms of education allow those who acquire them to participate in distinct social, economic, or political activities. Colonialism altered the economic and political landscape such that the kind of education being provided by missionaries and in colonial government schools allowed attendees to be active participants in the colonial state, while forms of education that predated colonialism were less equipped (or perceived to be less equipped) to prepare students to do so.

Over time, it became clear that the political and economic system had been permanently altered and that there was no going back to the political institutions that governed life before the arrival of and occupation by Europeans. Colonial territories, combining what were previously distinct and autonomous societies, became nation-states with fixed borders. This dramatic political transformation was not obvious at the outset of the colonial period. But by the time the reality of new, permanent African states became apparent to all, those who had been exposed to colonial schools early on had a considerable head start. The distribution of initial investments in colonial schools, which was in part a function of the extent of precolonial Islamization, and the association between these schools and Christianity, served as a critical juncture in the demand and supply of schooling going forward. This is a case of path-dependence,[13] where early investments and ideas set in motion a sequence of events which became impossible to reverse, and ultimately led to a large gap in educational outcomes across religious groups, and across areas with Muslim majority and minority populations.

---

[13] Mahoney (2000)

The Cases

Buganda and the Emirates serve as a particularly useful comparison for understanding how the extent of precolonial Islamic influence shaped colonial rule, and ultimately the Muslim–Christian schooling gap, because they are otherwise similar on several dimensions. Both were colonized almost simultaneously and colonial governance heavily influenced by a particular administrator, Frederick Lugard, who has been referred to as the "father of indirect rule." Even though both Buganda and the Emirates were centralized,[14] hierarchical, and considered by the British as two of the most "advanced" societies in Africa, British administrators applied different strategies of colonial rule. Since key colonial administrators overlapped to a large extent, differences in colonial policy can be more easily attributed to how administrators perceived differences in the context between the two cases, rather than differences in the administrators themselves.[15]

The Emirates also provide a quasi-counterfactual for what Buganda might have looked like had complete conversion to Islam taken place. Islam arrived in West Africa centuries before its arrival in Buganda, and the Emirates had experienced widespread conversion to Islam by the time the first British envoys set foot in the area in the late nineteenth century. Islam was part and parcel of governance in the Sokoto Caliphate, with the power and legitimacy of political leaders derived in part from a religious basis of authority, and with the adoption and application of Islamic law and jurisprudence.

By contrast, Islam arrived in Buganda in the mid nineteenth century, just decades before the first Christian missionaries and European explorers reached the area. As a result, only partial conversion to Islam had taken place and no comprehensive Islamic basis for governance had been established upon the arrival of British colonizers.[16] While there are many geographic differences between the land on which the Emirates and the Buganda kingdom sit, both are sufficiently far inland that they are not particularly easily reached by outsiders. The fact that both are located quite far from the coast alleviates the concern that British colonizers or Christian missionaries treated these areas differently because one was

---

[14] Müller-Crepon (2020) finds that the British devolved more power to centralized polities.
[15] A list of key administrators and their overlap in these two territories can be found in Table A.12.
[16] Kasozi (1986)

easier to access than another. In fact, if anything, the Emirates should have been somewhat easier to reach due to its proximity to the Niger River, and is closer to the coast than Buganda. Given the trends in Islamization in Buganda in the second half of the nineteenth century, one could argue that if Islam had arrived earlier, or colonialism and missionaries had arrived later, the kingdom would have become an Islamized political system like the Emirates. In the next section, I discuss how the extent of Islamization at the time of colonization affected colonial governance.

Islamization Shapes Colonial Governance

Islam has a long history in what is now northern Nigeria,[17] and the political entity that the British encountered at the start of colonial rule – the Sokoto Caliphate – was a case of consolidated Islamic political institutions. The Caliphate had been established a few decades prior to British rule by scholar and priest, Usman Dan Fodio, who led an Islamic reform movement. The goal of this and other Islamic reform movements at the time was to transform existing Islamic states into a more pure form of Islamic governance.[18] The Caliphate consisted of a set of semiautonomous Emirates and was headed by the Sultan (initially, Dan Fodio) in Sokoto.

By the start of the colonial period, the population of the Sokoto Caliphate was predominantly Muslim, though Islam was not universal. Religious demographics for the precolonial period are not available, but the 1931 Nigerian census shows that Muslims comprised more than 90 percent of the population in the states of Sokoto and Kano, and a majority in Zaria, Bornu, and Bauchi. In the first two decades of colonial rule there were an estimated six million Muslims,[19] out of a population of just over ten million,[20] living in the Emirates. Most non-Muslims lived in the southernmost emirates.

By contrast, Islam arrived much later in the interior of East Africa, where Buganda lies. Arab traders had been present in East Africa since the

---

[17] The Kanem–Borno states, which existed from around the ninth century, were perhaps the first major Islamic political structure to govern parts of modern-day Nigeria, and the Hausa, the predominant group in the area today, were Islamized around the sixteenth century (Sluglett and Currie 2015).
[18] Levtzion and Pouwels (2000)
[19] Perham (1968, p. 497)
[20] Population estimate of the Northern Provinces from the 1926 Blue Book for the Colony and Protectorate of Nigeria.

eighth century, but Muslim trading towns remained almost exclusively on the coast. It was not until the nineteenth century that Arab and Swahili traders began traversing the interior in earnest, reaching Buganda around the mid 1840s or 1850s.[21] There they found the king, Kabaka Suuna II, in the midst of this 24-year reign. Accounts from the time suggest that there were Muslim members of the Suuna's court, and that while Muslim traders' main purpose was not to convert the king or his subjects to Islam, they nonetheless began to introduce new religious ideas and practices.[22] Trade and the spread of Islam began to pick up considerably under Suuna's son and successor, Mukabya Muteesa I. By the mid 1870s, Muteesa is reported to have required all his subjects to practice Islam, including prayer, fasting, and adhering to particular methods of animal slaughter, and even put to death non-Muslims.[23] "One could say that Buganda had then become an Islamic state," suggests Kasozi.[24]

While the penetration of Islam in Buganda, both in terms of precolonial conversion and as incorporated into political institutions, was more limited than in the Nigerian Emirates, scholars have noted that the arrival of Islam to Buganda was, out of all of the rest of East Africa, the most similar to the arrival of Islam to the Central and West African states.[25] Had more time passed between the arrival of Arab traders and the arrival of Christian missionaries and the British, it is conceivable that the Buganda kingdom would have also fully consolidated as an Islamic political system, and perhaps even expanded to the broader interlacustrine region.[26] As it happened, the arrival of Christian missionaries and British explorers and administrators brought the spread of Islam to a halt.

Within the first few years of the twentieth century, both Buganda and the Nigerian Emirates found themselves under the thumb of imperial rule. But while in both the British found centralized and hierarchical political systems, the implementation of indirect rule differed in degree across the two polities. First, the British interfered far more with political institutions in Buganda than in the Emirates, maintaining a more active

---

[21] Kasozi (1986)
[22] Kasozi (1986, pp. 18–19)
[23] Although it has been argued that Muteesa I did not fully convert to Islam, he nevertheless began observing certain Islamic practices and implementing aspects of Islamic law (Fisher 1977). He oversaw the construction of mosques, began the practice of circumcision, observed Ramadan, began slaughtering animals according to Islamic law, and required his chiefs and members of his court to read the Qur'an in Arabic (Kasozi 1986).
[24] Kasozi (1986, p. 29)
[25] Fisher (1977)
[26] Hastings (1994, p. 375)

role in leadership selection, and greater fiscal control. Emirs were granted greater political and financial autonomy than was the Kabaka in Buganda. Second, while in the Emirates the British maintained and strengthened hereditary rule, in Buganda they promoted a more meritocratic system in which literacy and not lineage took primacy. These different forms of colonial engagement had the effect of limiting access to and depressing demand for colonial schooling in the Emirates, while expanding access and fueling demand in Buganda. In Northern Nigeria, the British invested less in the administrative apparatus, built fewer schools, and granted greater fiscal autonomy to Emirs than they did in Buganda.

While there are several reasons for the divergence in the practice of indirect rule, I suggest that the extent of Islamization – both of the population but also of political institutions – was an important factor. Because the British considered Islam more legitimate than traditional African religions and viewed Islamic political institutions as ready-made for indirect rule, they made fewer institutional changes in political institutions in the Emirates as compared to Buganda and restricted the activities of missionaries.

In the emirates, British Residents "were told that their duty was to act as advisers to the emirs, not usurp their functions."[27] The disparity in the colonial footprint can be seen in comparing the ratio of Native Administrations to population, as shown in Figure 3.3. Although Northern Nigeria is similarly populated to Western and parts of Eastern Nigeria

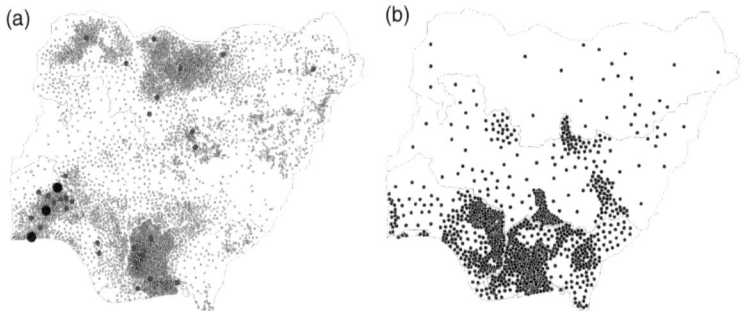

FIGURE 3.3 Native Administration and population in Nigeria in the mid colonial period. (a) Nigerian population, 1952 Census. Modifies from an original map by A. T. Grove with permission from his estate. (b) Native Administration, 1946–1947.
Source: Buchanan and Pugh (1955).

[27] Hailey (1951, p. 48)

(shown in panel (a)), there are far fewer Native Administrations (shown in panel (b)), demonstrating the extent of concentration of authority in the Emirs and the relative lack of administrative presence in the north.[28] Although the primary point of comparison in this section is with Buganda, it is clear that even within Nigeria there were dramatically different strategies of colonial rule. There was far greater British presence and interference in local institutions in the Southern as compared to the Northern Provinces, where the Emirates were located.[29]

In Buganda, by contrast, the political autonomy of the Kabaka was vastly diminished under colonial rule, and increasingly so over time. Further, unlike the Emirates, positions of political power below the king, such as the powerful county chiefs, were not hereditary, nor under control of the Kabaka as they had been in the past. These appointments were subject to approval by a representative of the Crown – in most cases, the Governor. A chief could be dismissed at any time if he was unable to fulfill his duties, including tax assessment and collection.

Thus, although the Kabaka was the most powerful traditional ruler in Buganda and arguably in the whole of the Uganda Protectorate, he could not override decisions regarding chieftaincy made by the colonial government.[30] This encroachment by the British on the authority of the Kabaka vis-à-vis his chiefs was not without friction. One observer at the time quoted a complaint from the kingdom to the Protectorate government which specifically noted the extent to which British colonial officers had taken over roles previously reserved for the Kabaka:

... the Provincial Commissioner in charge of Buganda appears to occupy the position which was intended for the Kabaka in the [1900] Agreement. The Provincial Commissioner is now the direct rule of the native chiefs of Buganda through his District Officers ... As a matter of fact, the direct and natural result of this practice has been that some of the more educated Chiefs of the young generation ... are now beginning to flout the authority of the Native Government of Buganda, and consider themselves more as Native Officers of the British Government to whom they are responsible for all their administrative duties ... [31]

[28] Maps recreated from Perham (1968).
[29] While the Igbo of the southeast were considered a decentralized group for which the creation of centralized authority might have been a relatively new institution, the Yoruba of the southwest were similarly centralized to Buganda or the Emirates, and also considered an "advanced" society by Lugard. The Yoruba, like Buganda, were only partially Islamized by the start of colonization.
[30] For example, archival evidence shows that the Governor made decisions regarding chief appointments and would not provide the Kabaka with a justification for his decision even when it was explicitly requested. C Series C.0836 II Buganda Native Government Appointments, p. 128., Entebbe Archives.
[31] Buell (1928, p. 577)

The conflict that began to emerge in this period would become much more severe, leading to the Kabaka's near deposition by the late 1930s.[32] This was averted only by his untimely death in 1939, likely not unrelated to the fact that throughout his time as Kabaka he was increasingly hemmed in by British authorities, and the earlier rights, privileges, and honors that came with his title all but eviscerated.

A second way in which the implementation of indirect rule was implemented differed in the Emirates as compared to Buganda concerned local revenue. Native Treasuries, held at the level of the province, provided emirs and other Native Authorities with sizable revenues, and at least some autonomy in their use. For example, in 1913, the Senior Clerk in the Nigeria Office, A. J. Harding, "Neither the Secretary of State nor the Governor has any legal or moral right to decide how the Emir of Kano or Sokoto spends his revenue. The resident and Governor may advise him how to do it and help him not to waste it – but it is the expenditure of his Government, not of theirs ..."[33] As this correspondence suggests, fiscal autonomy was greater in areas of more consolidated Islamic authority, a function of how the British perceived Islamic leadership and societies differently from others. The province of Sokoto, the seat of the Caliphate and of the nominal head of all the emirates, retained 75 percent of tax revenue, other Muslim emirates retained 50 percent, and "pagan" districts retained 25 percent.[34] Colonial records note that emirs had "considerable control over the preparation of Native Authority budgets," which amounted to up to nearly £1 million in the case of Kano Province.[35]

A third way in which the application of indirect rule differed between the Emirates and Buganda was in the promotion or undermining of hereditary bases of political authority. Political leaders in the Emirates were generally able to maintain hereditary rule, consolidating power within a set of ruling families. By contrast, in Buganda, the county and subcounty chiefs, as well as other administrative positions, could be accessed by those with skills in literacy and numeracy rather than being reserved for ruling families.

Not only did British rule preserve the authority of emirs, several contemporaries of the period suggested that under colonial rule emirs became

---

[32] Makubuya (2018, p. 86)
[33] Minute by Harding to Lugard on January 13, 1913, CO 446/107/39706, as cited in Carland (1985, p. 74)
[34] Carland (1985, p. 72)
[35] FCO 141-13367. 1952. Nigeria: Muslim Movements in Nigeria. Kew National Archives.

less accountable to the population than they had been before the arrival of the British.[36] Charles Lindsay Temple, who served as Resident in Sokoto, then as High Commissioner and Lieutenant Governor of the Northern Provinces, noted:

> The position of an Emir has, since the occupation, changed in one all-important feature. He is no longer subject to the influence of the public opinion of others of his kind, nor has he to trim his sails and to modify his actions accordingly. He is securely seated on his throne by a power operating from far and quite outside all local influence.[37]

Reflecting on this period, Lubeck (1986), a sociologist and scholar of Muslim societies and Nigeria in particular, similarly notes that the traditional checks on power that existed before colonialism disappeared under British rule, and that the political elite employed religion as a way to keep the British out of their affairs. Thus, the early British administrators of the Emirates not only maintained hereditary systems of political power, they also appear to have severed existing mechanisms of accountability between the ruling class and the masses. The evidence suggests that, if anything, British administrators delegated greater autonomy to the Emirs and Residents over time.

The cases of the Emirates and Buganda show that, despite having similarly centralized and hierarchical precolonial institutions, the practice of indirect rule was applied differently depending on the local context. As Low and Pratt note, "In the 1920s the tendency of the Northern Nigerian Administration to regard the Emirates as separate native states was a barrier there to the extension of central administrative controls. In contrast, in Uganda, though the constitutional status of the kingdom of Buganda was nearer to that of a native state than the Emirates, a different attitude towards the Native Government existed, and there was far less hesitancy to interfere."[38]

In the Emirates, where political institutions had an Islamic basis of authority, colonial officials insulated political elites, maintained a hereditary basis of leader selection, and were relatively uninvolved in the selection of political leaders during the colonial period. In Buganda, colonial officials were closely involved in the selection of political leaders, and increasingly so over time. The degree of competition for political

---

[36] Miller (1936, p. 63)
[37] Temple (1918, p. 67)
[38] Low and Pratt (1960, p. 303)

positions in Buganda, and the role of merit in selection, would increase elites' demand for colonial education, as well as its supply.

The Islamic basis of authority in the Emirates played an important role in the differential treatment of the Kabaka and the Emirs by the British. Low and Pratt make a similar comparison concerning Buganda and the Sultanate of Zanzibar. "The Sultan [of Zanzibar]," they wrote, "because of his Muslim and Middle Eastern connexions, was widely received as a genuine monarch, while the Kabaka tended, in contrast, to be treated as another tribal ruler."[39]

The Supply and Demand of Education in Buganda and the Emirates

The previous section demonstrated that the Emirates and Buganda experienced functionally distinct forms of indirect rule, even when governed by the same colonial administrators. In this section, I examine how the supply of colonial schooling, combined with the particular manifestation of indirect rule that they experienced, shaped demand for and norms about schooling, differentially so for Muslims living in Buganda and the Emirates.

The supply of colonial schooling was much greater in Buganda than the Emirates, primarily because Christian missionaries were allowed to operate in large numbers in the former, while their presence was restricted in Northern Nigeria. Muslims in Buganda therefore faced greater competition with Christians, not only for followers but also for political and economic power. The widespread availability of colonial schools and a relatively meritocratic civil service meant lower barriers to entry in the colonial state. This new form of schooling – increasingly a prerequisite for holding political office – quickly grew in demand. As elsewhere in Africa, Christians in Buganda had a head start, but Baganda Muslims responded by establishing their own schools, ultimately catching up to Christian schooling rates.

In the Emirates, the supply of colonial education was a fraction of that in Buganda despite having a much larger population. The colonial government established a small number of schools to train chiefs, but there were very few missionaries or missionary schools, and Muslims faced little to no competition with Christians either for converts or political power. The maintenance of the hereditary transfer of power and limited colonial schooling supply meant that, with few exceptions, only elites could access

[39] Low and Pratt (1960, p. 293)

this kind of school; it was not a pathway for the ordinary person to enter positions of political or economic power.

Unlike Buganda, Muslim leaders in the Emirates did not have strong incentives to provide mass schooling to their subjects. Limited colonial schooling strengthened their position vis-à-vis would-be political competitors, and there was already a large network of Qur'anic schools. Thousands of religious teachers and scholars had vested interests in maintaining the status quo. Colonial authorities were not keen to extend schooling to the masses either, as they believed doing so would disrupt social order. Overall rates of schooling among the – predominantly Muslim – population remained very low throughout the colonial period and up to the present.

Missionary Presence in Buganda and the Emirates

The first missionaries arrived in Buganda in the late 1870s, and by the early 1900s they had fanned out across the Protectorate. By 1914, there were 700 Anglican churches in Buganda, with an estimated 50,000 attendees. Catholics reported nearly twice that – 100,000 between their two mission bodies, the White Fathers and the Mill Hill Mission. The nearly simultaneous arrival of Islam, Catholicism, and Protestantism to Buganda, followed shortly thereafter by British colonialism, meant that the kingdom was split between the three factions.[40] It is remarkable how quickly conversion took place, and this was facilitated by the considerable missionary presence and in particular the establishment of hundreds of schools within a few decades.

Records from Blue Books, annual reports produced in each British territory, indicate that by the late 1920s nearly a quarter of all children in Buganda – approximately 50,000 – were attending school. There were more than 500 Anglican and more than 600 Catholic schools in a population of just under 800,000. Although there were relatively more boys than girls in school, this difference was not large – girls comprised about 40 percent of all students.[41]

---

[40] While Kabaka Chwa was Anglican, other members of the royal family were Catholic and Muslim. Of Buganda's twenty counties, Protestant chiefs headed ten, Catholic chiefs eight, and Muslim chiefs two.

[41] According to the 1926 Blue Book there were 554 Anglican primary schools, with over 15,000 boys and around 9,000 girls, with another nearly 7,000 adult pupils. In the 658 Catholics there were around 14,000 boys, 10,000 girls, and 900 adults. There were a further 118 nonmission schools, with approximately 1500 boys, 800 girls, and 1700 adults.

By contrast, missionaries had a minimal impact in Northern Nigeria, where missionary policy was influenced by colonizers' perceptions of how Muslims and Islamic authorities would respond to missionary presence, sometimes informed by earlier colonial encounters in Muslim areas.[42] In the Emirates, the British – and Lugard in particular – pledged to Muslim leaders that they would not interfere with religious practice. Missionaries were not completely barred in the Northern Provinces,[43] but the few granted access were not very successful in converting the population to Christianity.

The 1926 Blue Book for Nigeria indicates that the most successful mission in the Northern Provinces, the Church of England (CMS), had just over 120 churches and an estimated 10,500 followers. There were just under 27,000 followers across all the 25 mission bodies, and some missions reported only a single adherent.[44] Most mission stations were concentrated in the southernmost part of the Northern Provinces; there were almost none in provinces where Islam was strongest, like Sokoto.

The light missionary footprint had major implications for the supply of colonial schooling. Although the Northern Provinces had a population greater than ten times that of Buganda, they had a fraction of the number of schools and pupils. By the late 1920s, Buganda had seven times as many schools as the Northern Provinces, for a population one-twelfth of the size. Of the 185 schools in the Northern Provinces, about half were government schools, and the rest "Sundry Schools" (likely mission schools) which received no funding from the colonial government. In government schools there were a total of 3200 boys and just 11 girls.[45] In addition to these few colonial schools were over 30,000 Qur'anic schools with an estimated 390,000 pupils. Colonial records report that these Qur'anic schools, which constituted 99 percent of all schools in the Northern Provinces, were attended exclusively by boys.[46]

The comparison between Buganda and the Emirates is especially striking in comparing girls' schooling. A few decades into colonial rule, there

---

[42] Hastings (1994, p. 407)
[43] Though there is an oft-cited claim that missionaries were completely barred from the Emirates, Lugard himself made a point of stating that this was not quite the case, rather, "The Missions have always been at liberty to establish schools with the consent of the Emir." Comment by Lord Lugard in Murray (1935).
[44] Examples of these are the United Methodist Free Church, Church of Ireland, and Scottish Mission.
[45] In aided and unaided schools there were only slightly more pupils – about 3700 boys and 1000 girls.
[46] Colony and Protectorate of Nigeria Blue Books, 1926–1929.

were around 20,000 girls in school in Buganda compared to only 1000 in the Emirates. Of these 1000 girls, only 34 were in schools with government funding. Clearly, the few government schools in Northern Nigeria were not intended to provide schooling to the masses, and certainly not to girls. The British had neither the finances nor the interest to do so.

Figures from the Southern Provinces of Nigeria demonstrate that Nigeria as a whole was not treated differently than Buganda, but rather specifically the area under Islamic influence. In the Southern Provinces of Nigeria, where Islam had only partially penetrated by the start of colonial rule, there were 48 government schools, 208 aided missionary schools, and nearly 3000 "Other Private" schools, which, like the "Sundry Schools" in the north, were mostly likely unaided missionary schools. Across all of these there were nearly 150,000 students.[47] Although not as densely populated with schools as Buganda, the Southern Provinces of Nigeria demonstrate that the supply of schooling was much greater where missionaries were allowed to operate more freely.

Political Competition and the Demand for Schooling

The differential availability of colonial schooling in Buganda and the Emirates had implications for the skills expected of political leaders, as well as for who could aspire to positions of leadership. The widespread availability of missionary schools in Buganda allowed colonial authorities to set prerequisites for holding political office, and also to promote a meritocratic civil service instead of one based on lineage. Missionary schools, and the competition between religious bodies, not only changed the religious landscape of Buganda, but also the colonial-era political institutions.[48]

Colonial authorities in Buganda could refuse to appoint or approve the appointment of illiterate individuals, and they did. A quota system determined by the 1900 Uganda Agreement, which set the terms and conditions

---

[47] Figures from the 1926 Blue Book. In government schools there were about 9000 boys and 600 girls, in the aided schools 33,000 boys and 9000 girls, and in nonaided schools over 100,000 pupils. In the Northern Provinces, the category "Other Private" includes Qur'anic schools and so is not directly comparable with unaided schools in the south; no Qur'anic schools (called "Mohammedans") are recorded in the Southern Provinces. The total population of the Southern Provinces was close to 18.8 million.

[48] As Richards (1960, p. 68) notes, "The Buganda system of selection of chiefs cannot be described as democratic, but it has at least resulted in men of, relatively speaking, high education being drawn into the ranks of the Buganda Government service."

of colonial rule in Buganda, guaranteed the chieftainship of counties to be reserved for chieftainships for Protestants, Catholics, and Muslims, such that none was in danger of losing land and power altogether. However, it became increasingly clear that one needed to be able to read and write in order to hold political office. Further, the position of chief, whether at the county or lower level, was a career, rather than an office granted by virtue of one's birth or given out of loyalty to the king.[49]

A 1950 survey of chiefs in Buganda found that two-thirds of all chiefs – 80 percent of county chiefs and subcounty chiefs, and 32 percent of parish chiefs – had secondary or university education.[50] Moreover, most chiefs held administrative positions prior to their chieftaincy, indicating that chieftaincy was a promotion within the civil service. Ninety percent of county chiefs, 75 percent of subcounty chiefs, and more than 50 percent of parish chiefs held positions in the central government or African Local Government prior to their appointment. The rest had been previously employed in missions, European or Asian businesses, or self-employed as traders or businessmen.[51]

Acquiring colonial-style education became imperative for the elite in Buganda, regardless of religion. However, while Catholics and Anglicans had many government-recognized and aided schools at their disposal, Muslims initially did not. It did not take long for them to set up their own schools, however. This process was spearheaded by the Muslim elite, particularly members of the Muslim royal family in Buganda, and began with concerns over the education of a Muslim prince named Badru Kakungulu. Like other royals, it was expected that Kakungulu would attend colonial schools, yet his family rightfully feared that he would be converted to Christianity if he attended the elite missionary schools other royals attended. The imperative of colonial-style – but not missionary – education for Kakungulu prompted his guardian and the Buganda parliament, the *Lukiiko*, to establish a primary school in 1922 that specifically catered for the needs of children of prominent Muslim families. Though Kakungulu went on to attend missionary schools for his higher education, a foundation had been laid for Muslim schooling in Buganda and beyond.[52]

Muslim-founded schools established in the first half of the twentieth century, like the one established for Kakungulu, were supported by private

---

[49] Mair (1934, p. 198)
[50] Richards (1960)
[51] Richards (1960)
[52] Kasozi (1996)

funds and received no aid from the colonial government. This was because schools could only receive government funding if administered by an organization with financial institutions, and during the 1920s and 1930s, no such organization existed among the Muslim community. Instead, the Muslim elite established schools independently, the majority located in Buganda.[53] In the 1940s, however, Kakungulu, then the titular head of the Muslim community in Uganda, founded the Uganda Muslim Education Association (UMEA). This organization, still in existence up to the present, opened schools in Buganda and across the protectorate, and took over supervision of existing private schools owned by Muslim individuals and communities. In doing so, UMEA harmonized the decentralized efforts of Muslim individuals and communities to provide schooling for their members, centralizing their management, appointing head teachers, drafting syllabi, administering exams.[54] As a result of UMEA's efforts, by the early 1950s, there were more than fifty government-aided Muslim primary schools in the Uganda Protectorate, of which more than half were in Buganda and the Eastern Province.[55]

Census data suggest that rates of Muslim schooling in colonial Buganda were so high that it seems unlikely Muslim children attended only UMEA-managed schools, particularly since these efforts only got underway about a half century into colonial rule. Although relatively large in number, Muslim-founded schools probably do not fully explain the high levels of Muslim schooling in Buganda. It is likely that some Muslims attended mission schools despite their fear of conversion, underscoring how important they deemed this kind of education. Indeed, the county-level density of missionary schools is positively associated with Muslim education attainment during the colonial period.[56]

By contrast, in the Emirates, although Emirs had considerable resources at their disposal, there was no unified effort to provide mass schooling to the public, nor were Muslim civil society groups active in providing mass schooling.[57] Why didn't Muslim elites, whether political leaders

---

[53] By the early 1930s, there were ten private Muslim-founded primary schools, eight of which were in Buganda. Data from the 1933 Education Report of the Uganda Protectorate.
[54] Kasozi (1996, p. 113)
[55] 1951 Annual Report, Education Department Eastern Province. Minute Paper P/61/46, Jinja Archives.
[56] See Appendix A.4.
[57] Although at least one organization in Northern Nigeria was active in the education sector, the Northern Moslem Congress, the stated goals of this organization were the teaching of Arabic, improving Qur'anic schools, and providing scholarships for study in Muslim

3 The Colonial Origins of Inequality

or those in civil society, provide mass schooling in the Emirates? Some scholars argue that political leaders in Northern Nigeria actively opposed this type of education for the masses and even for their own sons.[58] Others argue that not only did Emirs send their sons, they also sought to develop more schools of this kind but were thwarted by British administrators.[59] Though the truth likely lies somewhere in between, it is probably reasonable to conclude that neither the Emirs nor the British imagined anything approaching mass schooling in the Northern Provinces, at least outside of the Qur'anic education system.

Investments in education that Emirs did make were small relative to the size of the population.[60] Moreover, while many or even most Emirs came to view colonial education as important for their descendants – particularly sons – they may have tried to limit access to it. For example, Tibenderana cites correspondence between colonial officials in which the Superintendent of Education in Zaria wrote of the Emir of Zaria: "He wishes his own sons and protégés to have the benefits of liberal education [but] he does not want the sons of rich traders, sons of men belonging to dynasties other than his own, or sons of men whom for various reasons he does not like, to have the same attainment as the sons of his own men."[61] Colonial reports also suggest that Emirs influenced the content of education in government schools because they were concerned Western education would "create a generation which will turn its back on tradition and on Islam."[62] Of girls' education, the 1934 Annual Report on the Education Department notes, "The delay in starting [girls' education] was due to the prejudices of the Mohammedan population which, until very recently, prevented any real expansion of education at all."[63]

---

countries. No other Muslim civil society group was reported to be explicitly engaged in the provision of nonreligious education in Northern Nigeria. CO 554-744. 1952. Muslim Influence and Problems in Nigeria, p. 21. Kew National Archives.

[58] Ozigi and Ocho (1981)
[59] Tibenderana (1983)
[60] For example, in 1934, the Sultan of Sokoto and the Emir in Gwandu provided assistants to two new girls schools, though the total number of pupils attending these schools was only around 60. CO 583-205 Education Department Annual Report for the year 1934, p. 16. Kew National Archives.
[61] Tibenderana (1983, p. 521)
[62] FCO 141-13367. 1952. Nigeria: Muslim Movements in Nigeria, p. 66. Kew National Archives.
[63] CO 583-205 Education Department Annual Report for the year 1934, p. 6. Kew National Archives.

British colonial administrators did little to expand access to schooling either, and some appear to have actively opposed any form of education that did not allow the "native to develop on his own lines."[64] The subject of how and where to organize education, and who should do it, was one of debate among key early administrators of the Northern Provinces, and one without agreement. However, it seems that in general, colonial perceptions of the "conservative" nature of the Emirs' rule may have affected their interest in extending schooling beyond the ruling class, and colonial authorities supported Emirs in their efforts to maintain schools that supported the political and religious status quo.[65]

Colonial correspondence also indicates that British administrators took into account the extent of Muslim influence in deciding where to place the few educational institutions that were established. The Secretary of State for the Colonies noted in an educational report from 1935 that he preferred a new college be established in Kaduna rather than Zaria, in part because of the extent of Muslim influence in the latter. He wrote: "Kaduna is situated not only in neutral ground (though it lies within the Zaria Emirate it is not under the immediate domination of an Emir) but is also more or less on the line which marks the southern limit of intense Islamic influence."[66]

On balance, it seems that the Emirs could have put more of their own resources toward mass schooling, but they were certainly not supported in this effort by all or even most of the British Residents who oversaw their work. While the Emirs had a relatively high degree of control over their finances,[67] they did not put much of it towards efforts to provide mass schooling, and colonial administrators were themselves hesitant to bring education to the masses.

Southern Nigeria again provides a useful comparison because, like Buganda, Muslim Yoruba living in the southwest were exposed to considerable competition with Christian missionaries and responded by establishing civil society organizations specifically designed to address Muslim schooling. Colonial reports suggest that some of the leaders of these Muslim organizations had been students in missionary schools, and

---

[64] Temple (1918, p. 222)
[65] Coleman (1958, p. 138)
[66] CO 583-205-5 Educational Policy of Nigeria, p. 3. Kew National Archives.
[67] Low and Pratt (1960, p. 309) note, for example: "In Northern Nigeria, the taxes continued to be levied in the name of the Emir and they continued to be paid into the Emir's treasury ... In consequence, the Northern Nigerian authorities thus had a much larger share of local revenue than the native authorities of other territories."

were motivated by political and economic competition with Christians to establish Muslim-founded primary schools with relatively little emphasis on religious education:[68]

> [Muslim leaders were] moved by the desire to see Moslems play a part in economic, administrative and political affairs, commensurate with their numbers in the West. They have taken as a model the Christian Mission schools and have sought to provide the same educational facilities as exist in the schools of the unbelievers. Religious teaching, as in the schools directed by the missionaries, takes a secondary place.

In this way, the self-provision of mass schooling by Yoruba Muslims looked very much like Buganda around the same period. The fact that there was successful self-organization of the Muslim population in both Buganda and in southwestern Nigeria suggests that the lack of self-provision of mass schooling in the Emirates was not the result of the Muslim elite being unable to provide this type of education, nor that this type of education was anathema to Islam as a religion. Rather, the Emirs had fewer political or economic incentives to invest in mass schooling, a function of their numeric dominance, differential treatment by colonial administrators, and lack of competition with Christian missionaries.

The overall argument, derived from these two cases, can be summarized as follows. The extent of Islamization in the precolonial period, with respect to religious demographics and political institutions, affected two aspects of colonial rule. First, the extent of Islamization affected Christian missionary presence and investments, particularly in the area of education. Those places with Islamic political institutions (like the Emirates) experienced relatively lower exposure to Christian missionaries than those with indigenous institutions, where colonizers and missionaries alike felt no need to limit missionary activity on account of preexisting religious ("pagan") beliefs. Second, Islamization affected the extent of colonial interference in local institutions generally, with Islamic political institutions left relatively more intact, and their hereditary systems of rule bolstered, which had the effect of limiting political competition.

For these reasons, areas without Islamic institutions tended to experience relatively more religious and political competition. The provision of mass schooling also had the effect of raising the prerequisites for holding political office in the colonial administration – namely higher levels of

---

[68] FCO 141-13367. 1952. Nigeria: Muslim Movements in Nigeria, p. 60. Kew National Archives.

schooling. This in turn affected demand for schooling. Many Africans ended up converting to Christianity, but Muslims who did not convert faced a choice either establishing their own system of mass schooling or maintaining existing Qur'anic schools. Religious and political competition, as well as demand for mass schooling, shaped the extent to which Muslim elites invested in mass schooling or religious schooling. Where they invested in mass schooling, the Muslim–Christian gap was considerably smaller than where they invested in religious schooling.

The Buganda kingdom and the Nigerian Emirates were considered by the British as two of the most "advanced" societies in Africa, yet, as this chapter has shown, despite their similarly centralized and hierarchical political institutions, British administrators applied quite different strategies of colonial rule. Emirs were granted a relatively high degree of autonomy, while the Kabaka was increasingly fenced in until he was little more than a figurehead in comparison to the rights and privileges the position featured prior to colonization. The divergent response by British administrators across these two settings – in some cases the same individuals – was driven by the relative deference and wide berth given to Islamic as compared to indigenous political authority. This differential treatment played an important role in the distribution of educational investments by Europeans, affecting the supply of colonial schools, religious and political competition, and ultimately demand for this new form of education.

4

The Limits of Existing Explanations for Persistence

Buganda and the Emirates serve as useful cases to examine the origin and colonial-era magnitude of the Muslim–Christian schooling gap, a function of the extent of Islamization in the precolonial period that affected the distribution of colonial schools and demand for these schools among Muslim communities. Despite being governed by some of the same British administrators, the implementation of colonial rule looked quite different in the Emirates as compared to Buganda. In Buganda, where Islam had only just begun to spread prior to colonial rule, the British allowed missionaries to work in large numbers, and religious and political competition with Christians led Muslims to establish their own schools. In the Emirates, the existence of Islamic political institutions led the British to implement a more extreme form of indirect rule, maintaining a hereditary and hierarchical political system, and limiting the work of missionaries. Nothing resembling mass schooling took place in the Emirates, and levels of schooling remained low, with the exception of the Muslim elite and the very few people who converted to Christianity.

Why did these initial gaps in schooling persist into the postindependence period, decades after the end of colonial rule, and why does the Muslim-Christian schooling gap tend to be largest in Muslim majority areas today? These are the questions to which I now turn. Nigeria and Uganda represent the extremes of the degree of colonial investment and religious competition, which is reflected in the magnitude of the schooling gap in each case. Nigeria has among the largest schooling gaps while Uganda has among the smallest. To explain the persistence of the Muslim-Christian schooling gap I focus on a third case, Malawi, which falls in the middle of the spectrum regarding the colonial-era and contemporary education gap. Like Nigeria, Muslims in Malawi were concentrated in a particular region of the country, but unlike the Emirates, they were not governed by Islamic political institutions. Islam arrived relatively late, as it had in Buganda, and while it spread among the population, particularly among the Yao, the structure of political institutions was a set of chiefs whose power was not primarily religious in nature. Malawi (then, Nyasaland), like Uganda, experienced a large influx of missionaries during the colonial period, both Catholic and Protestant. British colonial officials did not restrict missionaries from working in the Muslim areas of southeastern Malawi as they had in the Emirates, but missionaries were not very successful among Muslim communities and invested more heavily in other parts of the Nyasaland Protectorate, particularly the north of the territory.

Malawi is an ideal case to examine the persistence of the Muslim–Christian schooling gap, and in particular, why Muslim schooling tends to be lowest in areas where Muslims are a majority. First, in Malawi it is possible to compare communities where Muslims are a minority with those where Muslims are a majority, while holding constant ethnicity and geography. Southeastern Malawi is home to the majority of Muslims in Malawi, but within this area the distribution of Muslims and Christians varies. However, since the majority of Muslims are members of the Yao ethnic group, differences in norms or behavior across communities is unlikely to be related to ethnicity, since this is held constant. By contrast, in Uganda Muslims are a minority almost everywhere, while in Nigeria, Muslim majority areas are mainly in the north, which are areas inhabited by different ethnic groups from those in the south. Moreover, as shown in the previous chapter, the implementation of colonial rule differed in the north and south of Nigeria. Malawi allows for a cleaner examination of why Muslims living as a majority tend to have particularly low rates of schooling, holding constant other factors that may explain differences in education or the distribution of educational resources such as ethnicity or geography. To be clear, these other factors do matter, and do help explain the gap in some places. But the schooling gap exists even within ethnic groups and subnational regions, and explaining the persistence of the gap in general requires understanding why Muslim majority status is negatively correlated with Muslim educational attainment.

Second, Malawi is a "hard case" theoretically. Three decades of democratic governance and free primary education should have in theory gone a long way in reducing inequality in schooling across groups, and yet the Muslim–Christian schooling gap has proven stubbornly persistent. Among Malawian adults there is a two year gap in years of education, which is around the median for African countries. While educational attainment has been increasing for both Christians and

Muslims in the postindependence period, a substantial gap remains among school-age children today, and is largest in census tracts where Muslims are a majority.[1] In what follows, I introduce the historical and institutional background in Malawi, and then use evidence from surveys and administrative data to cast doubt on several plausible but ultimately insufficient explanations for the persistence of the Muslim–Christian education gap.

Historical and Institutional Background in Malawi

Like Uganda and Nigeria, Malawi was colonized by the British, and was administered as the Nyasaland Protectorate from 1889 until the country gained independence in 1964. While most ethnic groups in Malawi practiced indigenous religions prior to colonialism, one group, the Yao, had begun to convert to Islam by the 1870s and continued to do so throughout the early colonial period.[2] By the time of the 1931 census, Islam was the largest religion in the southeastern areas where the Yao lived, particularly the district currently known as Mangochi, where 45 percent of the population were Muslim. Nearby districts also had substantial Muslim populations, ranging from 8 to 38 percent of the population.

Today, Malawi is more than 85 percent Christian, and about 13 percent Muslim. The majority of Muslims are Yao, and the majority of Yao – three-quarters – are Muslim. As during the colonial period, the Muslim population, and the Yao, are concentrated in the southeast of the country, as shown in Figure 4.1.[3] Mangochi district, the second largest district in the country with a population of over 1.1 million, is more than 70 percent Muslim. It is home to one-third of the total Muslim population, and is the primary site of the fieldwork presented in this and subsequent chapters.

Like Nigeria and Uganda, Christian missionaries played a central role in providing education in colonial Malawi, and were hugely successful in converting the population to Christianity. By the early 1900s, missionaries from seven different bodies had already established 720 schools in the Protectorate, which had a population of less than a million inhabitants. However, these schools were unevenly distributed, with relatively fewer schools in Muslim areas. In 1904, the area comprising present-day Mangochi district had a total of 12 primary schools for a population of

---

[1] See Figure A.9.
[2] Bone (1982)
[3] Members of other ethnic groups in Malawi also converted to Islam, especially those living near Lake Malawi or in urban areas, but no other ethnic group converted in such large numbers, and no other major ethnic group in Malawi today has a Muslim majority.

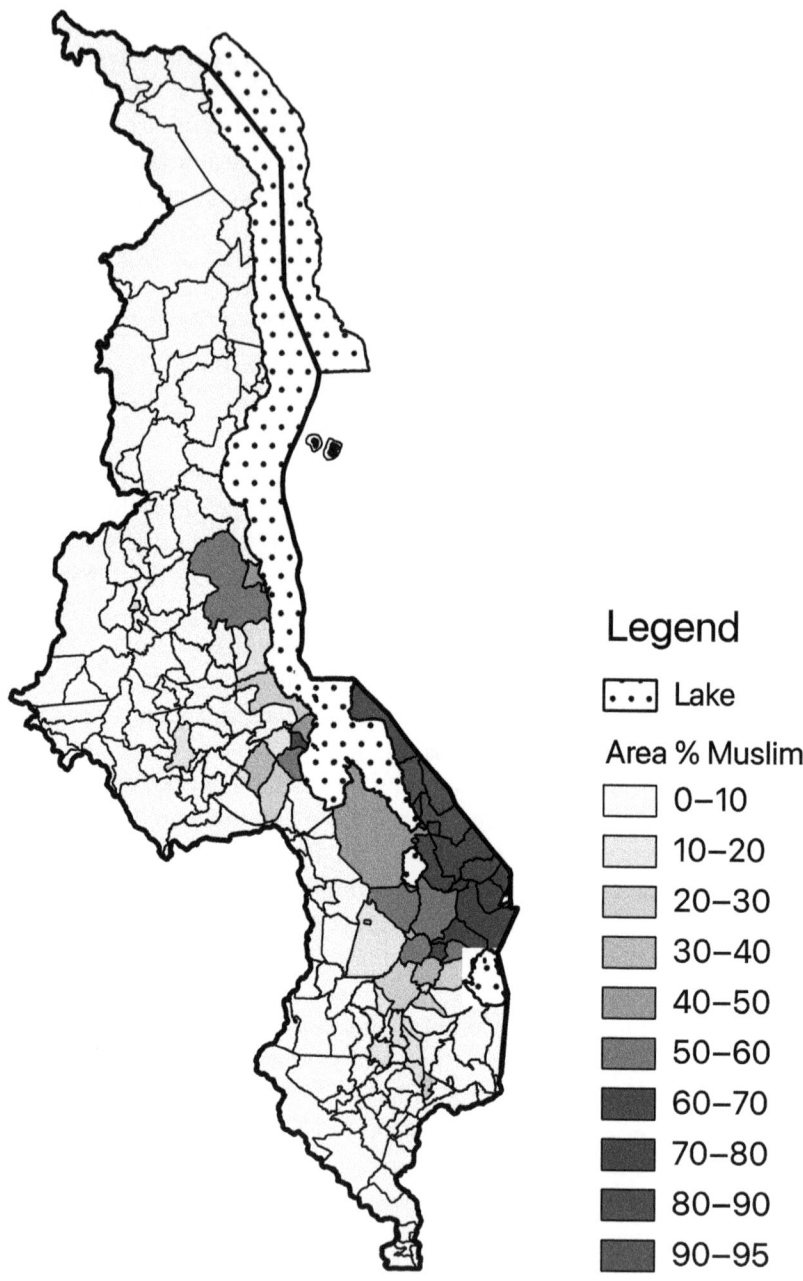

FIGURE 4.1 Distribution of Muslim population in Malawi, by administrative area.
Source: Malawi 2008 Census.

4 The Limits of Existing Explanations for Persistence 85

62,000 people, a ratio of greater than 1:5000. In the same year, the area comprising present-day Mzimba and Rumphi districts in the north had a total of 234 primary schools for a population of about 180,000, a ratio of about 1:800.[4]

Until 1927, all primary schools in the Nyasaland Protectorate were run by Christian missionaries. Although the colonial government did not prevent missionaries from working in southeastern Malawi, where the Muslim population was concentrated, those that operated in this region were not very successful. For example, between 1910 and 1930, five missionary bodies had established over 100 schools in southeastern Liwonde district, but each school had only about 30 students, and Muslim communities avoided them altogether. After decades of work, there were only 3000 converts to Christianity out of a population of 55,000.

British administrators noticed that Muslims were not attending mission schools, and unlike the Emirates, tried to encourage demand for schooling. One such effort involved establishing three "model" schools in Muslim areas, about which the Governor of the Protectorate wrote: "It is hoped that such an improved type of school will create amongst the natives a demand for a better type of school ... I feel that this introduction of Government schools into the Protectorate, and more especially the attempt to provide for Mohammedans, is pregnant with vast possibilities."[5] A Special Warrant released £180 – over US$16,000 in today's dollars – for teacher salaries, classroom construction, and equipment in three schools located in Kawinga, Jalasi, and Mponda, all Muslim areas in southeastern Malawi.

In just two years, however, inspection reports indicated low attendance, poor learning outcomes, and rundown facilities. Communities were not contributing to the maintenance of school buildings and property, and didn't seem very interested in sending their children, especially girls, to school. An inspection report from 1932 indicated that only 5 of 38 pupils were present in class, and Kawinga's school failed on virtually all metrics in the report.[6] At another of the model schools, the teacher reported that

---

[4] Nyasaland Blue Book 1904.
[5] S1-1067-28, Educational Facilities for Mohammedans, Zomba National Archives. Letter from Governor Bowring to Amery, August 1928.
[6] The school inspector, Ernest Bowman, commented that, among others: "Pupils dirty and uninterested" "Brick buildings, gloomy, untidy, walls dirty, white ants busy in one building which is quite unused" "No equipment save desks (mostly unused), forms, 1 table and 3 blackboards" "No records of work" "Physical training and games space cleared between buildings but all very purposeless" "Code not being followed". Bowman also noted that

he couldn't get children to come to school, and the headmen said the community "had no control over their children in this matter."[7]

One month later, Kawinga's school was closed, and its equipment redistributed to mission schools. While there are few if any accounts of the first-hand perspective of Muslim leaders and communities from this time, the colonial records suggest there was little demand for these demonstration schools. The failure of these first forays into providing government schools for non-Christians, and especially Muslims, seem to have led colonial officials to lose interest in pursuing the project further. By 1941 there was still only a single government school in Nyasaland, compared to the more than 4000 schools established by 15 missionary societies.[8] By 1954, just a decade shy of independence, there were only three government primary schools, two government assisted schools run by Muslim communities, and twelve Native Authority and community schools. Nearly all of the 4671 primary schools in the Nyasaland Protectorate were missionary schools, 84 percent of them unaided by government.[9]

By independence in 1964, there were nearly 370,000 children enrolled in primary schools, of which 39 percent had been operating without financial assistance of the Protectorate government and thus almost entirely in the control of religious organizations. Sixty percent were run by religious organizations with the assistance of grants from the government. Only 1 percent of primary schools – 17 out of 2667 – were government schools unaffiliated with any religious institution.[10]

What were the implications of such extensive reliance on religious organizations to provide education services? First, the development of schools was uncoordinated, decentralized, and determined largely by religious organizations rather than the colonial government. Therefore, plans to establish schools were not necessarily based on population or need, but rather the interests of the missionaries.

---

the school's teacher "appeared completely disheartened" and was putting little effort into teaching. S1-1067-28, Educational Facilities for Mohammedans, Zomba National Archives. "Inspection at Kawinga's School," July 26, 1932.

[7] Superintendent concluded: "It seemed to the District Commissioner and myself that while the Acting Principal Headman was interested in the school, neither the Acting Local Headman nor the people of the village had much interest, and that they did not intend to do anything to improve school attendance or to provide a decent building."

[8] Nyasaland Blue Book 1941, p. 72.

[9] CO 1015-151, Annual Education Report Nyasaland, 1954. Kew National Archives.

[10] Ministry of Education Annual Report 1963, p. 43.

4 The Limits of Existing Explanations for Persistence   87

Second, colonial-era schools and curricula in Malawi were heavily influenced by and associated with Christianity. The association between Christianity and education meant that, among Christians, school attendance was considered appropriate and even a key component of the process of conversion and socialization for those who converted to Christianity. Among those who had already converted to Islam, however, school attendance posed a threat to religious identity. Muslims were often not allowed to practice their religion or were required to participate in Christian religious practices, such as church attendance and prayer.

Although there are some historical accounts of Muslims' fear of conversion in Christian schools from the archival and secondary literature from Malawi and beyond as discussed in Chapter 2,[11] I collected additional first-hand evidence about the types of beliefs Muslim communities held about schooling during the colonial period through a set of focus groups with Malawians who were born and grew up in the late colonial period.

The focus groups were conducted in predominantly Muslim areas of southern Malawi in 2018, and all respondents were at least 60 years old at the time of the discussions, implying that they would have been of primary school age prior to independence. In a sample of nearly 40 older adults, every single one recalled hearing at least one negative thing about attending school. Often the source of negative beliefs about schooling came from parents and religious leaders. Through these first-hand accounts, as well as the secondary literature, it is clear that there was widespread fear among Muslims about attending school, precisely because of the threat such education posed to their religious identity. The following is a sample of some of the things respondents reported being told about attending school during the colonial period:

- "What we heard was that if we go to school we will be converted to Christianity."[12]
- "My parents were saying that we should not go to school because we will not be able to be in heaven paradise."[13]
- "For the people who didn't have any religion or any religious belief it was easy to join church or enroll in school without a problem, but Muslims had their beliefs and told their children not to go to school

---

[11] Lamba (1984), Bone (1982).
[12] Focus group MMS, Respondent 3, April 27, 2018.
[13] Focus group CKM, Respondent 4, April 27, 2018.

because either you will eat haram food or be converted to Christianity. As a result their children didn't go to school."[14]
- "My father was saying that I should not go to school and was discouraging [me] because he was saying that with school I will not go to heaven..."[15]
- "The sheikh was telling us that we must be devoted and serve Allah rather than going to school and end up in hell."[16]
- "Sheikhs discouraged their followers from going to school"[17]

Education Policy in Postindependence Malawi

Christian missionaries played a central role in education in Malawi until independence in 1964. Around that time, several major policy reforms affected the financing and governance of education, including greater responsibility of local government in the development of the education sector. But although these policies reduced the influence of Christian missionaries, a decentralized system of education governance and financing may have inadvertently exacerbated inequalities that emerged during the colonial period between Muslim and Christian areas.

First, in 1962, the Education Ordinance established the Local Government Authority as the Local Education Authority (LEA), which effectively decentralized the management of schools and placed the primary responsibility for establishing and maintaining schools with local authorities. In most cases, the LEA was the District Council.[18] Second, the postindependence National Development Plan (1965–1969) placed greater priority and devoted more government resources for development projects for secondary and technical education than for primary education. Under this plan, only 6 percent of the £5.5 million for capital expenditure was allocated to primary schools, and even this amount was intended only for a handful of government schools and schools located in urban areas. The 1964 annual Ministry of Education report notes that this distribution of expenditure "pre-supposes that the development in rural areas will depend on self-help and initiative and the ability and willingness of the Local Education Authorities and communities to make the necessary provision."[19]

---

[14] Focus group MNS, Respondent 7, April 28, 2018.
[15] Focus group MNS, Respondent 3, April 28, 2018.
[16] Focus group MMS, Respondent 2, April 27, 2018.
[17] Focus group CKM2, Respondent 1, April 27, 2018.
[18] Ministry of Education Annual Report, 1963, p. 10.
[19] Ministry of Education Annual Report, 1964, p. 1.

4 The Limits of Existing Explanations for Persistence 89

Thus, not only was governance devolved to the local level, but so too was the financing and development of new and existing schools. These policies likely served to lock-in inequalities in both the distribution and quality of primary schools that existed at the time of independence. Further, the increased expenditure at the secondary level would have primarily benefited those who had already had access to primary school. Because predominantly Muslim areas had low access to school to begin with, and because of the negative association with school in predominantly Muslim areas, these areas were poorly equipped to take over the responsibility of developing, maintaining, and financing local schools.

In the early 1990s, there were growing efforts to expand primary education, with significant donor support. In 1992, the Ministry of Education began distributing fee waivers for girls of primary school age. This program was a stepping stone on Malawi's path to becoming the first African country to completely waive primary school fees. Nationwide free primary education (FPE) was introduced in 1994, following the first democratic elections, in which Hastings Kamuzu Banda was unseated after a thirty-year reign. The removal of school fees led to massive increases in student enrollment – an increase of one million students, about a 50 percent increase – in the first five years of implementation.[20]

This policy also produced a tremendous increase in the establishment and construction of new schools. Figure 4.2 shows the growth of schools over time by proprietor, with a large spike in school establishment corresponding with the implementation of FPE in 1994.[21] There are very few Muslim-founded schools in general, and those that exist were not established until the 1940s – a half century after the first missionary schools were established. Moreover, as in Buganda and southwestern Nigeria, the first Muslim-founded schools were established not in Muslim majority areas, but rather where Muslims comprised a minority.[22]

Despite making schooling more accessible to the general population, per capita spending on students remained uneven across the country in the years after FPE was introduced. The northern region – which had the highest rates of missionary exposure and thus schooling historically – had lower student–teacher ratios and higher per capita education spending

---

[20] Al-Samarrai and Zaman (2007)
[21] This figure was creating using the year of establishment in a 2015 school dataset. There were many missionary schools during the colonial period that did not survive to the present, but there are no data on names or locations that would allow us to put together a comprehensive dataset linking the current and colonial data.
[22] Lamba (1984)

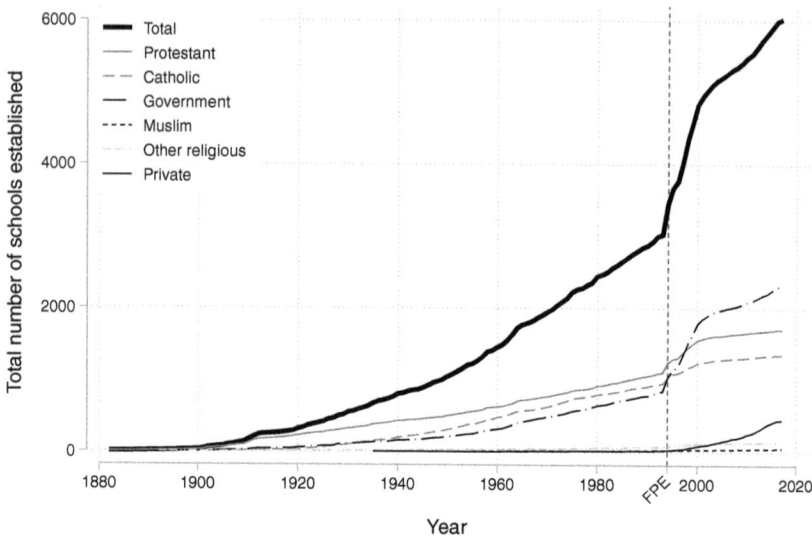

FIGURE 4.2 Cumulative number of primary schools, by proprietor, Malawi. *Source*: Malawi Education Management Information System.

than the southern region, where most Muslims lived.[23] And while attrition was a challenge everywhere, it was especially high in the southern region. As of the late 2000s, for every 1000 children who entered primary school in Malawi, only 400 would complete primary school and only 40 would complete secondary school.[24]

Today, although Malawi's government is centralized financially, local governments and local institutions such as Area and Village Development Committees (ADCs and VDCs), parent–teacher associations (PTAs), and school management committees (SMC) play a central role in school management and maintenance. These local-level institutions create their own development plans but are almost entirely dependent on the central government for funding as they do not raise enough revenue to be self-sufficient.[25]

---

[23] Al-Samarrai and Zaman (2007)
[24] Frye (2012, p. 1578)
[25] Development planning takes place from the ground-up, with Village Development Committees generating an initial development plan for each village. These are then passed on to Area Development Committees, who report to district local governments. Local governments then decide upon the priorities for the district, given available resources.

Although Malawi devotes 18 percent of government spending and 5 percent of GDP to education, which is higher than the average for the region, the education budgets that districts receive are very limited and are not able to fulfill maintenance needs. Malawi's GDP per capita in 2024 was about $550 (constant 2015 US dollars), ranking among the lowest globally. In 2022/2023, Malawi's total primary enrollment was over 5 million, and secondary enrollment over half a million.[26] Per capita spending is around US$50 per primary school student, and the majority of the government education budget is spent on the wage bill.[27] Because central government funding is insufficient to cover basic needs, district governments rely on communities and local institutions to mobilize resources and resolve problems.

For example, community members are asked to provide supplies and labor in the event that new infrastructure is needed, such as additional classroom blocks, teachers' houses, or latrines. If a school wants a school feeding program, which provides meals to students during the school day, the surrounding community must seek fertilizer and seeds from the local government, and then must find a plot of land on which to grow crops like maize, which is a staple food. Many schools also charge parents an additional fee on a per-pupil basis to cover expenses such as utilities, security, and other school development projects. In addition to teachers and school administrators, local leaders and organizations, such as village chiefs, PTAs, school management committees (SMCs), and mothers' groups, are tasked with monitoring schools, managing school development funds, and reporting to local government institutions in case of emergencies or other problems that are outside the scope of what the community can resolve. Thus, the governance of primary schools, including financing for school maintenance, relies heavily on local-level institutions and on community members themselves. Communities may not be equally equipped or interested in participating and contributing to school management and projects, which can directly affect the quality of the school and the quality of education their children receive.

Casting Doubt on Economic, Structural, and Religious Explanations

Having provided an overview of the historical and institutional context in which schooling takes place in Malawi, I now turn to a set of potential

---

[26] Malawi Education Statistics Report 2023, page xxi. Ministry of Education.
[27] 2024/2025 Malawi Education Budget Brief, page 3. UNICEF.

explanations for the persistence of the Muslim–Christian schooling gap. I show, using evidence primarily from Malawi but also from the broader region, that a set of economic, structural, and religious explanations do not fully or even well explain the Muslim–Christian schooling gap, and particularly why Muslim schooling tends to be lowest where Muslims are a local majority.

To investigate these explanations I use administrative and census data, the Demographic and Health and Afrobarometer surveys, and original surveys conducted in Malawi in 2014 and 2018. The first of two original surveys and the primary source for this section was conducted with 600 parents who had children between the ages of 6 and 13. This survey took place in two districts, Mangochi and Chiradzulu, which are 70 and 10 percent Muslim, respectively.[28] I selected these two districts because they vary on the outcome of interest, the Muslim–Christian schooling gap, while holding constant several potentially relevant factors, including subnational region, and to a large extent, ethnicity, while varying the concentration of Muslims within the district.

Data from the 2008 Malawian census showed that Muslim adults in both districts were less likely to be literate and less likely to have attended school than Christian adults. Among children, the gap appears to have closed in the Christian majority district, but not in the Muslim majority district. In the Muslim majority district, 80 percent of Christian children between age 8 and 12 were in school, compared to 59 percent of Muslim children. In the Christian majority district, the percentage of children in school is just under 90 percent for both Christians and Muslims. The second original survey was conducted in a set of ten Muslim majority and ten Christian majority villages in Mangochi, again with the goal of comparing behavior and beliefs across areas with differing religious demographics. Although this second survey was designed to measure schooling norms, and is discussed at greater length in Chapter 6, I present some of its findings regarding economic explanations for the Muslim–Christian schooling gap in the sections that follow.

---

[28] The majority of Muslims in both districts are members of the Yao ethnic group, while Christians are members of a wider variety of ethnic groups.

Economic Explanations

Perhaps the most obvious explanations for variation in educational attainment are economic. If Muslims are poorer, they may face greater barriers to school attendance and greater opportunity costs. Attending school not only results in private costs for school inputs, but also involves the opportunity cost of foregone income had a child begun working instead of attending school. The work–school tradeoff is likely more severe among the poor, since there is a time dimension with regard to return on investment – attending school brings uncertain returns at some future date, while child labor brings relatively certain returns in the present period. If Muslims are poorer on average, then poverty could affect educational outcomes through its effect on child labor.

Several pieces of evidence cut against poverty being the main, or even a significant, contributor to the Muslim–Christian schooling gap, and in particular the low levels of schooling among Muslims where they are a majority. First, as shown in the introduction, the Muslim–Christian schooling gap remains after controlling for wealth. Including wealth as a covariate in country-level regressions reduces the magnitude of the negative coefficient on Muslim in some cases, but a significant and substantial gap remains. Moreover, in some countries, the inclusion of wealth and urban residency as covariates actually flips the sign of the coefficient on Muslim religious affiliation from positive to negative. Examples of these inlcude Uganda, Rwanda, and Burundi. In these cases, Muslims are a minority, and tend to live in parts of the respective countries that are relatively better off. For this reason, at the national level, Muslims appear to have higher levels of education than Christians. However, after controlling for wealth and urban residency, and including region and ethnic group fixed effects, a negative gap once again emerges. These results demonstrate that it is not the case that levels of education among Muslims are lower than Christians simply because of a wealth or income differential. There are countries where Muslims are poorer on average, or live in more economically disadvantaged places, but these factors only accentuate an already existing gap rather than explaining it in its entirety.

Second, while Muslims in sub-Saharan Africa are, on average, somewhat poorer than Christians, this difference does not seem to be very large, and it does not increase with the Muslim percentage of the population in the way that educational outcomes do. Rather, both Christians and

Muslims living in areas with larger Muslim populations are somewhat less well off than those living in Christian areas.[29] The minority religious group tends to perform better in a given region – Muslims are somewhat better off than Christians in the regions with the largest percentage of Christians, while Christians are somewhat better off than Muslims in regions with the largest percentage of Muslims. Those living in Muslim areas are less wealthy than those living in Christian areas, but Christian households look similar to Muslim households in Muslim areas, except in regions where Muslims are a supermajority (greater than 90 percent of the population). Even then, however, Christians are not as well off as Muslims in Christian majority areas.

Third, recent work on the long-term effects of missionaries finds a more robust relationship of the effect of missions on education[30] than on income, particularly at the microlevel. For example, Jedwab, Selhausen, and Moradi (2021) find suggestive evidence of the effect of missions on literacy rates in Ghana, but no impact on local economic development. Similarly, Wietzke (2015) finds little evidence of economic impacts of missionary schooling in Madagascar. Thus, the link between education and income, or education and local economic development, may be more complex than typically theorized.

Another channel through which a work–school tradeoff could operate is through differential job opportunities that vary with respect to educational requirements. Labor market differentiation between Christians and Muslims in Africa has been noted historically, where Muslims have long been associated with trade and business, often inherited within families, due to the way in which Islam arrived and spread within Africa by Muslim traders. Further, early educational advances among Christians and recruitment into the colonial civil service meant that Christians and Muslims continued engaging in distinct labor markets during the colonial period. Labor market segregation along religious lines could be persistent if and when social networks, an important component of access to employment,[31] remain religiously homogeneous. Recent research has shown that inequalities in job recruitment between groups, such as men and women, can persist due to social network characteristics even when no intentional

---

[29] See Figure A.6, which uses DHS data to show a household's predicted wealth quintile across 28 African countries.
[30] See, for example, Nunn (2014), Amasyali (2022), Cogneau and Moradi (2014), Waldinger (2017), and Calvi, Hoehn-Velasco, and Mantovanelli (2022).
[31] Granovetter (1973) and Calvó-Armengol and Jackson (2004)

4 The Limits of Existing Explanations for Persistence

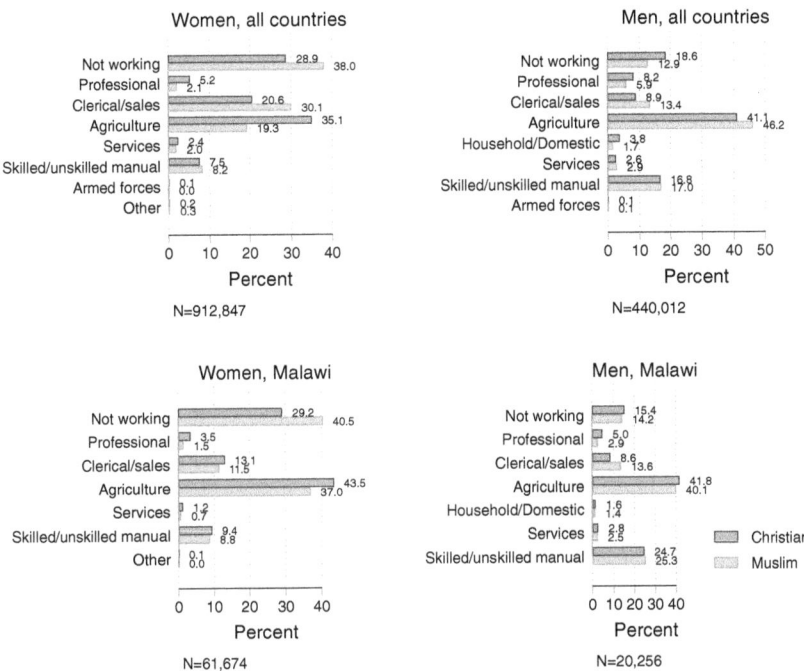

FIGURE 4.3 Occupation by religion and gender in Malawi and 28 African countries.
Source: DHS.

discrimination exists.[32] Social networks are especially likely to be religiously homogeneous where religious groups comprise a majority.

However, survey data show that while there are some differences in occupation across religious groups, their implications for educational investments are not obvious. Figure 4.3 shows the distribution by religion and gender across occupations in Malawi and in a set of 28 African countries, using data from the Demographic and Health Surveys. Among women, the main differences in occupation across religious groups are that Muslim women are substantially more likely than Christian women to report that they are not working, and Christian women are more likely than Muslim women to report working in agriculture. Among men, there are smaller differences, which show the opposite pattern as compared to women – Christian men are more likely than Muslim men to report not working and are less likely to be working in agriculture. Muslims

[32] Beaman, Keleher, and Magruder (2016)

across both genders are more likely than Christians to report working in sales work, which may reflect the historical involvement of Muslims in business. While Christians are more likely than Muslims to report working as professionals, the only category for which formal education is a definite prerequisite, this job category comprises a very small percentage of the total population – less than 5 percent for women and less than 10 percent for men. The majority of respondents are engaged in employment which probably does not require formal education in a strict sense. In Malawi, the majority of working respondents, regardless of religion or gender, are involved in agriculture and manual labor.

Another potential economic explanation is that there are different expectations about the economic returns to schooling across religous communities. Work in the field of behavioral economics has shown that a lack of information explains some of the underinvestment in welfare improving goods and services, such as health and education, and perhaps Muslims living in Muslim majority areas have less access to information about economic returns.[33] Evidence from the surveys I conducted in both 2014 and 2018 suggest this is not the case.[34] As shown in Figure 4.4, all respondents perceived a large difference in returns to schooling given the completion of secondary school compared to all levels below, but there were no significant differences in expected returns at any level of education between Christians and Muslims or between Christian majority and Muslim majority areas.[35] The average estimated monthly income for someone with no formal schooling was around US$20, and for someone who had completed secondary school was around US$60.[36] When asked what kind of jobs they expected their children to have if they completed secondary school, two-thirds of all respondents expected their child would get a job in the formal sector, an expectation which was similar across religious groups and in Muslim majority and Christian majority areas.[37] In a related survey experiment, I examined whether

---

[33] Dupas (2011), Jensen (2010)
[34] Returns to education modules were included on surveys in 2014 and 2018, with similar results. The results from the 2018 survey, discussed at greater length in Chapter 6, conducted in Muslim and Christian villages in Malawi, are presented here.
[35] To estimate expected returns, respondents were asked to estimate monthly income for an individual at each level of education, as in Jensen (2010). For details, see Appendix A.7.
[36] At the time of the survey, the exchange rate was approximately 715 Kwacha to the dollar.
[37] 2014 survey. Formal sector is defined from the answer choices, where teacher, civil servant, policeman, and military are included as formal sector job.

4 The Limits of Existing Explanations for Persistence

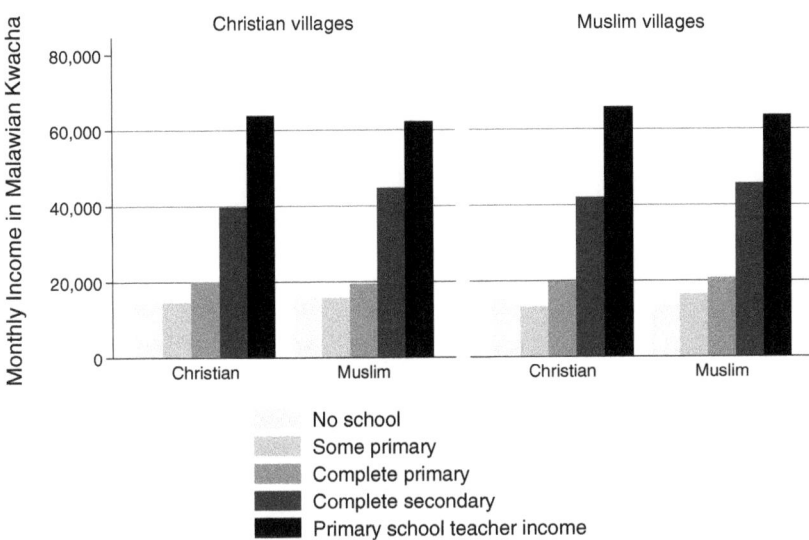

FIGURE 4.4 Mean expected income across levels of schooling, by religion and village type.
Source: Malawi 2018 Survey.

Muslims perceived discrimination in the labor market, which could in theory affect their educational investments, but found no evidence that this was the case.[38] Altogether I find little evidence to suggest that any of these economic factors are the primary explanation for the Muslim–Christian gap or for particularly low educational attainment among Muslims in Muslim majority areas.

Structural Explanations

Another set of potential explanations are structural in nature. Perhaps Muslim majority areas are worse off in terms of schooling infrastructure, quality of schooling, or educational resources than areas where Muslims are a minority. This kind of explanation is not particularly satisfying for two reasons. First, Christians living in Muslim areas achieve similar levels of schooling as they do in areas where Muslims are a minority, suggesting that the factor driving educational attainment patterns is operating through people rather than area- or region-level investments. Second, factors like the quality of schooling can be endogenous to the average

[38] See Appendix A.7.

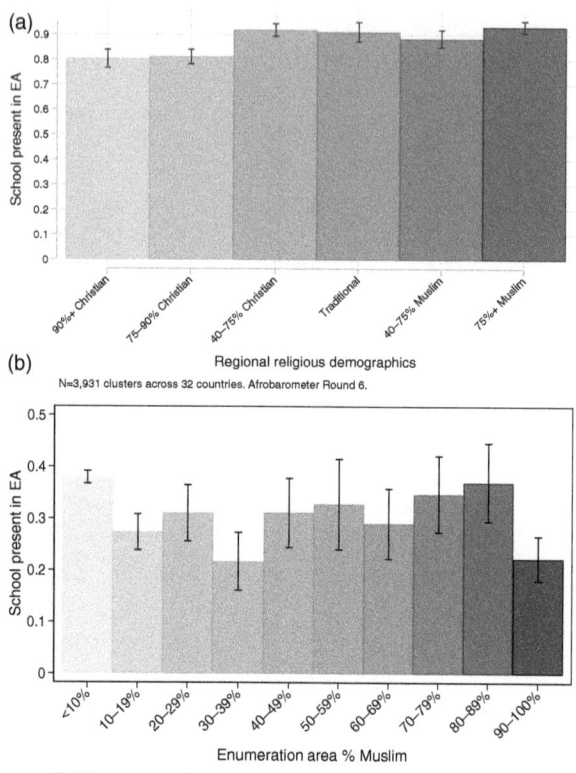

FIGURE 4.5 Availability of school infrastructure by subnational religious demographics. (a) Subnational regions across 32 African countries. (b) Enumeration areas within Malawi.
Source: Afrobarometer Round 6, World Religions Database, Malawi National Statistics Office.

level of schooling, a possibility I examine in more in detail Chapter 5. In areas where average levels of schooling are low, it may be difficult to mobilize parents or communities to contribute to the maintenance and monitoring of schools, either because people don't have experience with these institutions or because they do not have much interest in doing so.

Nevertheless, I use Afrobarometer data from 28 African countries and administrative data from schools across Malawi to examine whether there are structural differences in areas with a larger percentage of Muslims. Specifically, I examine whether there are differences in the likelihood

4 The Limits of Existing Explanations for Persistence 99

that a school is present in an enumeration area.[39] Figure 4.5a shows the mean school presence by subnational religious demographics, using Afrobarometer Round 6 data, and subnational religious composition from the World Religions Database. This figure does not suggest that Muslim majority areas are less likely to have school infrastructure. If anything, it appears that areas with large Christian majorities are less likely to have schools than areas with large Muslim majorities.

Figure 4.5b shows mean school presence across enumeration areas in Malawi, which are presented by percent Muslim, binned in ten percentage point increments. In Malawi, it does appear that enumeration areas with the largest Muslim majorities (over 90 percent Muslim) are less likely to have a school than other areas, but the overall relationship between religious demographics and school presence is not clear. For example, areas that are 30–40 percent Muslim look similar to those that are 90–100 percent Muslim, while those areas between 70–90 percent Muslim look similar to or even more likely to have schools than those that are 10–30 percent Muslim. Thus, while it may be the case that areas with the largest Muslim populations are among the places least likely to have a school present, the overall pattern does not match schooling outcomes – the likelihood of school presence does not decrease as the percentage Muslim increases. Moreover, as noted above, the fact that Christians living in all areas have similar levels of schooling suggests that physical access to schools is not the primary constraint to school attendance today. Using data from the Malawi Educational Management Information System (EMIS) from 2016, however, I find that predominantly Muslim areas do tend to have higher student–teacher ratios, which may impact the quality of teaching. Data from Afrobarometer surveys from across countries also suggest that areas with very large Christian majorities (90 or more percent Christian) are less likely to report teacher absenteeism, poor facilities, or overcrowding than other areas, but that there are no major differences between majority Muslim areas and Christian areas without supermajorities. Together, this evidence suggests that areas greater than 90 percent Christian may have better educational access and higher quality schools than elsewhere, but this does not fully explain why Muslim majority areas perform more poorly than even mixed areas.

---

[39] The data come from Round 6, which is the most recent survey for which I could access georeferenced data. Comparing rounds is difficult because the countries covered change in each round, and generally increase over time.

Religious Explanations

Finally, I examine a set of religious explanations. First, it could be that Muslims living as a majority are more likely than those living as a minority to invest in religious as opposed to secular education. Across the Muslim world, and across African countries, there are many varieties of Islamic religious education.[40] Students attending schools providing religious instruction, some starting at a very young age, are generally taught by religious scholars. In some places these schools effectively constitute an alternative school system, in others, they combine religious education and mass schooling, and in others, they complement mass schooling, such that children attend both.

A trade-off between religious and mass schooling is not a particularly compelling explanation for the persistence of the Muslim–Christian schooling gap because only a minority of Muslims report attending Qur'anic school at the exclusion of mass schooling, and the overwhelming majority of children at least start primary school. In other words, schooling patterns suggest children today are not opting out of school altogether, rather, they simply do not attend for very long. However,

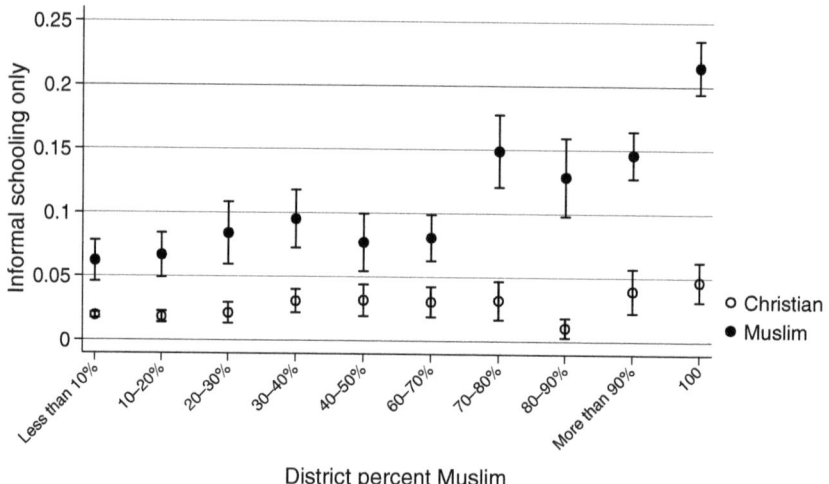

FIGURE 4.6 Informal schooling by administrative area percent Muslim.
Source: Afrobarometer Rounds 2–6, census samples from IPUMS International.

---

[40] Launay (2016)

Afrobarometer data do show that there is a relationship between the relative size of the Muslim population and the percent of the adults who report attending informal school only. Figure 4.6 shows the likelihood that a respondent reports attending informal school only, which includes Qur'anic school, as the percentage Muslim of the administrative area in which they live increases, with the highest levels of attendance in districts where Muslims comprise 90 percent or more of the population.[41]

Nevertheless, while a tradeoff between religious and mass schooling was a consideration historically in some parts of Africa, and while Qur'anic education remains an alternative mode of schooling in some places, this is not a particularly compelling explanation in the case of Malawi. Unlike parts of West Africa or even coastal East Africa where Islam had been present for centuries, by the time of colonization there was not a well-established Qur'anic schooling system in southeastern Malawi.[42] In Malawi today, as in many African countries, Qur'anic schools comprise a complement rather than a substitute for the public education system, and they are designed so that their hours do not conflict with the timetable of the country's primary schools. While it is certainly possible that individuals or families may choose to invest relatively more in religious schools, or, conversely, invest relatively less in primary school, it does not appear to be the case that they are opting out entirely. Indeed, over 90 percent of all children attend at least some primary school. Moreover, the surveys I conducted revealed that, if anything, Muslims living as a minority were more likely to report attending Qur'anic school and were more likely to be able to speak Arabic than those living in Muslim majority areas.

A second kind of religious explanation relates to differences in family structure, namely, the hypothesis that Muslim families have more children, on average, than Christian families, or that the practice of polygamy is more common. If this is the case, Muslim families may have fewer

---

[41] District percent Muslim is binned in increments of ten percentage points and is calculated from IPUMS census samples.
[42] In parts of Africa where these were present, they were noted and efforts made to quantify them in colonial records. For example, Blue Books for Nigeria and Sierra Leone both provide estimates of the number of Qur'anic schools (labeled as "Mohammedan") as well as estimates of the number of pupils in these schools. No such records are available in the Blue Books for Nyasaland, nor are Qur'anic schools mentioned in colonial education reports. As shown in the previous chapter, colonial authorities were aware that Muslims were not attending colonial schools – whether mission or government – in southeastern Malawi, but they did not mention Qur'anic schools as an alternative to these schools.

resources available per child, given the larger size of family on average, which could in theory affect their ability to support children through school. Yet using census data from across the continent, Alesina et al. (2023) find that while Muslim households are larger, on average, than Christian households in African countries, this explains only a fraction of the gap in intergenerational educational mobility.

A third explanation in this vein is that Muslims discourage schooling specifically for girls – due to doctrinal or other reasons. While I do find some differences in schooling norms by gender (reported in Chapter 6), there is also a large schooling gap between Muslim and Christian men, demonstrating that the gap is not being driven by low levels of schooling among Muslim women only. In fact, Muslim men have on average lower levels of schooling than Christian women. However, as Chapter 3 demonstrated, during the colonial period, boys' schooling rates were higher in places like Northern Nigeria than girls' schooling rates. Because Qur'anic schooling historically was mainly attended by boys and men rather than girls and women, particularly at higher levels, it could be that in places with longstanding Qur'anic education system there are differences in norms about schooling by gender that have carried over to mass schooling. If there are differences in expectations for Muslim girls and boys, however, they are not universal. As I will show in Chapter 6, in countries like Uganda, there are no differences in expectations about girls and boys schooling among Muslims or Christians.

It could also be that Muslims living as a majority hold different beliefs and preferences about other factors that might matter for schooling, such as age of marriage and childbearing, or hold stronger in-group preferences. Survey evidence from Malawi suggests there are some differences in the religious beliefs and practices among Muslims living in Christian majority and Muslim majority areas, but these do not necessarily align with the schooling gap. For example, there are no differences in the ages that people report as ideal for women and men to get married and have their first child.[43] Muslims in the Muslim majority area are more likely to say that girls should get married after getting their menstrual period (which would mean cutting short schooling), though this difference is not large (only 7 percent report agreeing or strongly agreeing in the Muslim majority area, compared to 5 percent in the Christian majority area).

---

[43] See Table A.7 for a means comparison between Muslims living in the Muslim majority and Christian majority district, taken from the 2014 survey.

4 The Limits of Existing Explanations for Persistence

Still, it could be that milestones like beginning menstruation are more meaningful markers of age in this context than age in years.

On religious practice, the results are somewhat mixed. On the one hand, Muslims in the Muslim majority area report higher rates of fasting during Ramadan, but on the other, Muslims in the Christian majority area report praying more frequently, and are much more likely to have attended Qur'anic school. The gap in Qur'anic school attendance is especially large among women. More than two thirds of women in the Christian majority area reported attending Qur'anic school, compared to less than a third in the Muslim majority area. There is no difference across the two groups in the frequency of mosque attendance (almost all attend at least once a week), in giving zakat, or in the total years spent in Qur'anic school, conditional on attendance.

There are several measures on which Muslims in the Muslim majority area appear to have stronger in-group preferences. For example, they report higher levels of trust in religious and traditional leaders, and are less likely to say they would allow their son or daughter to marry outside their religious faith or ethnic group. It is worth noting, however, that even though there are differences across groups in marriage preferences, a majority reported that they would allow their daughters and sons to marry outside their religious faith and ethnic group. Together, some of these differences across groups hint at the possibility of differences in within-group beliefs and practices among Muslims living in Muslim majority versus Christian majority areas, but not that Muslims living as a majority are trading off religious education and mass schooling. If anything, attendance of religious and primary school are correlated.

THE CHILDREN DON'T WANT TO GO

If not these economic, structural, or religious explanations, what else might explain the persistent differences in schooling across religious communties? Having hit a dead end, I returned to a simple question on the first survey of parents in Malawi, which asked them directly why their children were not in school. This survey had revealed that nearly 90 percent of respondents' children had attended primary school at some point, but Muslim children were far more likely to be out of school where they were a majority. Almost half of Muslim respondents in the Muslim majority district had at least one child who was not in school, as compared to around 30 percent all other respondents. These respondents were also more likely to have a child who had not attended school the previous term, or were not planning to attend the subsequent term. When asked directly, the most common explanation given by parents as to why children are not in school was that they "did not want to go." Illness or injury was the second most common explanation (around 20 percent), and only 7 percent of those with children out of school cited school fees as a constraint.

The fact that most children start school, and that most who drop out say they "did not want to go," suggested to me that low attainment was in part a function of parents' and communities' interest or ability to enforce attendance. In fact, even beyond Malawi recent surveys from Nigeria and Sierra Leone also suggest that "dispositional factors" are at least as common as situational factors (e.g. lack of money), and certainly more common than institutional factors (e.g. distance to school) in the reasons parents cite as to why their children are not in school.[44]

Having cast doubt on a number of plausible explanations for the persistence of the gap, and taking seriously parents' own explanation for why their children were not in school, between 2016 and 2018 I conducted over one hundred interviews with parents, teachers, religious leaders, and political leaders in Muslim majority and Christian majority areas to learn their own rationales for schooling decisions. This inductive exercise, the results of which are presented in Chapter 5, formed the basis of the main argument for the persistence of the Muslim-Christian schooling gap that I present in this book, which is that social influence – in the form of norms about school attendance held within religious communities and derived from the historical link between mass schooling and Christianity – matters for schooling behavior, and helps explain the persistence of the Muslim–Christian schooling gap in Africa.

---

44 UNESCO (2021)

5

Education as Seen from the Ground

Let's return to Margaret, from Kutambua village, whom I introduced in Chapter 1.[1] I ended up on Margaret's doorstep precisely because the most obvious answers – those that were economic, structural, or religious in nature – did not fully or even well explain the persistence of the Muslim-Christian schooling gap, and in particular why Muslims living in Muslim majority areas tended to have worse educational outcomes than those that did not.

To be clear, it is not that these factors, economic or otherwise, do not matter for schooling. Nor can we assume that the findings from Malawi, for example, that beliefs about the economic returns to education are similar across groups, will necessarily hold elsewhere. The point is not to rule out these explanations in their entirety. Rather, the goal is to develop a more complete picture of the factors that are shaping school attendance once we take into account the most common barriers, including financial constraints and physical access to school. Doing so is not only of theoretical interest. Many recent policies to increase schooling have been premised on the idea that economic factors drive schooling patterns. Some of these policies, like free primary education, have had a tremendous impact on school attendance.[2] Obviously, financial constraints matter. But in Malawi and elsewhere, millions of children start but do not complete

---

[1] Throughout this section I sometimes use the term "we" instead of "I" when describing interviews and encounters. This "we" refers to myself and Shem Yuda, who served as an invaluable research assistant and without whom this work would not have been possible.
[2] For example, see Lucas and Mbiti (2012) for impacts on enrollment in Kenya; Kadzamira and Rose (2003) in Malawi; Kan and Klasen (2021) in Uganda.

primary school, even after decades of free primary school policies. Africa is the only region where the number of children out of school is on the rise.[3]

After an initial survey and examination of continent-wide survey data cast doubt on some of the most obvious explanations for the persistence of the Muslim–Christian schooling gap, I returned to southeastern Malawi. Over the course of two years I conducted interviews, focus groups, and participant observation to learn from parents, teachers, and local leaders, and to hear their own explanations as to why children were or weren't in school. These interactions formed the basis for the main argument for the persistence of educational inequality presented in this book: Community-level beliefs and expectations about school attendance play an important role in schooling decisions, and the strength of these norms has varied across religious communities in Africa due to the association between mass schooling and Christianity historically.[4] In this chapter I share findings from these interviews and discussions, which demonstrate that in Muslim areas in southeastern Malawi, there are only weak expectations that children will persist in school. In the subsequent chapter, I report findings from a survey and set of coordination games designed to measure schooling norms empirically.

Kutambua was one of five Muslim majority villages I studied in depth during this period, and Margaret was the first parent I met.[5] Margaret was Muslim, like most others in the village, and she had never been to school, nor attended Qur'anic school. All of Margaret's older children had left school after a few years, and only one six-year old child was in school at the time of my visit. Resources were certainly a constraint for Margaret, but it wasn't clear they were the main reason her children weren't in school. Margaret said her thirteen-year-old son didn't like school, and would avoid attending during final exams, which forced him to repeat the same class several times. Margaret estimated that most girls in the village left school between year three and five to get married.

Although the school serving the Kutambua is Christian-founded, Margaret was not worried about the religion of the teachers or her children losing their faith or identity. "Faith and school are two different things," she explained. She thinks going to school is a good thing, on balance.

---

[3] UNESCO (2021)
[4] A complete list of interviews conducted in Malawi between 2013 and 2019 can be found in Table A.5.
[5] I selected five Muslim majority and five Christian majority enumeration areas, using the 2008 census, each in a different Traditional Authorities area – an administrative unit equivalent to a county, each with a traditional leader as its head.

5 Education as Seen from the Ground

School records from the year I visited showed that there were nearly 400 students in Standard 1 and only 18 – 16 boys and 2 girls – in the final year of primary school. Clearly, only a tiny fraction of children in this and neighboring villages would complete primary school. Far from being outliers, the schooling experience of Margaret and her children was the modal outcome.

In fact, it was not obvious how different life would be for Margaret's children in the unlikely event that they did finish primary school. Kutambua is a rural, agricultural community where only a fraction of children completes the eight years of primary school, fewer still finish secondary school, and one of the few formal sector jobs is in the school itself. While the income and quality of life of teachers posted in Kutambua is probably higher than average for the village, it may not be so by much.

In Kutambua children grow up, find partners, work in gardens or fish in the nearby lake, and have children of their own. The difference between two and eight years of primary school on one's overall life trajectory is not clear. Indeed, the initial survey suggested that no one perceived a difference in economic returns between zero and four years of school, and only a small increase in returns between four years and completing primary school. Moreover, there did not appear to be social repercussions for dropping out. On the contrary, leaving school to get on with your life – particularly family life – was quite expected.

From discussions with Margaret and over a hundred other parents, community leaders, religious leaders, and teachers across these villages, some of which I followed over the next few years, several themes began to emerge. First, there was a tenuous link between schooling and later employment. The purpose of school attendance, at least at the primary level, was not to get a job in the formal sector. Second, school attendance did not seem to bring much in the way of social status. Adolescents looked forward to recognition as an adult, but this came not with completion of schooling but with finding a partner and starting a family. The kinds of skills considered useful in the community had more to do with farming, fishing, starting a business and managing a household than those being taught in school. Third, it became clear that in communities with lower levels of schooling on average, and where expectations about school completion were low, the local organizations that play an important role in school management and fundraising were dysfunctional, and schools were sometimes even predatory. In such contexts, the quality of education provided was poor, which dampened demand, producing a feedback cycle of poor quality and low demand.

Finally, what was notably absent from these conversations were explicit references to Islam or religion as important for schooling decisions. In these Muslim majority communities fear of conversion did not keep children away from school. Rather, the expectation of school attendance and persistence in school was simply not very strong. Without obvious economic benefits and no social imperative for attendance, what became more puzzling was why anyone *stayed* in school. In the remainder of the chapter, I elaborate on the core themes that emerged from the interviews and participant observation in southeastern Malawi.

The Tenuous Link between Schooling and Employment

While many parents talked favorably about school, they almost never had direct experience with formal sector employment. When asked about the benefits of school, Margaret herself suggested that it would "help a child to have a good future, for example to be a doctor, and going to South Africa to work." She didn't know the process for becoming a doctor, however, explaining, "I am illiterate." Parents were usually unclear about the qualifications and path to, for example, becoming a medical professional. Instead, there was a general sense that for some types of jobs, you need to have at least completed secondary school. But these jobs tended to be abstract ideas.

The detachment between attending primary school and obtaining a job for which schooling is a prerequisite is reinforced by the fact that this connection is rarely observed in practice. First, in communities with low levels of this type of education historically, there are few examples of those who completed secondary school or university, whether or not they are successfully employed. Second, those few who do complete higher levels of education are either successful in acquiring a formal sector job, in which case they almost necessarily leave their communities and their success is not directly observed, or they are unsuccessful, in which case they remain in their communities and their inability to obtain such a job is highly visible to others. One woman noted, "In this whole area we have been talking about education, but nobody has achieved the success...Most children are learning and will still be learning, but no one I know is employed in a company or the NGOs which are working in our area."[6]

Even those members of a community in the formal sector who are visible – particularly teachers and health workers – are not especially

---

[6] Participant observation in TA Chowe, 2018.

5 Education as Seen from the Ground

well-off, and may not be better off than others who do not have formal sector employment. One teacher recounted the story of a former student who had gone to South Africa and when he came back, mocked the teachers, saying "what is the benefit of school? I left you with same tie on your neck, and today you are having the same without changing. Look at me, I did not finish primary school but am driving today, I have got money and houses."[7]

This interaction demonstrates not only that students may not be motivated to acquire formal sector employment, but also that they aspire to other things in life. In a survey conducted in twenty villages in Mangochi district, discussed at greater length in Chapter 6, respondents were asked the name and occupation of their role model. The modal response for Christians, and for Muslims living in Christian majority villages, was a person working as a public sector mid level professional – usually a teacher or health worker. Among Muslims living in the Muslim majority villages, the modal response was a trader, hawker, or vendor. The level of schooling of the role model was also lower, on average, for Muslims in the Muslim villages. More than 40 percent of Muslims living in these areas reported that their role model had never attended school or had attended only at the primary level.[8] These responses suggest that aspirations are shaped by what individuals are able to observe, but also that aspirations can differ systematically across religious groups, even within the same village.

Indeed, although there were no differences in the distribution of occupations between Christian and Muslim respondents, they perceived Muslims and Christians to be engaged in distinct kinds of work. Nearly 40 percent of respondents thought most Muslims in their district were traders or shop owners, while 50 percent thought most Christians were mid or upper-level professionals. In fact, fewer than 3 percent of Christian respondents were professionals, and only 15 percent of Muslims were in trade or retail. The vast majority of all respondents, regardless of religion, were engaged in agriculture, fishing, unskilled manual labor, or piecework (working for a large landholder). These findings demonstrate misperceptions among both Christians and Muslims about the relationship between religious affiliation and occupation.

---

[7] TA Jalasi, Village K1, 2016.
[8] Fewer than 30 percent of all other respondents reported similarly low levels of schooling among their role models.

Conceptions of Childhood and Future Aspirations

A second theme that emerged from interviews had to do with the concepts of childhood and adolescence, and what is considered useful education in these communities. Among the Muslim communities I visited, most children attended at least the first year of primary school, but stopped after a few years. Attending school is a part of childhood in these communities, but a brief one.

Even then, "going to school" is not the regular, daily attendance for nine months of the year that may be imagined from the perspective of someone who is used to a context with universal primary schooling. Rather, attendance waxes and wanes throughout the year. Many children start the school year but peter out over time. Some come to school during seasons of food scarcity, particularly if schools have feeding programs. Students may also stay home and help their families plant or harvest crops at regular intervals throughout the year.

Starting school at age eight or nine, rather than six, is common. So is repeating a class, due in part to the on-and-off nature of school attendance, but also due to high student–teacher ratios, teacher absenteeism, and lack of basic supplies. As a result, teenagers who persist in school often find themselves amidst younger children. It is not uncommon for a 12- or 13-year-old to be in lower primary – perhaps grade two or three – even though based on age they should be completing primary school.

The mixing of ages can be awkward, and reinforces the idea that school is a thing for children, not a place to be if you want to make your mark on the world. As one man noted, "… when our children start school in standard one, on average you can see at the age of eight or nine a child is starting school. How can you expect that child to complete school? At the age of sixteen, they are in standard 5 and already started sexual relationships."[9]

Parents, grandparents, and guardians frequently talk about school attendance as a function of children's interest. How far a child will go in school is dependent on how far they want to go, how much they want it for themselves. Some children are interested, of course. They are eager to go, find the challenge exciting, dream of the next step. Many others, perhaps most, do not.

Parents often noted that their children were not interested in school. When asked why, one explained, "I don't know. I have been forcing him

---

[9] Participant observation in TA Chowe, 2018.

to go to school, even denying him eating lunch or supper, but he goes to the lake with friends to play or do piece work there at the lake to have money ... Masauko just runs away, he comes here late in the evening only to sleep, we don't see face to face."[10]

Indeed, the experience of going to school is often not particularly pleasant. Language can be a problem, where the language of instruction may not be spoken at home. As is the case the world over, teachers can make or break the experience. A bad teacher can turn a child off a subject, or off school altogether. Classrooms are crowded, and even the best teachers will have trouble helping everyone, perhaps focusing their attention on the most promising students, or those with the most invested parents.

Under these circumstances, even basic literacy and numeracy may be a higher bar than what most parents have in mind. When asked about the benefits of school, one parent noted, "[so that the child is] able to read the notice board, and they cannot lose direction wherever they go."[11]

Even when children are interested in continuing school, some parents are not supportive. One teenager noted, "Here we have parents who don't value education and when a child begs them school materials or uniform they don't feel good, thinking that the child is a troublesome child. And these parents force boys when grown up to marry by saying 'look you are now grown up, be like your friend, he is married, and he helps himself and has a child. Why not you?' "[12]

By the teenage years, the thing young people look forward to is becoming independent – like teenagers everywhere. They seek some distance from their parents, and look for their own space. With independence typically comes having a partner, and having children. These markers indicate that you are now an adult, and will no longer be treated as a child. To do these things is to be respected by your friends and peers. They are also what is generally expected by others in the community.

As one young man noted, "It is our custom for a child whether a boy or girl when grown up not to live under the same roof with their parents. It's not respectful. I left school in standard 3 when I was 15 years, and I felt shy in my class I was over age, and my mother forced me to stop going to school and be married, but I just stopped going to school and not married up to date."[13]

---

[10] Parent 2, TA Mponda.
[11] Parent 2, TA Katuli, Village L1.
[12] Participant observation in TA Chowe, 2018.
[13] Participant observation in TA Chowe, 2018.

One solution to those seeking independence is to live with friends, siblings, or cousins outside of their family home. However, if this happens, parents are even less able to monitor and influence children's behavior, and teenagers may enter into relationships that ultimately form the basis of their own family life. Teenage pregnancy is quite common, even among those who are in school.

One 18-year-old man we met described how these living arrangements worked. Unusually, he had started secondary school, but had dropped out after one year because he couldn't pay the fees. At the point we met he was learning to become a builder, starting with his own home, or shelter, as he called it:

> I am building a small house that boys will be using as their shelter. I do not charge any money, but they can give anything as a thanks giving because we are acting brotherly. I will not sleep alone, there could be three or five boys in one shelter. And each is preparing himself for adulthood and discussing how to be a responsible man. All of us here (three boys) are having girlfriends except this young guy (12 years old). He is young. What is he going to do with a girl? Girls come to our shelters during the night after we take them from their shelter, or they visit us themselves. We make shifts so that we give our friend a chance to chat with his partner while the rest of the boys go out to play at a far distance.

In another village, as we introduced ourselves to the village chief, his school-age grandchildren gathered around to watch. The local primary school was less than 500 meters away, and it was mid morning. When we asked why the children weren't at school, one replied that she was sick, while another said his clothes were torn. This was a common scene throughout the interviews – children of all ages playing in and around the village during school hours, usually in the presence of parents and local leaders.

There was no opposition to school reported, but neither were there any apparent social costs to dropping out – no one would look at you askance if your children were running around the village on a school day. On the contrary, in places where it is rare to complete primary school, and even more so to complete secondary school, dropping out was simply a step in the process of growing up. Many people didn't seem too worried about what people would think of their education credentials, but rather their success in marriage and child-rearing. One respondent explained:

> Here we have some cash crops which we plant and sell ... we can pay school fees, but if you ask someone they will tell you that we don't have money for school fees. But what they [really] want is for their children to get married ... marriage here is like a competition. A role model is one who married and gave birth, and

the minimum age for those marriages is 12 to 20 years ... a boy or a girl who has not married or gotten pregnant is teased and named bad names [about their fertility].[14]

Thus, the expectation for children is not that they will finish school, but rather that they will get married and have children, often at a very young age. As the above quote suggests, there are social costs to deviating from this set of expectations, including teasing and potentially the inability to find a marriage partner. When asked what makes one successful in life, respondents replied "have a family," "have enough food in the household," and to have "daily cash in hand."[15]

One young man, noted "It is good to start life together with a wife whilst young," while another explained the goal of his 16-year-old friend who was trying to make a marriage proposal was to "bathe with warm water and [have] an independent life with his wife."[16] What is seen as desirable, appropriate, and normatively good for young people in these areas was to start adult life – marriage and children – as soon as possible, after which point the man would be tasked with providing for the family and the woman with raising the children. One teenage girl told us that since she had matured physically, it would be childish to put on a uniform and continue going to school.

The beliefs and expectations about what children and teenagers will and should do are not centrally about attending school. Looking around, both children and parents see that most children go to school for only a few years. Those who are esteemed in the community are not those who have extensive education of this type. In fact, those who have been to school for many years – including the teachers in the school – are often not substantially better off than everyone else. Many who have struggled to get through secondary school have been unable to find jobs. Those who have been least successful are those who are most visible, because they are the ones who have returned to the village, those for whom school seems to have been a futile effort. An 18-year-old woman, who had become pregnant in Standard 5 and subsequently stopped going to school, said, "I do not regret dropping school, because no one proceeds with school."[17]

Together, these discussions began to paint a different kind of understanding about childhood and what is considered a useful education.

---

[14] Participant observation, TA Jalasi, Village M1, 2017.
[15] Various respondents, TA Jalasi, 2018.
[16] Participant observation, TA Jalasi, 2017.
[17] Participant observation, TA Chowe, 2017.

Current paradigms of economic development place the attendance of primary – and increasingly, secondary – school as the centerpiece of childhood and adolescence. The idea, espoused by international organizations and national governments, is that children spend many of their waking hours within the walls of an institution regulated, if not run, by national and local governments. Within these schools, they cover a curriculum established or regulated by these same entities.

The presence and attendance of these schools dramatically alters the understanding of what childhood is, what children are being taught and prepared for, and implicitly or explicitly, what goals they should aspire towards as adults. Prior to this paradigm shift of mass schooling, there were alternate understandings of childhood and adolescence, which varied across and within countries. The entry of this new, seemingly universal, conceptualization of childhood does not fill a void, but rather complements or sometimes competes with existing conceptions. Nor does this new conceptualization of childhood necessarily alter the expectations of what is to come after childhood – what men and women strive to become. It is perhaps not surprising, then, that simply constructing a building called a school, or removing school fees, does not necessarily mean that children will begin attending, much less persist in attending for the next six to eight years.

To be sure, the removal of primary school fees produced a dramatic increase in rates of schooling in many African countries, Malawi included. This increase is strong evidence of a demand for primary school, and the idea that school attendance is sensitive to the economic costs of schooling, a finding which has been amply demonstrated in a variety of settings.[18] Nevertheless, it does not follow that the removal of school fees replaced existing conceptions of childhood overnight, nor overturned long held ideas about what it meant to be a respected community member. In other words, the removal of school fees did not necessarily change aspirations of parents or children and what it meant to live a meaningful life.

Economic models of the demand for schooling typically center around the returns of schooling, realized many years after the investments made in education. These economic returns come by means of earning more for one's labor than would have been possible with less schooling, and surmounting the income foregone while attending school instead of working.

---

[18] J-PAL Policy Bulletin. 2017. "Roll Call: Getting Children into School." Cambridge, MA: Abdul Latif Jameel Poverty Action Lab.

The idea is that becoming a teacher, civil servant, doctor, lawyer, or similar is more desirable than working in agriculture, as "unskilled" labor, or other jobs for which schooling, at least within the walls of a classroom, is not strictly required. Thus, we might assume that a goal, if not the goal, of schooling is to increase the chances that one obtains a higher paying job than would have been the case in the absence of schooling. But the provision of free primary education did not change the opportunities for formal sector employment that were available, nor provide information about how to access these opportunities. If anything, free primary education drove up the supply of potential workers while leaving demand stagnant.

Moreover, transitioning to formal sector employment as a replacement for land- and agricultural-based subsistence marks a drastic departure from how most rural communities work. Land ownership is not only meaningful, working the land also provides an insurance policy against hunger. In a context where government cannot be relied upon to provide basic necessities in times of crisis, it makes sense to have a fallback plan which allows you and your family to weather crises independently.

If the "ends" of mass schooling are a formal sector job, these ends are not universally desirable, and the means required to get there – the process – is not well-known. Further, while primary school is free, secondary school is not, and access to secondary school is often contingent on passing a primary school-leaving exam. Given the very large hurdles in accessing secondary school, one may reasonably ask whether the point of attending primary school is a formal sector job. Without secondary school, these jobs are unattainable. The calculation of (economic) returns to schooling hinges both on believing that these types of employment are attainable, on the one hand, and that they are preferable to the alternatives, on the other. As the above discussion makes clear, the provision of free primary education did not necessarily alter beliefs for either of these two components.

What then is the purpose of primary school? Some may hold out hope that they will be among the few who are both able to complete school *and* obtain a formal sector job. From a rational perspective, this outcome in the context of rural Malawi is so unlikely that it probably is not the motivating factor driving primary school attendance.

There are three other reasons for attending primary school, under conditions where postprimary education is unlikely: (1) the desire to learn skills such as literacy and numeracy, (2) being legally compelled to do so, with a credible threat of punishment, and (3) nonmaterial benefits, including social status, social pressure, and personal conviction that going to school is what children *should* do, in a normative sense.

The first reason – skill acquisition – is certainly a motivating factor, but the quality of schooling is frequently so poor, and time spent in school so short, that many children are unable to read or write after having attended several years of primary school.[19] The second reason – legal enforcement of attendance – is rarely a motivating factor in contexts such as rural Malawi because the government's ability to monitor compliance and enforce attendance is weak. I suggest that it is primarily the third reason — nonmaterial, social benefits – that plays an important, yet underappreciated, role in school attendance at the primary level in rural Malawi.

Of course, many people in rural communities do attend school, and for much longer periods of time than Margaret's children. Is this because they have different expectations about what school attendance will yield? Is the schooling–employment link stronger for them? What else could drive children in these communities to spend so much more of their lives in school?

Most Christians we spoke to in predominantly Muslim villages stayed in school until late primary school and often secondary school, even when they were surrounded by – and even friends with – Muslims who did not. In a focus group of young men in a Muslim majority village, composed mostly of Muslims but also a few Christians, religion was a near perfect predictor of educational attainment – the two with any secondary school were both Christian, while those with primary school or no schooling were all Muslim. A focus group with young women in the same village revealed the same pattern – the only one to have reached secondary school was Christian.[20]

The economic chances of both Christians and Muslims in this area were quite similar – in this rural and remote village, several hours from the district headquarters on a nearly impassable road – even those with secondary education were farmers or self-employed. Yet despite similar economic conditions and similar beliefs about the expected economic returns of schooling, Christians in Muslim majority areas consistently stayed in school longer than their Muslim neighbors. There seemed to be some

---

[19] As of 2024, less than 1 in 5 Malawian children of primary school age had foundational literacy skills, and less than 1 in 7 had foundational numeracy skills (UNICEF 2024).
[20] Focus groups conducted in Mangochi, March 2018.

5 Education as Seen from the Ground

other motivation driving their attendance – the sense that they *should* go to school as far as they could, regardless of the economic outcome.

In Christian majority areas, both Christians and Muslims attended school in large numbers. There were no children hanging around the village during school hours, none leisurely walking along the footpaths – everyone was in school. Respondents here reported that Muslims attended school to access economic opportunities as well as to fit in with the majority Christian community. One village leader in a Christian majority district reported, "now they [Muslims] have realized that school and religion are different, and here in Chiradzulu parents are now forcing their children to school to be like their fellow Christians."[21] A Muslim mother replied, "here in Chiradzulu everyone knows that if you don't go to school you will be living in the remote area for the rest of your life."[22]

When asked to reflect on the differences in schooling behavior in areas where Muslims were a majority or minority, respondents frequently cited social pressure, seeing the example of Christians, and wanting to copy Christians as explanations for why Muslim schooling rates were higher. For example, one head teacher explained, "I think because of the environment they are in ... they are dominated by people who are interested with school and I think they have been mocked if they don't go to school ..."[23] A Muslim religious leader similarly noted, "here [Muslims] are surrounded by Christians who went to school in order to have a bright future."[24]

Our driver throughout these interviews was himself a Muslim who lived in a Christian majority area, and expressed shock upon visiting the Muslim majority areas. Where he lived, he explained, "if you don't go to school, people will laugh at you." These accounts suggest that in the Christian areas, there are social benefits of going to school, and social costs to dropping out. Going to school is part of what it means to be successful, while to drop out is a failure.

MFANO SCHOOL: FEEDBACK LOOPS

Schooling norms not only affect the schooling behavior of children, but also the quality of schools, which in turn affects demand for schooling.

---

[21] TA Kadewere, M1 Village, February 2017.
[22] TA Likoswe, K1 Village, February 2017.
[23] Head teacher, Nanyumbu. Interview on March 3, 2019.
[24] TA Likoswe, K1 Village, February 2017.

This feedback loop became particularly clear in the case of a school I followed over the course of several years.

Mfano school was one of several schools I visited within Mangochi, located in TA Jalasi, a predominantly Muslim traditional authority, where 95 percent of the more than 75,000 inhabitants are Muslim. While there were many villages in this TA we could have visited, I chose an area near a primary school that, according to government records, was Muslim-founded – a rarity in a country where the majority of schools were originally founded by churches. What made inhabitants of this area decide to build their own school, and how well was it functioning?

Like Kutambua, Mfano was at least an hour's drive from the district headquarters, but it was only a few kilometers from the main road. While the road to Kutambua could become impassable in heavy rain, and cut off from the rest of the country, Mfano could be easily reached at any time of year. As was the case in all villages, the village headman, or chief, was the first point of contact. His name was Abdula. Abdula was 67 years old when we met, which meant his childhood had overlapped with the late colonial period in Malawi.[25] As a child, his parents told him he should not go to school, and that he would be given *haram* food if he went. He never attended. "Most people my age are not educated, I am still regretting," he explained.

Things are different today – all three of Abdula's youngest children attend both madrasa and primary school, and they like school. "I encourage them to be fully committed to education, because now the world is still advancing," he says. But only one of Abdula's children is in the grade level he should be according to age. The oldest, age 12, is in Standard 4 when he should be in Standard 6. The youngest, age 10, is in Standard 3 when he should be in Standard 4.

The chief's children are not alone. The official age for starting primary school is six, but the average age for first-year pupils in Mfano school is eight. Mfano school records show that only a quarter of the children in Standard 1, the first year of primary school, are the appropriate age. Part of this discrepancy is due to those who repeat a grade – each year, up to 30 percent of children in Standard 1 are those who are taking it for a second or third time.

Even more striking is the attrition rate. During the 2016/2017 school year, when I first visited Mfano, the number of pupils in Standard 2 was

---

[25] Interview conducted on November 24, 2016.

half of that in Standard 1. Though there were over 400 children in Standard 1, there were only 12 pupils in Standard 7, the penultimate year of primary school, and the highest level offered at Mfano. In other words, only about 3 percent of students at Mfano were making it to Standard 7, and even fewer of those end up making the trek to the nearest school that offered Standard 8 – several kilometers away.

Enrollment at Mfano school throughout the 2010s had been steadily increasing, but high rates of attrition did not budge. According to Malawi's official education statistics, a "dropout" is a child who stops mid year. This means that if a child finishes the first year of school and never comes back, this kind of attrition is not captured. As a result, official dropout rates vastly under-estimate the rate at which children leave school.

Prior to the establishment of Mfano, the closest school to the village was Choyamba Primary School, a Roman Catholic school built in 1973. Initially, Roman Catholics had a plan to build another school close to Mfano village, since it was hard for children to reach Choyamba on foot. At the time, however, Muslim leaders were uncomfortable with the idea of a Catholic school in Mfano. Instead, they preempted the Catholics, constructing two thatched shelters as classrooms. It remained a makeshift building with a single teacher until 1995, when it was constructed as a Local Education Authority (LEA) school. The school today is made of brick and iron sheets.

By the time we reached Mfano Primary School, classes had ended for the day. We spoke with three of the six teachers on staff, as well as the head teacher, hoping to learn why so few students made it through primary school in this area. John, a Standard 4 teacher, explained that when students reach Standard 6 or 7, they often go to South Africa looking for work, or get married. "Parents don't pressure students to go to school," he explained. This is especially so, he says, if the parents themselves have not been to school: "They don't have the spirit to motivate kids."

At the time, John was new to Mfano, and said the school desperately needed more teachers. There were two teachers assigned to Standard 1 – with more than 400 students – but one of them hadn't been showing up to teach. The Head Teacher, Mr. Chitinji, said he told the local Primary Education Advisor (PEA), who oversees Mfano and other schools in the area, that the school needed more teachers. But even if more teachers came, there was no place to house them. There were no teachers' accommodations, so teachers lived at the nearby trading center and had to travel several kilometers to the school each day, usually by bicycle.

Apart from the funds the school receives from the government, the school asks parents to contribute 150 Kwacha per year per student (about 20 cents in US dollars), as well as to contribute labor and materials to mould and burn bricks for teachers' housing, latrines, and classroom blocks. In 2016, the first year we visited, Mr. Chitinji reported that only 250 of the 860 students paid these fees, and that it is "very difficult to get people to participate" in making bricks.

Despite these challenges, Mr. Chitinji said things were much better than when he began at the school in 2001. "[Back then] most parents were not sending learners." Chitinji said that to most parents, "going to school is nothing compared to business." Even the children of village leaders rarely complete primary school.

Mr. Chitinji is the only teacher at the school who is Muslim, but the teachers' religious affiliations don't seem to matter to parents. Emily, a mother of seven living in Mfano explained, "they only went there for schooling, I don't want my children to use their thumbs when marking their names because of illiteracy." Even so, Emily's two oldest children (18 and 15) stopped attending after Standard 1.

Mfano is a window into the dynamics of how schooling norms can reinforce and be reinforced by local institutions, including schools themselves and the organizations tasked with monitoring them and coordinating teachers and communities. Those who invested in schooling early on – namely Christians – did so because school attendance was not just useful but normatively good, an important part of being Christian. Those who invested early were also well-placed to organize and marshal scarce resources to make their schools better, thereby fueling demand.

Those who did not invest in schooling early on – including many Muslim leaders and communities, especially in Muslim majority areas – made this decision not irrationally, but because initially the schools available were a threat to religious identity and even to existing institutions. Areas with low initial investment in schools were also those whose local institutions and political leaders were unable or unwilling to mobilize resources to strengthen what few schools were established, or to take the initiative to build their own.

Here, Mfano is somewhat exceptional, as local leaders did take it upon themselves to construct a school – as a direct result of religious competition that resembles that in Buganda – but it was barely functional for many years. As can be seen in the case of Mfano, school quality suffers when local institutions and leaders do not actively work to strengthen and support schools. In some cases, schools deteriorate to the extent that attending them is a waste of time, further deflating demand.

I observed this feedback loop in real time in the case of Mfano. Less than a month after my first visit to Mfano school, a message popped up on my phone. It was John, the Standard 1 teacher. I stared at the screen, which showed a photo of the brick classroom block and a heap of iron sheets piled at the side. The wind one day had blown the roof right off.

John reported that the school management committee (SMC) and parent–teacher association (PTA) were communicating with "relevant stakeholders" about the incident, though he didn't specify exactly who these were. A few days later, the head teacher of the school called a meeting with the local chiefs and PTA to try to figure out a plan to repair the classroom.

Two more months went by, and this time it was I who messaged John. The roof was still off, he explained, though the Member of Parliament (MP) for the area had promised to fix it. In another two months, John messaged again. Still no roof. They were waiting for the MP to do something. There seemed to be considerable confusion over who was responsible for fixing the roof, for notifying relevant authorities, and for mobilizing the resources to fix it. Meanwhile, classes were severely disrupted in a school that already struggled with retention.

In a follow-up visit to Mfano a few months later, villagers reported that the SMC and PTA were generally dysfunctional, despite the critical role they were meant to play in school management and development. The chair of the SMC reported that his own committee was not active, and that the PTA had never held a meeting since being elected. A teacher at the school explained:

The PTA and SMC leaders don't know their roles and responsibilities. For example, after the school block [roof] blew off it took almost three months before the PEA, MP, and the T/A knew that. It was the Head teacher who informed them all during the school zone meeting after the MP asked each of the participants (Head Teachers) at that meeting the problems faced by the schools. That is when our Head teacher said about the incident and the MP promised to come, and he did so, only that he came during weekend on Saturday, and he didn't find any teacher here but met PTA chairman, because we [teachers] all live at the trading center ... I am sure if it happened that the Head Teacher didn't raise that issue, all of them could not know that issue.[26]

---

[26] Teacher, Mfano school, June 2017.

A community member noted, "our school committees, PTA and SMC are not active, and they don't know their roles and responsibilities, they only show up when the village headman called them or telling them what to do." Another type of local organization, the Mothers Group, which also serves as a liaison between schools and parents for girls education in particular, faced resistance from community members.

One Mothers Group member explained:

> To be honest, in this area everything is not working, the big problem is education but also health, and I know the root cause of all this is parents here are not educated and are illiterate. They don't know the benefit of education in real sense, they just heard from other people. But in them, they don't value it as a key to development and success. And early pregnancy and marriages ... youth become parents before they become adults, [they] drop out of school in the classes between [Standard] 3–6 and no one completes Standard 8, you can go around the village you will not find one ... these children who stop going to school and marry and become a parent after giving birth – do you think this same parent can force her/his own child or young sibling to school? ... Teachers have been sending names of children to us, the Mothers Group and the chief for follow up, but when we visit these homes most parents do not welcome us, instead they start shouting at us, exchanging with us bad words or even abusive words and intimidate us in the presence of their children, so how can we convince such a parent or child to go back to school?

Even members of school committees had relatively little experience with this type of education. Half of the members of the PTA and school management committee had never attended school.[27] There were also reports that the previous village chief had undermined the authority of the local education committees, which may in part explain their dysfunction. For example, the chairman of the PTA said that the previous chief told the committees to stop forcing parents to send children to school, which "demoralized us the school committees." But that chief had since died and was replaced by a woman who seemed more interested in encouraging children to attend school.

In fact, during one of our visits to Mfano the new chief was holding court, solving a variety of issues in the village related to early marriages and pregnancies. However, she was now having problems exerting her own authority, at least with respect to matters concerning children and parenting. She explained,

---

[27] See Table A.6.

Here in my village everything is not going well, young girls are being married early. Imagine at the age of 10 years [a girl] gets pregnant and parents force that child to get married to that man responsible for that pregnancy. When our community policing forum or Mothers Group goes to that house to meet with the parents, most of them try to exchange bad words with these people by saying: "don't interfere in my household issue, who are you? Are you the one who takes care of all my children? Mind your own business in your homes or if you don't have anything to do, just go and raise up your children."

On the issue of schooling specifically, she explained:

When the other children who are in school see the other grown up children stop going to school and just playing or chatting at home, ...they get tempted to follow what these drop out children are doing, and they think that they are enjoying, so they again stop going to school with the influence of out of school children, and most parents don't force them to school. The number of children who are in school is very small, and they are also very young to defuse the peer pressure. As a result, they end up of being out of school, but others do go back in and out each year. ...

It is very difficult to find a child completing Standard 8. Both parents and other children are not educated and don't value education and are not interested about that, and their children you will find them at the mini market just hanging around without anything to do.

The management and monitoring of schools and school attendance involved a complex web of institutions that relied centrally on the cooperation of ordinary community members, and especially parents. There was little expectation among community members and children themselves that children in Mfano village would complete primary school. In the event that individuals, such as the new chief or the Mothers Group member, tried to alter the status quo, they met resistance from parents. The PTA and school management committee were dysfunctional, which meant that when problems arose, such as the roof blowing off, they were unable to effectively or efficiently solve these problems. As a result, the quality of the school itself suffered, making it an even less attractive place for children to spend time.

John continued to send me updates on how things were going. The roof was finally fixed. But in February 2018 he messaged me again, this time to report that many girls at the school had become pregnant. In July of that year, we went back to try to understand what had happened, and to see how things were going in general at Mfano school. The pregnancies certainly seemed a setback for schooling in the community.

There were eleven girls between the ages of 13 and 17 who had become pregnant at Mfano during the 2017/2018 school year. While a few planned to return to school, most did not, with the sentiment being that they were now "over age" or that because they were now mothers there was no need to return to school. In most cases, the fathers of the children were also boys and young men from the village, some of whom had since gone to South Africa to work.

Despite this news, there were also positive developments in the school, most of which had been spearheaded by Mfano's teachers. One of the challenges Mfano had faced was there was no Standard 8 class, which meant that the few students who persisted up to Standard 7 could not complete primary school, and thus had no chance to continue onto to secondary school. The closest school offering Standard 8 was several kilometers away.

The teachers had held a meeting with the PTA, SMC, Mother Group, and chiefs from surrounding villages, to inform them that the teachers wanted to add a Standard 8 class. All the committees agreed, and they wrote a letter to inform the district education office. Two months later they received a positive response, and had begun teaching.

The first class of Standard 8 pupils sat exams in 2018, and John was their teacher. In January 2019 he informed me that there were 21 students in his class, 9 girls and 12 boys, up from 15 the year before. All 21 students had progressed from Standard 7 the previous year.

Mfano was improving, in fits and starts, with numerous setbacks along the way. While Mfano is not meant to be representative of all schools in Malawi, or even all schools in predominantly Muslim areas, what this case makes clear is that school quality is a function of the participation of the community, the efficacy of local institutions like the PTA and SMC, and the commitment of the teachers.

In a context with extremely limited government funding for education, and low oversight capacity – Mangochi district alone has over 300 primary schools with more than 265,000 students – communities and local institutions play essential roles in school management, maintenance, and fundraising. If dropping out before the completion of primary school is seen as normal and expected, communities will be less invested in maintaining school quality.

Where parents have little to no experience with this type of education themselves, and where most children attend for only a few years, the incentives to participate in these institutions are few. Members of these institutions are selected by communities and by the schools' founding institutions. For example, a school originally founded by the Catholic Church will have representatives of the church on one or both of these committees. Representatives may or may not be selected based on merit or experience. Often PTAs and SMCs are inactive, and meet only at the encouragement of the teachers when an urgent issue arises.

This in turn places a great weight on the role of teachers regarding school governance and quality. In these villages, teachers are rarely from the community in which they work, precisely because so few students ever make it through secondary school and obtain the requisite education to become a teacher in the first place. Without teachers' houses, teachers live farther from the school and are more likely to come late in the absence of close monitoring and sanctioning. When calamities arise, such as a roof blowing off, it takes months to fix, leaving students to study outside or in makeshift structures. If this happens during the rainy season, as it did in Mfano, this may discourage students from attending altogether, potentially permanently affecting their education. Falling behind in class due to such disruptions may discourage them from continuing the next year.

In the best case scenario, teachers are dedicated, and trying their best under difficult conditions – schools are located far from towns, teacher housing is of poor quality when it is provided at all, teachers live far from their extended families, and they teach large classes with few supplies. In spite of all this, these teachers are able to make incremental improvements in the school – fixing a roof, constructing teacher housing, repairing a latrine. In the worst cases though, school staff become predatory, demanding monetary contributions from students and families or else sending them home, and then making it impossible to account for how this money has been spent. Even if parents know that it is their right to insist that children attend school, they may not be in a position to do so.

Individual teachers and headteachers in such circumstances often have far more education and experience working with government than community members or members of the local institutions. They may in fact be the only ones with the means to communicate with local governments, and as was seen in the case of Mfano, teachers may be the ones to mobilize the very institutions that are meant to be monitoring them. Despite its challenges, Mfano seems lucky, because it has ended up with teachers like John.

To make matters worse, it is difficult for local government officials like the District Education Manager (DEM) to tell when schools are failing. The official education report from Mfano school in 2016, when we first visited, says that the SMC met 11 times – this is the information that received by the district education office. But by all accounts from the ground – including from the SMC chairman himself – no such meetings were held.

In fact, out of the 262 schools included in the 2016 education report to the district, which is also compiled across districts and sent to the Ministry of Education, only two schools reported that no SMS meetings were held. How this misreporting occurs is not clear, but it does not seem in the interest of the SMC itself to report that it has never met, and confirmation that meetings took place are likely difficult to verify, especially for school inspectors tasked with monitoring dozens of far-flung schools.

I observed similar dynamics playing out in other schools in Muslim areas in Malawi, sometimes with teachers who were much less dedicated than those I met at Mfano. One school, which I'll call Mwindaji school, stood out in particular. The school was in the mountains, so close to the border with Mozambique that the cell phone coverage would occasionally revert to the Mozambican network. Many people worked for a multinational corporation growing coffee and macadamia nuts. The school signpost even had the company's name, proudly boasting the financial support the corporation had provided.

One might think that a school with such financial support would be particularly high quality. However, several teachers reported that the head teacher demanded fees from the children attending the school, and if families could not or did not pay, she would send the children back home. These fees, usually called "contribution fees" or "development fees" are common in primary schools in Malawi, and are meant to cover costs in school maintenance and equipment not fully covered by the meager resources sent by the central government. However, these fees are not a legal requirement for attending school, and not a basis on which children should be allowed to attend or not. Moreover, the fee reported at this particular school was 1300 Kwacha, a relatively small amount but about four times as much as the fees reported at other schools.

Several parents corroborated the teachers' reports that children were out of school because they could not pay the school "development fee." Preventing children from attending school for not contributing these fees is illegal, but most of the parents had no experience with the education sector and most likely did not realize that these fees were not a basis upon which the school could decide whether their children would attend or not.

On our visit to the school, the head teacher herself was nowhere to be found. The teachers reported that she often left the area to attend "workshops and meetings" for days at a time, which negatively affected the quality of the school. Why didn't the school management committee, which should have been tasked with monitoring school performance, complain about the development fee? To this, the teachers simply replied, "they are illiterate."

Moreover, the teachers themselves were not happy with their posting, it being far from any kind of urban center and without transportation that would allow them to easily travel to and from the school. In fact, three teachers had transferred away in the previous year, leaving only seven teachers in a school where there were over 250 students in Standard 1 alone. Ideally at least three teachers should have been devoted to a Standard 1 class of that size (which even then would have meant a student–teacher ratio of 80:1) but this was not possible given the staffing constraints. These dynamics are all too familiar in the schools I visited, revealing vicious cycles of low attendance and poor quality schooling.

Schooling Norms as Key Drivers of Behavior

It was no longer a mystery why children like Margaret's stopped school after a few years. The mystery, if there was one, was how children made it through primary school and on to secondary school at all. Walking to school every day, spending much of your waking hours throughout childhood and adolescence in school, these are huge investments. To make this decision to step out of home and into the classroom every day is either to buy into the idea that is simply what one does, to believe in the long-term rewards (tenuous at best), or to be required to do so.

This suggests that among some families and communities there are greater social rewards – there are strong norms – for attending school, separate from the economic returns to schooling. The historical relationship between missionaries and mass schooling created a set of normative expectations about the attendance of school among Christians and those living in predominantly Christian communities. However, the social costs of school attendance were once very high for many African Muslims – often prohibitively high – as Muslims feared school attendance would mean conversion to Christianity.

While a number of institutional and policy changes have reduced these social costs, the social *benefits* of school attendance have only slowly, and recently, been increasing among Muslims. Muslims living as a minority behave differently from those living as a majority because they have faced greater incentives to fit in socially and compete economically with Christians. Both of these factors have meant that the social benefits of school have "spilled over" to a greater extent among Muslims who live as a local minority.

The interviews and observations presented in this chapter formed the basis of an alternative explanation for the Muslim–Christian schooling gap, and why it has tended to be so much larger in Muslim majority areas: the role of community-level norms in shaping schooling behavior. Using insights from these interactions, I developed a survey designed to measure norms across communities empirically, the results of which I present in Chapter 6.

6

Empirical Evidence of Schooling Norms in Malawi

The interactions and interviews with parents, teachers, and community leaders discussed in Chapter 5 suggest that a distinct set of expectations about schooling exist between Christians and Muslims in predominantly Muslim and predominantly Christian communities in southern Malawi today. Among Muslims in predominantly Muslim communities, it is expected that children will start school, but very few will finish primary school, much less secondary school. Parents often talk vaguely about the benefits of school. Some children are particularly interested and self-motivated to go to school, but if they are not and one day stop attending, this does not seem to raise eyebrows. Indeed, it seems to be the norm that one stops attending school by the early teenage years at the latest, and thereafter begins looking towards starting and supporting a family.

Meanwhile, Christians living in Muslim communities typically persist in school longer than their Muslim neighbors, as do Christians and Muslims living in predominantly Christian communities. This is not to say most Christians or most of those living in Christian communities finish secondary school – completing secondary school is rare everywhere. But the expectation among Christians, regardless of whether they live in a predominantly Christian or predominantly Muslim community, seems to be that children stay in school as long as possible.

In this chapter, I use a combination of coordination games and survey evidence to examine the extent and strength of schooling norms empirically among Christians and Muslims living in a set of Muslim majority and Christian majority villages in southern Malawi. I show that, in general, Christians exhibit stronger schooling norms than Muslims, and that the gap in empirical and normative expectations is particularly large in predominantly Muslim areas. A survey with traditional leaders, who play a key role in local governance, reveals that these leaders also perceive differences in schooling norms between Christians and Muslims.

Measuring Norms

How do we measure norms? I begin by discussing some considerations and strategies in eliciting these sorts of beliefs. Norms are made up of a set of expectations about what others will do – empirical expectations – and what others think should be done – normative expectations. These expectations are second-order beliefs, they are beliefs about others' beliefs. They are distinct from personal beliefs, which are about one's own preferences. Second-order beliefs are important to understand because they can shape behavior independently of personal beliefs, and one's personal belief may differ from one's expectations of others' beliefs.[1]

First I discuss survey approaches to norm measurement, which form the basis of the approach I use in the context of Malawi. There are several ways to measure second-order beliefs. Regarding empirical expectations, we could ask respondents what they expect is the most common behavior in a particular domain (e.g. what level of education do you think most people complete in the neighborhood where you live?), or ask them to estimate the percentage of people that behave in a certain way (e.g. what percent of children in your neighborhood complete high school?). Regarding normative expectations, we could ask for a respondent's expectations about what most other people think *should* be done, in addition to what they think people would actually do.

While individuals are usually reasonably confident in their personal beliefs, there is often some degree of uncertainty about others' beliefs, and the extent of uncertainty can help us understand the strength of a norm. For example, imagine you are standing outside your office or apartment building on a typical day, watching people come in and out. Out of every ten people who enter the building with someone following close behind, how many do you think would wait and hold the door? How many out of ten do you think would say that one *should* hold the door in such a circumstance?

If you said nine or ten for one or both of these questions, this would suggest your belief in a fairly strong norm that one should hold the door.

---

[1] Cialdini (2007); Bicchieri (2016)

If you said five or six, this would be evidence of a weaker norm, and if you said zero or one this would indicate you think there is definitely not a norm of door-holding. Values toward the middle of the spectrum indicate greater uncertainty than those at the extremes.[2]

Uncertainty in others' beliefs is also likely to produce greater variation in expectations within a community. It could be the case that your expectations are closely aligned with those of others, or it could be that they are very far from the average expectation. To get a good sense of the norm in the community as a whole, you would want to go through the exercise of eliciting second-order beliefs with a representative sample of people for whom the behavior applies (in the door-holding case, for example, those who use the building).

The strength of the norm is therefore indicated not only by the average expectation – say, on average people who use the building think nine out of ten people would hold the door – but also the dispersion of these responses. It could be that all those surveyed guessed the same number, nine out of ten, or it could be that half guessed ten, another quarter guessed eight, and another quarter guessed between one and seven. A larger dispersion indicates greater uncertainty about the norm within the community, and thus a weaker norm. If there is not a common understanding of what constitutes appropriate behavior, norms about that behavior are relatively weak. For example, Prentice (2012, p. 27) present the thought experiment of two hypothetical communities, one in which the expected range of schooling is seven to nine years and another where it is four to twelve years. In both cases, the average expected years of schooling is eight years, but "the norm for how much to educate children is likely to have a much stronger influence in the first community than in the second."

Finally, you might expect that others' beliefs and behavior vary, on average, across identity groups such as gender, ethnicity, or religion. In order to gauge whether people expect differences across groups, you could elicit second-order beliefs for different groups (e.g. beliefs among women compared to men).

I administered questions like these in a survey in Malawi, discussed in greater length in the sections that follow. However, there are also limitations to a survey approach that informed my decision to also include a

---

[2] These example values are provided to demonstrate the variation in the strength of a potential norm, not to provide cut-points of what constitutes a norm or not.

set of coordination games designed to measure second-order beliefs about schooling. First, it may be difficult to estimate the beliefs of an abstract group of individuals, even when the boundaries of the group are clear (e.g. beliefs among members of a particular village). Indeed, in the process of piloting questions designed to elicit second-order beliefs, I found that respondents often experienced difficulty in estimating percentages about characteristics of community members. While ideally a respondent would be able to provide an estimate of the percentage of people in their village whom they believe will do or think a particular thing, this was quite difficult to do in practice, perhaps especially so in contexts with relatively low levels of numeracy.

Second, it could be that social desirability bias affects survey responses.[3] In the context of schooling beliefs, perhaps respondents feel that enumerators – who have higher levels of education than themselves – would want them to say that education is important to members of their community. In other words, perhaps they are telling us what they think we want to hear, or they want to portray their group in a positive light.

To address these limitations, in addition to a survey, I conducted a set of coordination games that were designed to make it easier for respondents to provide estimates of others' beliefs by making the "others" more concrete, and to reduce the likelihood of social desirability bias. First, the games brought respondents into physical proximity with one another, so the "others" whose beliefs they were estimating were more tangible. Second, since we were able to measure the beliefs of all the participants, we were able to know the "truth," at least as they reported it to us, about their beliefs. Because we knew the true value of the modal response, we could monetarily incentivize respondents to provide accurate responses, reducing the likelihood of strength of social desirability bias, a strategy that builds on work by Krupka and Weber (2013). Note that this does not fully avoid the possibility of social desirability bias, particularly if respondents believe *others* will exhibit social desirability in their responses. Nevertheless, providing a monetary incentive may reduce the likelihood that social desirability is affecting responses.[4] Finally, in the games, respondents provided responses privately instead of directly to enumerators, which may further reduce the likelihood of social desirability bias.

[3] Zizzo (2010)
[4] Bicchieri (2016)

Evidence from Malawi

To measure beliefs about school attendance and persistence in school, I conducted surveys and coordination games with over 700 respondents in 20 villages, half of which are predominantly Muslim and half predominantly Christian. I compare beliefs about schooling between Christian and Muslim respondents across the two types of villages. The villages are all within Mangochi, the Muslim majority district that was the site of the majority of the interviews presented in the previous chapter. By focusing on a single district, I am also able to hold constant the overall capacity of the local government, particularly with respect to the quality of school inspection and the efficacy of district education officers.[5] Mangochi is also a particularly important district, being the second largest in the country, with a population of over 1.1 million. More than 70 percent of the population of Mangochi are Muslim, and it is home to one-third of the total Muslim population in Malawi.[6]

The 20 villages in the sample were located in 10 randomly selected enumeration areas where Muslims comprised 5 to 25 percent of the population (Christian majority), and another 10 where Muslims comprised 75 to 95 percent of the population (Muslim majority). As this was a model testing exercise, I selected villages well-predicted by the best fitting model.[7] Specifically, I selected villages for which the rate of Muslim school attendance was close to that predicted based on the percentage Muslim of the area. Figure 6.1 shows the relationship between percentage Muslim and Muslim school attendance for all the enumeration areas in Mangochi district, where the sampled enumeration areas are symbolized with a black dot.[8]

In each village, a set of 36 respondents, half Christian and half Muslim, participated in a set of games designed to measure second-order beliefs regarding school attendance. Each respondent was also administered a one-on-one survey. Additionally, I collected observational data about public goods and collective action in the villages and interviewed each of the village chiefs.

---

[5] The choice of focusing on a particular district prioritizes internal over external validity. At the end of the chapter, I take up the question of the generalizability of the argument.
[6] 2018 Malawi Census.
[7] Lieberman (2005)
[8] Further details of sample selection can be found in Appendix A.7.

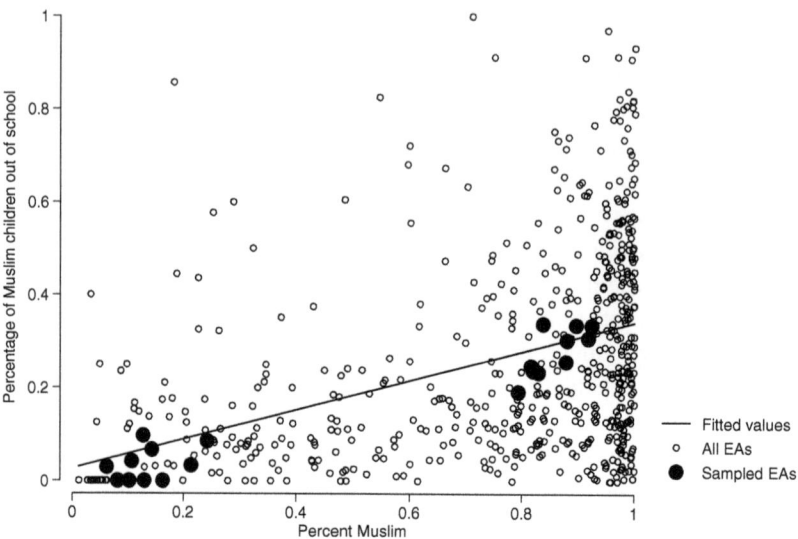

FIGURE 6.1 Sampled enumeration areas.
Source: Malawi 2008 Census.

Altogether, 720 respondents participated in the survey and games.[9] Their average age was 37 years, and 60 percent were female. Three-quarters of respondents were married, with an average of nearly four children. In this rural setting, 94 percent of respondents lived in homes without electricity, though 65 percent reported owning a mobile phone, and nearly 90 percent reported owning land. Over 80 percent of all respondents reported working in agriculture, as hawkers/vendors, fishing, or unskilled manual labor. Fewer than 2 percent reported working in the formal sector. Christians were slightly more likely to own assets like a bicycle or mobile phone.

The survey confirmed that there are differences in the educational attainment of Muslim adults living as a majority and minority, as well as compared to Christians. Like the census data shown in earlier chapters, the survey data show a negative relationship between literacy and the

---

[9] Respondents were mobilized the day before the research activity, and were approached using a combination of guidance about the locations of religious groups in the village from the village headman, followed by a random walk procedure in each village. Every effort was made to achieve gender balance, but in practice this was quite difficult, as men were more likely to be away working during the day, when the data collection took place. Unfortunately, this was particularly true in Muslim majority areas. As a result, there are more women than men in the sample.

6 *Empirical Evidence of Schooling Norms in Malawi*

local share of the Muslim population among Muslims, a relationship not observed among Christians. The magnitude of this effect is large – among Muslims living in Christian areas, 58 percent were literate, compared to 39 percent of Muslims living in Muslim areas. This gap persists after controlling for age, gender, and reported household income.

As shown in Table 6.1, there are also differences in educational attainment among Muslim children across the two areas, but not for Christians,

TABLE 6.1 *Summary statistics of respondents' children.*

	Muslim children (18 and above)		
	Majority Christian	Majority Muslim	p-value
No school	0.02	0.18	0.00***
Years of education	7.55	5.49	0.00***
Ever repeated	0.78	0.89	0.39
Attended madrasa	0.63	0.51	0.03*
N	164	164	
	Muslim children (age 6–17)		
	Majority Christian	Majority Muslim	p-value
Child in school	0.94	0.89	0.06+
Will attend next year	0.93	0.86	0.01**
Ever repeated	0.76	0.71	0.18
Attended madrasa	0.68	0.54	0.00**
N	308	270	
	Christian children (18 and above)		
	Majority Christian	Majority Muslim	p-value
No school	0.07	0.07	0.86
Years of education	7.43	7.21	0.56
Ever repeated	0.64	0.85	0.12
N	230	145	
	Christian children (age 6–17)		
	Majority Christian	Majority Muslim	p-value
Child in school	0.97	0.94	0.25
Will attend next year	0.96	0.93	0.10
Ever repeated	0.64	0.64	0.91
N	280	270	

Note: + $p < 0.10$, * $p < 0.05$, ** $p < 0.01$, *** $p < 0.001$.

confirming that this education gap is indeed persisting up to the present day. Among respondents' adult children (age 18 and above), Muslims living in Muslim areas were more likely to have never attended school and had fewer years of education on average. Among respondents' children of school-going age (age 6–17), Muslim children were more likely to be out of school and less likely to report planning to attend the subsequent year.

Among both adult and school-age children, Muslim children living in Christian areas were more likely to attend madrasa than those living in Muslim areas, suggesting, as in the earlier survey, that madrasa is not serving as a replacement for formal education in this setting. These figures confirm that there continue to be worse educational outcomes for Muslim children living in Muslim areas, even within the same district.

Are Christian and Muslim majority villages different on other important dimensions that could affect schooling outcomes? The fact that Christians and Muslims living in the same village experience different schooling outcomes in the Muslim areas suggests that it is not a village-level factor that is affecting schooling outcomes but rather something specific to Muslim or Christian inhabitants of the village. Nevertheless, I collected a variety of village-level measures to examine whether and how Christian and Muslim villages might differ in ways that could be affecting the schooling gap. Specifically, I collected observational data about public goods located in the village and interviewed the village chief about his or her perceptions of the village. Although the sample of villages is too small to pick up all but large differences across village types, summary statistics suggest that the two sets of villages – majority Christian and majority Muslim – are quite similar to one another on a variety of dimensions.

First, these sets of villages look quite similar in terms of public goods available. If anything, the Muslim villages seemed slightly better off on a few dimensions. All but one village (a Christian village) had a government primary school, and about half of Muslim and half of Christian villages had a nursery. Secondary schools were rare in general. Three Christian villages and two Muslim villages had a secondary school.

In terms of infrastructure, Muslim villages were more likely to be connected to the electricity grid (four of ten Muslim villages compared to one of ten Christian villages), and enumerators assessed the road quality as similar. Muslim villages were more likely to have a government health center (three of ten Muslim villages compared to one of ten Christian villages), and slightly more likely to have a market (eight of ten Muslim villages compared to six of ten Christian villages). There were more functional water points and latrines in the Muslim villages as well. Not surprisingly, Christian villages had more churches, while Muslim villages had more mosques.

Second, both sets of villages look similar in terms of their overall level of social capital. Social capital is often thought to be important for public goods provision, of which education is one. On its face, social capital may seem conceptually similar to the way I have defined culture. For example, Putnam, Leonardi, and Nanetti (1993, p. 167) write: "social capital ... refers to features of social organization, such as trust, norms, and networks that can improve the efficiency of society ... " Nevertheless, the argument presented here and the evidence from the interviews with parents and community members is not that inhabitants in Muslim areas are less able to solve collective action problems or are more inefficient *in general*. It is specifically the strength of schooling norms that differ between Muslim and Christian areas, not differences in social capital generally.

To assess overall levels of social capital, we asked the village chief to assess cohesion and cooperation of the community, including how well the village works to solve problems, and whether villagers contribute money, labor, or in-kind goods to village projects. The chiefs' responses suggest that there are no differences in general social cohesion or collective action. Chiefs reported that inhabitants contribute to projects at similar rates across village types, and assessed communities' abilities to solve problems similarly. If anything, the leaders in Muslim villages rated monetary contributions to village projects as slightly higher than those in Christian areas.[10]

Schooling Expectations

Next, I turn to both empirical and normative expectations about schooling in Muslim and Christian communities using survey data. Completion of primary school is a relatively rare event in southern Malawi, particularly in Mangochi district. Among respondents' children, Muslim children living in Muslim villages were more likely than those in Christian villages to be out of school, and not plan to attend the following year. Twice as many Muslim children living in Muslim areas did not plan to attend school in the coming academic year as compared to Muslim children living in Christian areas and Christian children living in Muslim areas.

---

[10] Table A.8 shows summary statistics by area type for a variety of village-level outcomes.

Respondents are clearly aware of the differences in persistence in school across religious groups. Most respondents believe that there is a gap in schooling outcomes between Christians and Muslims. A first assessment of empirical expectations was to ask respondents whether they thought Christians or Muslims were more likely to complete primary school. Across both types of villages, most respondents reported a belief that Christians are more likely to complete primary school than Muslims. Christian respondents perceive a particularly large gap, and the perceived gap was larger in Muslim villages than Christian villages. Close to 80 percent of all Christian respondents said that Christians were more likely to complete primary school than Muslims (83.8 percent in Muslim villages and 78.1 percent in Christian villages). The majority of Muslims also believed that Christians were more likely than Muslims to complete school (66.3 percent in Muslim villages, and 50.3 percent in Christian villages).

Figure 6.2 shows the distribution of responses to the question of who is more likely to complete primary school, presented by religion and village type, demonstrating the widespread empirical expectation that there is a gap in persistence in school across religious groups. Those who deviate from this expectation almost universally say that Christians and Muslims

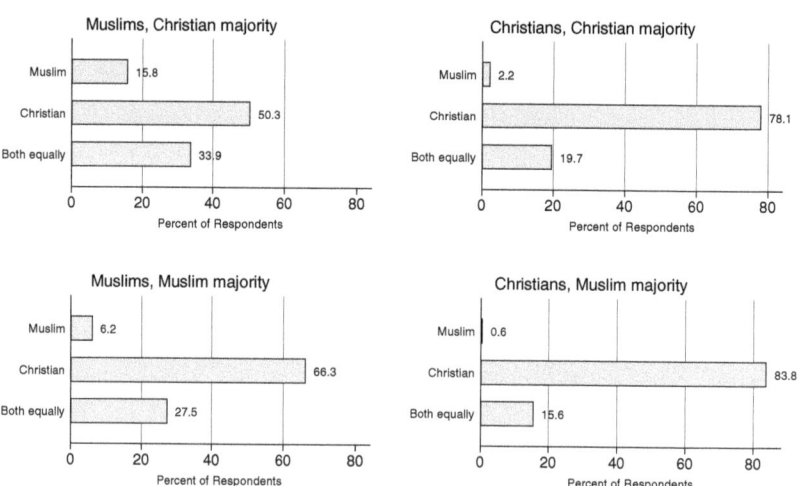

FIGURE 6.2 Distribution of responses to the question, "Who is more likely to complete primary school?" by religion and village type.
Source: Malawi 2018 Survey.

6 Empirical Evidence of Schooling Norms in Malawi 139

are equally likely to complete school. Only a small minority of respondents say that Muslims are more likely to complete primary school than Christians.

In a follow-up question, respondents were asked to explain their answer as to whether Muslims or Christians were more likely to complete primary school. While respondents gave a variety of answers, those who believe Christians are more likely to finish school tend to explain that this is due to parenting, such as parents' encouragement for children to attend and children listening to parents, or values and culture, including Muslims valuing business over education, Muslims valuing marriage over education, and Muslims valuing madrasa over formal education.

A number of respondents specifically invoked the term "culture" to explain differences. This included a culture of schooling among Christians, and the importance of other activities besides schooling among Muslims. One Christian respondent explained, "It is because of the cultural values among Christians and the belief in business among Muslims" (Christian, Christian village). Another also noted the role of business, namely that "Christians have a good background of school than Muslims who have the culture of doing businesses. Hence, Christians work harder to achieve their goals than Muslims who easily drop out and start business or other things." Yet another said that "It is like Christians' culture to go to school while Muslims encourage their children to go to South Africa or to go fishing" (Christian, Muslim village). Another simply explained, "Mostly it's because of the culture we believe in" (Christian, Christian village).

Muslims also frequently described differences in how Christians conceived of education. One Muslim respondent noted, "Christians take education as culture, for example in their family have role models that inspire them to continue education," and another that "Christians value school more than everything" (Muslim, Muslim village). Muslims tended to note things that they considered to be "cultural" that were at odds with or clashed with schooling, and some thought that Muslims preferred or prioritized madrasa. One explained, "Muslim culture doesn't push children for education" (Muslim, Christian village).

Concerning parenting, many reported differences in parenting styles and emphasis across religious groups. Muslims reported that "[Christian] Parents make effort to chase them to school" (Muslim, Muslim majority area), "Muslim parents still have mentality that children should not be educated like them so make no effort to send them to school" (Muslim,

Muslim village), and "Most of the Muslims they don't force their children to go school" (Muslim, Christian village).

A number of Christians expressed a similar sentiment, that "[Muslim] Parents don't encourage their children to go to school" (Christian, Muslim village), "Christian parents focus on education a lot than Muslims... Education is a major key to Christians" (Christian, Muslim village), and "Most Christian parents encourage their children to go to school as compared with the Muslim parents who push their children into marriage" (Christian, Muslim village).

Together, these responses show both widespread recognition in the differences in levels of schooling attained by Christians and Muslims, but also in how these groups conceive of schooling. This brings us to a closer investigation of normative expectations. In addition to perceiving differences in the actual levels of schooling achieved – beliefs which are also accurate empirically – do respondents also perceive there to be differences across groups in what level of schooling is considered *appropriate*?

In the survey, we asked respondents to state the level – in terms of grade year – at which most Muslims and most Christians think it is appropriate to stop schooling. When asked this question, I find that the average level of schooling that Christians say other Christians deem appropriate is significantly higher than the level reported among Muslims about other Muslims. Further, Muslims living in Muslim villages report lower levels of schooling as being appropriate than Muslims living in Christian villages. Figure 6.3 shows the estimated level of schooling that Muslims and Christians in each type of village report as being the appropriate level at which to stop schooling for their own religious group.

There is another feature of the responses to this particular question that sheds light on the *strength* of these normative beliefs. As noted at the outset of the chapter, one measure of the strength of norms is the degree to which there is a common understanding about what others expect. I find that the variation in responses among Christian respondents is significantly less than among Muslim respondents, indicating a greater degree of coordination in second-order beliefs about schooling among Christians as compared to Muslims. Christians are much more certain of other Christians' beliefs about appropriate levels of schooling than Muslims are of other Muslims' beliefs.

Respondents were also asked what they thought the appropriate level of schooling was for members of the religious outgroup (i.e. Muslims' beliefs about Christians' expectations and vice versa). In general, Christians reported lower expectations about Muslims' schooling rates and

6 Empirical Evidence of Schooling Norms in Malawi 141

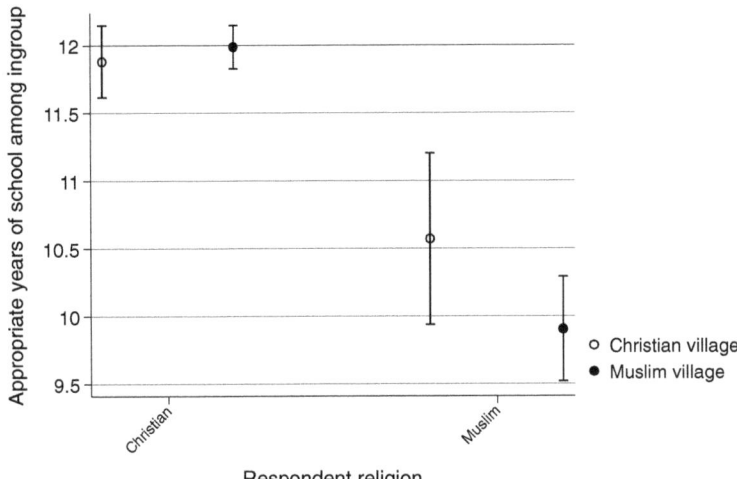

FIGURE 6.3 Level of schooling considered appropriate among ingroup, by religion and village type.
Source: Malawi 2018 Survey.

normative beliefs about schooling than Muslims did of themselves. This may in part reflect stereotypes among Christians about Muslims' schooling levels, or a tendency for Muslims to report more favorable perceptions of group members than they actually believe, or both. Muslim respondents also reported slightly lower expectations of Christians than Christians did about themselves, but these expectations were still higher than their expectations of other Muslims' beliefs.

These findings show that first, both Christians and Muslims perceive higher levels of schooling as being appropriate among Christians, and second, the gap in normative and empirical expectations is larger in Muslim as compared to Christian villages. As shown in Figure 6.4, there are relatively larger gaps in normative expectations in the Muslim villages as compared to Christian villages, and the gaps were larger among Christian than Muslim respondents. For example, Christians living in the Muslim villages perceived a difference of about three and a half years in the levels of schooling considered appropriate by Christians as compared to Muslims. These surveys provide evidence in support of the idea that both normative and empirical expectations differ in Muslim and Christian villages, and particularly so among Muslim respondents as compared to Christian respondents in Muslim villages.

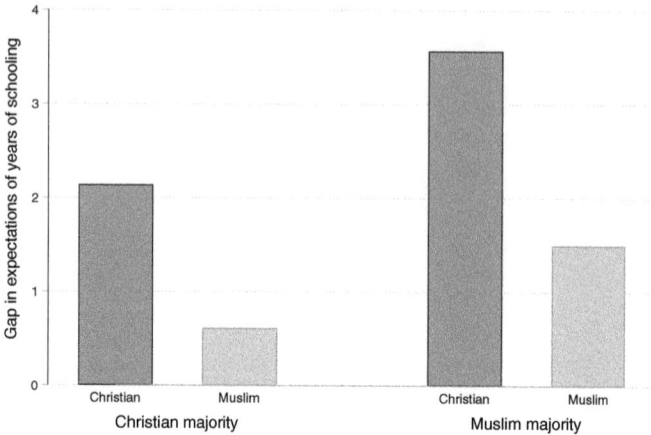

FIGURE 6.4 Gap in expected years of schooling between Christians and Muslims. *Source*: Malawi 2018 Survey.

Coordination Games

Owing to the potential limitations of measuring norms through surveys, I used two games to provide an alternative measure of normative beliefs about schooling. Respondents in each village were randomly assigned to participate in a religiously homogeneous (Muslim only or Christian only) or religiously mixed (half Christian, half Muslim) session.[11] In each village, three sessions ran concurrently, with twelve respondents each. In each session, the respondents sat together in a community space such as a classroom or meeting area. Respondents were given a pen and a clipboard with a set of data collection sheets on which they would privately mark their own responses, with the idea that the opportunity to answer in private would reduce the likelihood of social desirability bias that might emerge in interacting directly with enumerators. Of the various second-order beliefs respondents provided over the course of the games, five were randomly selected and respondents received 200 Kwacha for each correct response (a response that matched the modal response of other respondents in that session) of the selected questions. Further, all respondents received 500 Kwacha (about US$0.70) for participating.

---

[11] During the introduction of the activity within the group, the religious composition of the group was made salient, with respondents being informed that the members of the group were either all Christian, all Muslim, or half Christian and half Muslim. Since all respondents live in the same village, it is likely that they already knew this information, but reminding them made the religious composition of the group more salient.

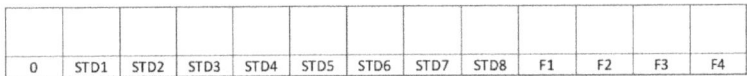

FIGURE 6.5 Timeline tool.

The Timeline Game
A first game, called the timeline game, provided a parallel to one of the survey questions, where respondents were asked to indicate the level at which they thought others in their session would think it was appropriate for a boy and girl, respectively, to stop attending school. Specifically, they were asked to mark on the sheet what they thought the most common response would be among other members of their session. The data collection sheet that respondents used is shown in Figure 6.5. This sheet shows all the levels of primary school (Standard 1 to Standard 8, written in as commonly abbreviated) and all the levels of secondary school (Form 1 to Form 4). *Please indicate the class at which you think most people in this session think it is appropriate for a [BOY/GIRL] to stop attending school.*

The results of the timeline game were similar to those from the survey. The majority of respondents in all groups thought that others believe completing secondary school was the appropriate level to stop school. However, Muslims in Muslim villages were more likely than others to say that some primary or complete primary was the appropriate level of schooling to attain, and the differences were particularly pronounced when providing estimates of expectations for girls' schooling.

For example, a quarter of Muslims in Muslim villages thought that a girl dropping out during primary school or not attending at all would be considered appropriate. Nearly 40 percent thought that a girl completing primary school or less would be considered appropriate. Among boys, expectations were somewhat higher, though one-quarter of Muslims in Muslim villages thought completing primary school or less would be considered appropriate. Thus, while the majority of Muslim respondents report that the appropriate level of schooling is completing secondary school, a substantial minority report much lower expectations, particularly so in Muslim villages.

Figure 6.6 shows the predicted values for the expected years of school considered appropriate by village type and respondents' religious affiliation. This figure reveals that first, regarding the appropriate level of school, Christians have higher expectations of other Christians than

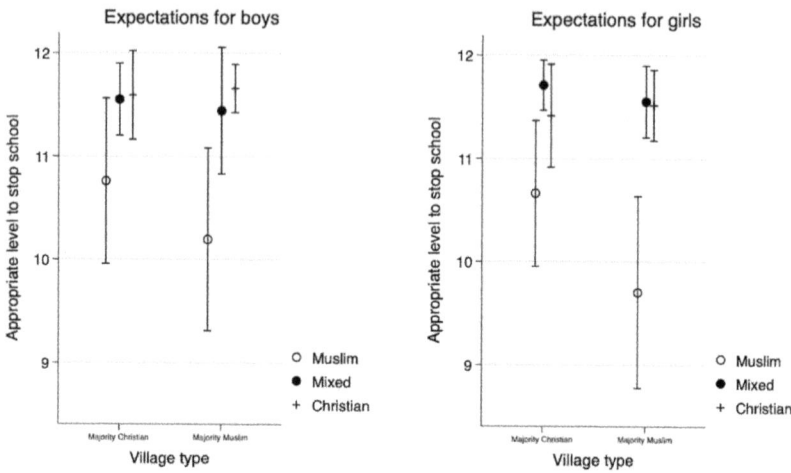

FIGURE 6.6 Expected level of schooling, normative beliefs.
Source: Malawi 2018 Survey.

Muslims do of other Muslims, regardless of village type. Second, in comparing the confidence intervals, we can see that there is greater precision for the estimates of Christian as compared to Muslim responses, indicating less variance in the former. As with the survey responses, this suggests that not only is the average expectation about the appropriate level of schooling higher, there is also greater consensus about this estimate, indicating a stronger norm.

Third, the estimates for the appropriate level of schooling are lower among Muslims living in Muslim villages than those living in Christian villages. While these patterns are present for estimates of girls' and boys' schooling, the interaction between Muslim and village type (Christian or Muslim) is significant only for estimates of girls' schooling. This may in part be a reflection of a lack of statistical power to detect a difference, particularly given the variance in Muslims' responses. However, it could also be that norms about boys' and girls' schooling are somewhat different among Muslims. Additionally, the variation among Muslims in Muslim-only groups once again underscores the degree of uncertainty Muslims have about other Muslims' schooling beliefs, and provides further evidence of relatively weaker norms.

6 Empirical Evidence of Schooling Norms in Malawi

Fourth, estimates of beliefs in the mixed groups are significantly higher than those in the Muslim groups, and are similar to those in the Christian groups. This provides additional evidence that respondents are aware of the differences in beliefs across religious groups, and perceive that the modal response regarding the appropriate years of schooling will be higher in a group where there are Christians.

Social Appropriateness Game

In a second set of games, respondents were read a set of actions that someone could take – for example, a boy stopping school after completing primary school – and were asked to guess the modal response for participants in their session regarding the degree of social appropriateness for each action. There were four answer options they could choose from: very inappropriate, somewhat inappropriate, somewhat appropriate, and very appropriate.

To play the game, respondents were asked to mark on their response sheet (see Figure 6.7) the face indicating the degree of social appropriateness of each behavior described by the enumerator. Respondents were asked to select the answer that they thought would be the modal response for the group – that is, what other people think, rather than their personal opinion. The key behaviors in question were stopping school after completion of various levels (e.g. some primary, complete primary, some secondary) as well as stopping school for specific reasons, such as after

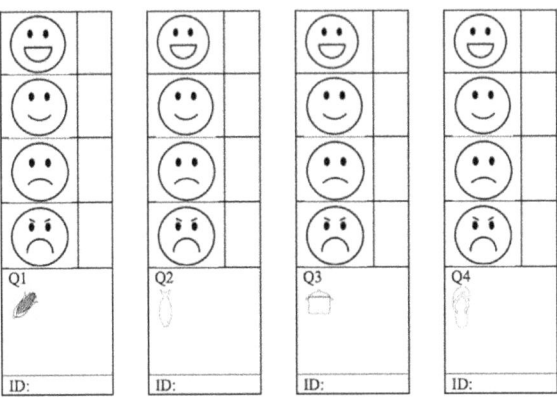

FIGURE 6.7 Social appropriateness response sheet.

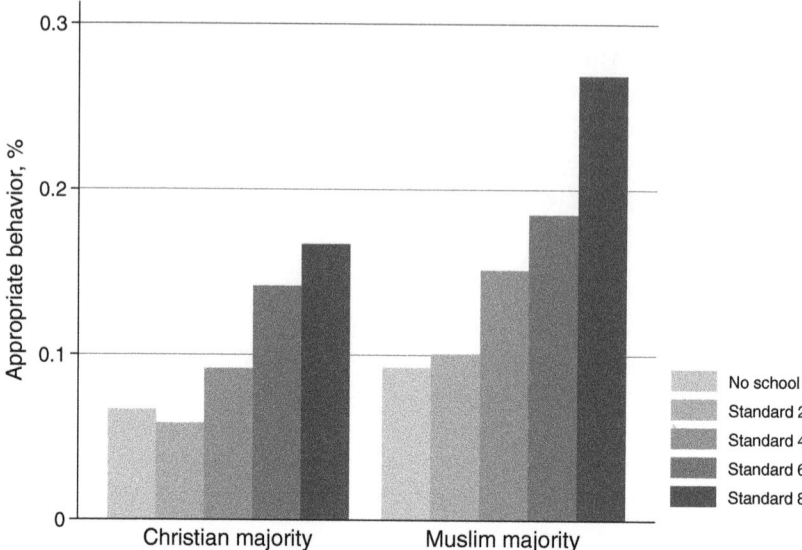

FIGURE 6.8 Percentage of Muslim respondents who believe other Muslims think it is appropriate to leave school, by area type.
Source: Malawi 2018 Survey.

having learned to read and write, to help their family with planting, or to start work or a family.[12]

The goal of the response sheet was to allow respondents to make their choices privately, without revealing their beliefs to others. In practice, however, this game was quite challenging for many respondents, particularly those who were illiterate, and the idea of making a mark with a pen was intimidating to some. Ultimately, the survey (administered by enumerators) and the coordination games yielded similar results, but high levels of illiteracy mean that efforts to measure norms using techniques such as these games should be complemented by strategies that do not require respondents to write.

Figure 6.8 shows the percentage of Muslim respondents, by area type, who believe others think it is "somewhat appropriate" or "very appropriate" to leave school after two, four, six and eight years of primary school, or to never have attended at all. For example, 9 percent of Muslim respondents in the Muslim area and 6 percent of Muslim respondents

[12] Each card indicates the question number and respondent ID, and symbols are used to help respondents ensure they are on the correct question, as many respondents were illiterate.

in the Christian area think other Muslims deem it appropriate to never attend school.

As might be expected, the appropriateness of leaving school increases with the level of education in question – respondents are more likely to think others will approve of dropping out after completing primary school (Standard 8) as compared to leaving after completing only two years, for example. However, at all levels, Muslims living in Muslim areas are more likely than Muslims living in Christian areas to think other Muslims consider leaving school appropriate. The gap in beliefs is largest at higher levels of schooling. Muslims living in predominantly Muslim villages are 40 percent more likely to think other Muslims believe it is appropriate to stop attending after completing primary school than Muslims living among Christians. There is also a large gap in beliefs between Christians and Muslims living in Muslim majority areas, where Muslims are far more likely to believe that others perceive leaving school as appropriate behavior.[13]

Respondents were also asked about the appropriateness of leaving school for particular reasons, and about other behaviors that might interfere with school completion. Some of these included leaving school to help the family plant crops, starting school late (at age nine instead of six, when children in Malawi are supposed to begin Standard 1), leaving school after learning to read and write, leaving school at puberty to work (in the case of a boy) or to start a family (in the case of a girl), for a girl to marry at age 15, or becoming pregnant before marriage. In general, there were not large differences in expectations about the appropriateness of these behaviors between Christians and Muslims or between those living in Christian versus Muslim villages.

Together, the coordination games and survey responses show that both Muslims and Christians expect Christians to persist in school longer than Muslims, an empirical expectation, and that they also perceive differences in normative expectations about persistence in school across religious groups. There was a high degree of coordination of second-order beliefs among Christians about fellow Christians, and much greater variation in second-order beliefs among Muslims about fellow Muslims. These findings suggest that schooling norms are stronger among Christians compared to Muslims, and normative and empirical expectations about Muslim schooling are particularly low in majority Muslim areas.

[13] See Figure A.12.

Beliefs and Perceptions of Traditional Leaders

While the survey and games focused on the beliefs of community members, it is also useful to consider the beliefs of local leaders. Leaders play a central role in local governance and can also influence the beliefs of their constituents. Using a survey of 62 Traditional Authorities (TAs), I find that traditional leaders hold broadly similar expectations about schooling expectations as their constituents. They expect Muslim children to complete less schooling than Christian children, and they perceive differences across religious communities about the level of education that is considered appropriate to complete. They also say that they infer nonattendance of school as evidence that parents do not value education, which may have implications for the extent to which they prioritize educational investments in their constituencies. Finally, with respect to TAs' own development priorities, those with lower levels of schooling themselves were less likely to propose spending new resources on an education project.

The constituencies of the 62 TAs surveyed were located in six districts in Malawi where Muslims comprise a substantial proportion of the population, shown in Figure 6.9. As in many other African countries, traditional leaders in Malawi play a central role in local governance.[14] In the context of Malawi, TAs are unelected, often hereditary leaders who

FIGURE 6.9 Sampled districts, Traditional Authority Survey.

[14] Logan (2009)

work closely with local governments to formulate and execute policy. Their authority is geographically demarcated, and "Traditional Authority" refers both to the individual and the administrative area they govern, which are akin to counties within a district.

Existing work shows that traditional leaders in Malawi can play a central role in shaping their constituents' behavior, for example, in the utilization of health services.[15] Additionally, TAs serve as advocates for their communities in relation to the district and central government, for example in lobbying for and mobilizing resources and securing development projects. TAs can also formulate and implement local bylaws, for example, requiring women to deliver in health facilities or prohibiting child marriage.[16]

Trust in traditional leaders by the Malawian public is quite high, especially as compared to elected leaders. In nationally representative surveys, 70 percent of Malawians report trusting traditional leaders "somewhat" (18 percent) or "a lot" (52 percent) compared to 51 percent who say the same of the national parliament and 55 percent who say the same of the elected local council.[17] As trusted leaders, TA beliefs – whether about schooling or other subjects – are likely to matter to their constituents.

The survey of TAs included estimates of educational attainment within the TA, their priorities over different types of development projects, how the schooling behavior of constituents shaped their beliefs about how much constituents value education, and their beliefs about schooling norms among Christians and Muslims. All TAs also had the opportunity to enter a lottery in which they could win US$500 to go towards a development project of their choice. This was meant to provide a semibehavioral measure of their preferences for education projects over other types of development projects.

Of the 62 traditional authorities interviewed, two-thirds were Muslim and one-third Christian, and 85 percent were men. Christian TAs were twice as likely to speak English as Muslim TAs (43 percent and 22 percent, respectively), and while all the Christian TAs had attended school, one-quarter of the Muslim TAs had never attended school. Thus, the Muslim–Christian schooling gap is present at the level of leaders as well as within the general population.

---

[15] Walsh et al. (2018)
[16] Maiden (2021)
[17] Malawi Round 6 Afrobarometer survey.

For the most part, the religion of the TA reflects the majority religion of the area. All the Christian TAs lived in areas where Christians were a majority, and where Muslims were less than a quarter of the population. The majority of Muslim TAs lived in areas where Muslims were a majority, though ten Muslim TAs presided over areas where Muslims comprised less than half of the population. As TAs are unelected positions, they tend to be held for quite a long time. On average, the TAs in our sample had been in their current position for twelve and a half years, with just under 20 percent serving twenty years or more.

The TAs are reasonably well-informed about their constituents, and if anything, somewhat underestimate educational attainment. For example, on average, Muslim TAs thought just over 40 percent of adults in their area were literate, when in fact the figure was around 55 percent. Christian TAs estimated just over half of adults in their area were literate, when in reality around two-thirds were. Muslim TAs believed the children in their area completed school at significantly lower rates than did Christian TAs.

The TAs also reported different empirical expectations for persistence in primary school among Muslim as compared to Christian children, as shown in Figure 6.10, which plots TA responses to the question: "I want you to think about the Muslim children who live in [TA name]. Out of 10 Muslim [Christian] children in [TA name], how many do you think finish STD8?" Expectations about the percentage of Christian children who would complete school were significantly higher than expectations about the percentage of Muslim children who would complete primary school.

The TAs were also asked directly whether they expected Muslims or Christians to be more likely to complete primary school, an empirical expectation that mirrored the question asked of respondents in the community member survey. Only a single TA reported that he expected a Muslim to be more likely to complete school than a Christian. A majority thought there was no difference, but a substantial minority – about 40 percent – thought Christians were more likely to complete school.

In addition to empirical expectations, TAs were asked what they thought their constituents believed regarding the appropriateness of school attendance and persistence in school, their normative expectations. Both Christian and Muslim TAs reported the appropriate level to stop schooling as lower among Muslims than Christians. For example, 90 percent of TAs think that their constituents believe completing secondary school (Form 4) is the appropriate level at which to stop for Christian

6 Empirical Evidence of Schooling Norms in Malawi

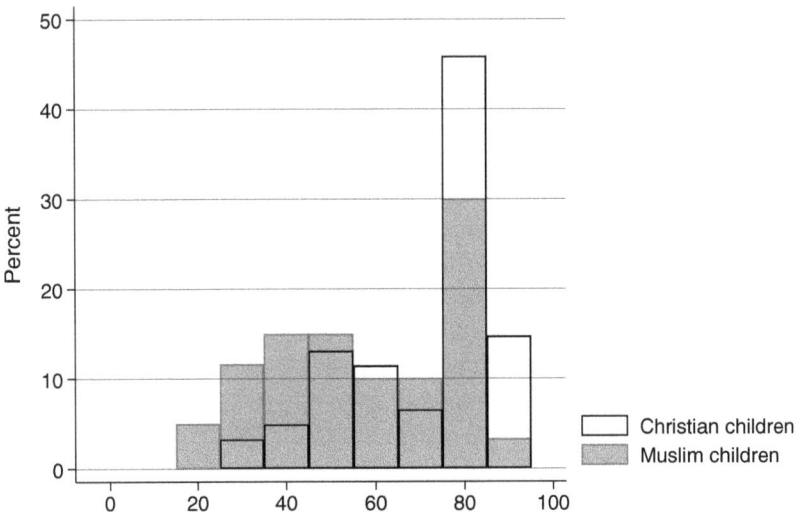

FIGURE 6.10 Traditional Authority (TA) empirical expectations about completion of primary school, by child's religion.
Source: Malawi 2019 TA Survey.

boys and girls. By contrast, more than a third think their constituents believe Standard 8 (complete primary school) or less is appropriate for Muslim girls, and nearly a quarter believe Standard 8 or less is appropriate for Muslim boys. This reflects the findings of the coordination games and survey, which are that people – both ordinary people and local leaders – perceive Muslims to have lower normative expectations than Christians for what level of schooling is appropriate to complete.

In addition, and also mirroring the findings of the coordination games, there was greater dispersion of expectations when considering the beliefs of Muslims than of Christians. There was a high degree of consensus about what Christians believe constitutes an appropriate level of schooling, while there was less consensus regarding what Muslims believe is appropriate, again indicative of a stronger schooling norm among Christians than Muslims.

Although there are clear differences in TAs' beliefs about normative expectations among Muslims and Christians, like survey respondents from the coordination games, they nonetheless report much higher levels of schooling being appropriate than what is actually observed. Only 35 percent of children nationally progress from primary to secondary school, so the idea that 90 percent of TAs think their constituents believe completion of secondary school is the appropriate level at which to stop (at least for Christians) does not align with actual completion rates, or with their own empirical expectations.

I therefore measured TAs' normative expectations in another way, in which I asked TAs to estimate the percentage of Christian and Muslim parents in their area who thought children "should" complete primary school. This question was asked of TAs and not in the general survey due to the aforementioned difficulty many respondents experienced in estimating percentages. Specifically, TAs received the following prompt: "I want you to think about the Christian/Muslim parents who live in [TA name]. Out of 10 Christian/Muslim parents in [TA name], how many think children should finish Standard 8?"

On average, TAs thought a lower percentage of Muslim than Christian parents think children should complete primary school. The TAs thought just under 70 percent of Muslim parents would think children should complete primary school, compared to nearly 80 percent of Christian parents. Once again, this suggests the schooling norm as perceived by TAs is stronger among Christian parents than Muslim parents. Together, this provides evidence that TAs' empirical beliefs about schooling and their perceptions of their constituents' normative beliefs about schooling differ across religious groups.

To what extent do TAs' normative and empirical expectations about their constituents affect TAs' behavior with respect to education? If leaders perceive that their constituents do not value education very much, will they be less likely to mobilize resources for education as compared to other sectors? In order to evaluate these questions, I asked TAs to report their interpretation of parents' behaviors. In particular, I asked how much they thought parents valued education in the case where a child never went to school, where a child attended until Standard 4 and then stopped (some primary), and where a child attended until Standard 8 and then stopped (complete primary).

The TAs were unanimous in their assessment that if a child never goes to school, they infer that the parents of the child "don't value education at all." Even for a child who stops halfway through primary school, which is probably the modal outcome in many of these areas, a majority of TAs infer from this behavior that parents "don't value education at all." If a child completes primary school, which is rare in general and especially in these areas, the modal response from TAs is that parents value education "a little." Considering that a large percentage of children never complete primary school, it seems likely that local leaders infer that many of their

6 Empirical Evidence of Schooling Norms in Malawi 153

constituents do not value education. Given the many development priorities – from water, to food security, to health – local leaders may choose to invest their limited time and resources elsewhere if they perceive low interest in education among their constituents.

To assess TAs' development priorities, we gave TAs the opportunity to enter a lottery worth US$500 to implement a development project of their choice, and asked them what this project would be. A quarter of TAs proposed a project related to education, and the strongest predictor of proposing an education project is the TAs' own level of education: TAs with higher levels of education are more likely to propose an education project. In fact, none of the ten TAs without schooling proposed an education project. The Muslim–Christian literacy gap was also a significant predictor – TAs were more likely to propose an education project in areas with larger gaps. The TAs' perceptions about how much their constituents value education and their perceptions about rates of completion do not seem to shape their project proposals.[18]

Together, these findings show that traditional leaders, among the most respected leaders in Malawian society, perceive differences in both actual rates of schooling among Christians and Muslims as well as in their normative assessments of persistence in school. They also report that they make important inferences about how much parents value education as a function of children's persistence in school.

Although TAs report that their constituents have relatively high expectations about the level that schooling children should attain, they are also aware that many children do not reach this level in practice. Further, leaders' own experience with education is correlated with at least one measure of educational investments – the likelihood of proposing a project to improve education in their constituency. Those with some or complete secondary education were also somewhat more likely to say that educational infrastructure was the most important service to people living in their TA.

While the survey of TAs does not allow us to test whether and how much these leaders directly impact the creation or maintenance of norms about schooling, it does demonstrate that there are broadly similar trends in both empirical and normative expectations among ordinary people and their leaders. These findings also provide suggestive evidence that leaders'

---

[18] Table A.10 shows differences across TAs that chose education versus other projects, while Table A.11 shows results in a regression framework, with the caveat that the number of observations is relatively small.

own experience with education can affect educational investments. Areas with low levels of schooling are likely to produce leaders with low levels of schooling. Leaders' educational attainment can, in turn, affect their own priorities and investments, and possibly their ability to execute projects. Those with no schooling may have less information about how the education system works, and what specific inputs are needed, lending further credence to the idea that feedback loops sustain differences in schooling and school quality across communities.

Contemporary Schooling Norms in Nigeria and Uganda

To what extent do the findings from southeastern Malawi travel to other contexts? In this final section I examine survey data that provides suggestive evidence that schooling norms differ in Buganda and Nigeria, the two cases I examined in exploring the historical roots of the Muslim–Christian schooling gap. Within Nigeria, the percentage Muslim of the population is a predictor of schooling beliefs, while in Uganda, Christians and Muslims report similar schooling beliefs.

Empirically, examining norms in a large number of cases is a challenge, particularly if one is interested not only in first-order but also second-order beliefs, which are almost never measured on cross-national surveys commonly used in the literature on culture and cultural persistence, such as the World Values Survey or regional public opinion surveys such as the Afrobarometer.[19] Moreover, in part because of the presumed universal demand for mass schooling, respondents are rarely asked about their beliefs about this type of schooling, whether first- or second-order.

However, although the most commonly used public opinion surveys are limited in their ability to measure the schooling norms I have described, there have been a few specialized surveys on education that ask

---

[19] Some existing work on culture as a mechanism of persistence uses historical exposure to an event, shock, or practice, and contemporary measures of first-order beliefs in order to make a case for the persistence of norms. A number of these studies use measures of trust as a type of cultural belief or norm. For example, Nunn and Wantchekon (2011) argue that slavery in Africa led to a "culture of mistrust" that has persisted across the centuries. To test this hypothesis empirically, they show that historical exposure to slavery is associated with lower levels of trust in local government and in other individuals (relatives, neighbors, and coethnics), as measured in contemporary public opinion surveys. Tabellini (2010) also uses survey data on generalized trust, the importance of respect for others, and one's sense of control to create a measure of culture, and demonstrates that early literacy and historical political institutions are predictive of this measure of contemporary culture.

6 Empirical Evidence of Schooling Norms in Malawi

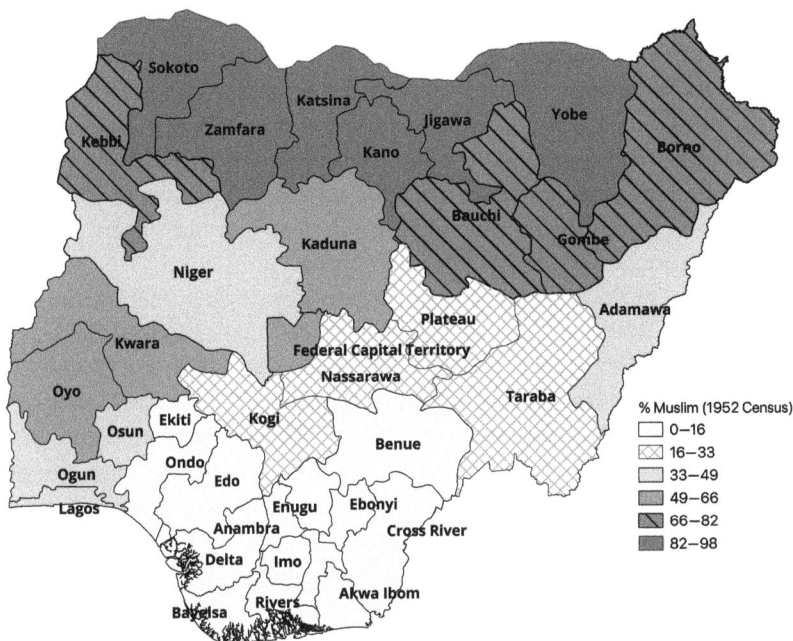

FIGURE 6.11 Percentage of Muslims by State in Nigeria.
Source: Nigeria 1952 Census.

detailed questions regarding beliefs about schooling as well as reasons why children might not be attending school. In this section, I present results corroborating the findings from Malawi using the EdData II survey in Nigeria, conducted as part of the Demographic and Health Surveys (DHS), as well as an original survey from Uganda.

The Nigerian EdData II survey was conducted in 2004 and covers all of the country's federal states. Although this survey lacks measures of second-order beliefs, it includes questions about parents' beliefs concerning education and their engagement with schools.[20] In terms of religious demographics, Nigerian states vary from about 0.1 percent to 98 percent Muslim. Figure 6.11 shows a map of Nigeria with the distribution of percentage of Muslims by state. These figures, except for the Abuja Federal Capital Territory (FTC) come from the Nigeria 1952 Census.[21]

---

[20] The EdData II surveys were also conducted in Uganda and Malawi, but in these samples, data on respondents' location are incomplete and the sample size by administrative unit is very small, which renders it difficult to examine how beliefs and behavior vary as a function of the local percentage of Muslims.
[21] The Nigerian census has not collected data on religion since 1963 and any current estimates are based on survey data, which are frequently not designed to be representative

The EdData II sample includes 3987 respondents, of whom almost exactly half are Christian and half are Muslim. Literacy rates among respondents were quite low: 50 percent of Christian respondents and 66 percent of Muslim respondents were unable to read the sentence administered in the literacy test, while 24 percent of Christians and 58 percent of Muslims said they had never attended school.[22] The average age was 43 years, indicating that the average respondent had been born around the time Nigeria gained independence in 1960.

The survey reveals several points that corroborate the findings from my own survey in Malawi. First, as in Malawi, there appear to be differences in schooling beliefs across Muslim and Christians, which are driven by Muslims living in areas where they are a majority. While the EdData II survey does not ask about appropriate levels of schooling within communities, which would be the ideal measure, it does ask about a number of beliefs with respect to schooling that pertain to gender as well as parental involvement in schools.

Regarding gender differences, the survey included questions about the prioritization of education by gender, as well as advantages and disadvantages of sending boys and girls to school. These data suggest that Muslims living in Nigerian states with larger Muslim populations have quite different views about girls' schooling than Christians and than Muslims living in states with fewer Muslims. In one survey question, respondents are given the following prompt: "I am interested in knowing your opinions about what makes primary schools good and the importance of schooling. Do you agree or disagree with the following statements?" There were four statements that followed, having to do with the quality of school structures, competing demands for child labor, skills taught in primary school, and the prioritization of school by gender. This last preference was phrased as follows: "It is more important to send a boy to school than to send a girl to school."

In the full sample, around 30 percent of respondents agreed, and 60 percent disagreed, that it was more important to send boys to school

---

at the state level. State-level religious demographics are similar across the 1952 and 1963 censuses.

[22] The school attendance was asked such that it included religious education that also included other subjects, but would have excluded schooling that was purely religious: "Now I would like to ask about your schooling. When we talk about schooling, it includes formal schools at the primary, secondary, and higher levels. Schooling also includes formal religious schools that teach academic subjects like mathematics, in addition to teaching religion."

6 Empirical Evidence of Schooling Norms in Malawi

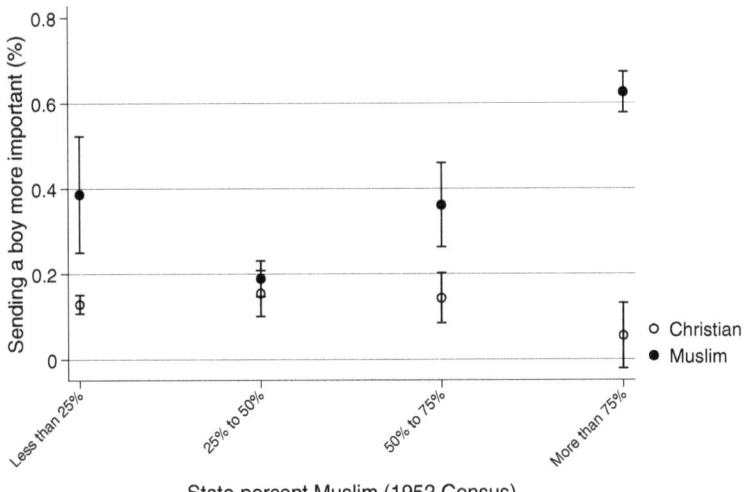

FIGURE 6.12 Predicted probability of agreeing that schooling is more important for boys than girls.
Source: Nigeria EdData II, 2004.

than girls. However, there was a large difference across religious groups. Only 14 percent of Christian respondents agreed, while nearly half – 48 percent – of Muslim respondents agreed. Further, the likelihood that Muslims agreed with the statement was much larger in states with a large Muslim population.

Figure 6.12 shows that the predicted probability that a Muslim respondent agrees with the statement that it is more important to send a boy than a girl to school is highest where Muslims comprise over 75 percent of the state.[23]

Another set of questions asked respondents whether they perceived any disadvantages of sending boys or girls to school. Although it was relatively rare, Muslims were twice as likely as Christians to say that there was at least one disadvantage of sending girls to school – 10 percent of Christians and 20 percent of Muslims noted at least one disadvantage. The predicted probability that a Muslim respondent mentions a disadvantage of sending

---

[23] This figure shows the results of a logistic regression where the outcome is whether or not a respondent agrees that sending boys to school is more important than sending girls and Muslim religious affiliation is interacted with the percentage Muslim of the state according to the 1952 Census, where the state percent Muslim is binned in quartiles. A model including ethnicity, urban/rural status, and respondent education yields a similar pattern, though the estimates are lower overall.

a girl to school increases from 8 percent to 25 percent as the percent Muslim of the state in which they live increases from less than 25 percent to more than 75 percent. The interaction is statistically significant, but not robust to the inclusion of ethnicity as a covariate.[24]

In addition to the fact that Muslims were more likely to mention disadvantages, the specific disadvantages parents cite also differed by religion. Among Muslims who mentioned at least one disadvantage, 55 percent noted concerns with marriage, including "later marriage" or that it would be "harder to find a husband." By contrast, only 2 percent of Christians listed marriage as a concern, instead citing factors such as "bad manners" and "leaving the village."

These survey questions are limited in their ability to establish respondents' second-order beliefs about other members of their communities. Nevertheless, they show there are differences in first-order beliefs about the importance and disadvantages of participating in mass schooling, particularly for girls. These responses thus provide suggestive evidence that schooling norms are weaker among Muslims living in Muslim majority areas of Nigeria. There appears to be greater variation in expectations about what constitutes appropriate behavior, with a nontrivial percentage of Muslim respondents reporting concerns about girls schooling, even at the primary level.

Another set of survey questions allows me to examine whether levels of parental engagement are lower in Muslim majority areas. Evidence from Mfano in Malawi suggested that norms about schooling, or the lack thereof, can enter a feedback loop that affects school quality. One of the ways this can happen is if parents are less engaged in school maintenance and management. In many low resource settings, funding provided by governments is insufficient to cover even basic needs, such as school infrastructure. Communities can step in by providing support for schools in the form of materials or labor.

According to the Nigeria EdData II survey, around 40 percent of parents reported contributing labor, money, or materials to support school buildings. However, Christians were much more likely to report making a contribution of some kind than were Muslims: 56 percent of Christians mentioned at least one form of contribution, compared to 36 percent

---

[24] In a model where state Muslim is binned by quartile, Muslims in the top quartile are substantially more likely to report at least one disadvantage than those in the second and third quartiles. Estimates for the first quartile are noisy due to the small size of the Muslim sample in this bin.

6 Empirical Evidence of Schooling Norms in Malawi

of Muslims. Further, Muslims were less likely to contribute in Muslim majority states. The likelihood of reporting any school contribution falls from 45 percent to just over 30 percent as the Muslim population of the state increases.

Muslim parents in Muslim majority states are also less involved with their children's schools. They are less likely to report having a parent–teacher association (PTA) and among those who do have one, they are less likely to have attended a PTA meeting in the 12 months preceding the survey.

Finally, Muslim parents living in Muslim majority states are less likely to engage with teachers or the school. The survey asked about three types of engagement in particular: attending a school event, meeting with a teacher, and picking up a school report card. Muslims living in Muslim majority states were less likely to have engaged in at least one of these activities than Christians and than Muslims living as a majority. Figure 6.13 shows that the likelihood of engaging in at least one of these three activities is lowest among Muslims where they comprise 75 percent or more of the state population.

A second finding that is in accord with the results from Malawi is that, despite the paucity of schools in Northern Nigeria during the colonial period, survey evidence suggests that physical access is no longer a major

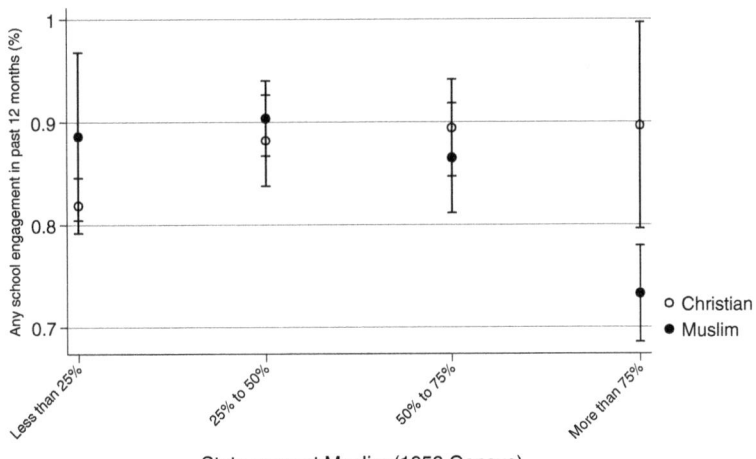

Engagement includes attending a school event, meeting with a teacher, or picking up a report card.

FIGURE 6.13 Predicted probability of engaging with children's school and teachers.
Source: Nigeria EdData II, 2004.

impediment to school attendance. There is no substantial difference in respondents' estimates of the distance to the nearest primary school by respondent religion or in Muslim majority areas as compared to Muslim minority areas.[25]

On average, Nigerian respondents estimated that walking to the nearest primary school would take 15 minutes. The average length of time to school in Muslim areas was shorter among Christians than Muslims – around 7–9 minutes, compared to 15–18 minutes. Nevertheless, this difference is not so large that this should constitute a major obstacle. Moreover, the average distance reported by Christians in Christian areas was also around 15 minutes on average, and school attendance in these areas is high. Estimates of distance using kilometers show similar patterns, and never exceed 1 kilometer on average.

Together, data from the Nigerian EdData II survey provides evidence that corroborates the findings from Malawi. First, norms about schooling seem to differ among Muslims in Muslim majority areas. The norms we are able to examine are those related to girls' schooling specifically, but nevertheless indicate that the norm of universal schooling is not as strong in these areas, certainly not with respect to girls. Second, there is evidence that parental involvement is lower among Muslims in Muslim majority areas. While there are no measures of school quality, it seems plausible that lower parental investment both in time and resources is likely to produce lower quality education. Third, there is no evidence that access to school in terms of physical distance is a major impediment to Muslim schooling, and thus is unlikely to explain the differential rates of schooling between Christians and Muslims in Nigeria.

In contrast to Nigeria, in Uganda the distribution of the Muslim population is much more diffuse, and an analysis using districts that is analogous to that using state-level percentage of Muslims in Nigeria is not possible. However, it is telling that in the Uganda EdData II survey, there were no differences between Christians and Muslims in beliefs about schooling for boys and girls. Ninety-eight percent of all respondents disagreed with the statements that "Girls do not need more than a primary school education" and "Boys do not need more than a primary school education."

---

[25] Distance to school is measured in two ways. One is parents' estimation of the distance in kilometers and the other is their estimation of the distance in minutes to the nearest primary school. Both these show a statistically significant but substantively small effect of the interaction between being Muslim and the percentage Muslim of the state on distance to school.

6 Empirical Evidence of Schooling Norms in Malawi

Ninety-five percent of all respondents said there were no disadvantages of sending girls or boys to school.

Indeed, in Uganda I would not expect to see differences in norms to the degree that I observed them in Malawi since Muslims are a minority almost everywhere. Nevertheless, I present some limited evidence from a survey conducted in Masaka, a district in central Uganda that is about 20 percent Muslim according to the 2002 Census.[26] The survey sample included 2447 individuals, of whom nearly 30 percent were Muslim. On average, women had completed about six years of school, and men between six and seven years. For both men and women the average years of schooling for Muslims was actually slightly higher than Christians. In other words, there was no Muslim–Christian schooling gap in this population. Over 95 percent of respondents said religion was somewhat or very important, with the majority of respondents falling in the latter category.

This survey was conducted prior to the fieldwork in Malawi, and thus was not designed with the goal of measuring schooling norms. Nevertheless, I did ask a number of questions designed to assess the first-order beliefs about schooling. First, about 90 percent of all respondents "completely agree" that sending boys and girls to primary and secondary school is important; 7–10 percent selected "somewhat agree" and a handful disagreed. There were no differences between Christian and Muslim respondents. Over 90 percent of respondents also said that they never keep boys or girls home from school, and those who do said that this was done only a few times a year.

Another question attempted to force a response with respect to gender preferences by asking the following, "If you had two school going children, a son and daughter, and you were only able to send one of them to school, who would you send?" Here, about half of respondents said a son and half said a daughter. About 10 percent said neither, or that it depends on ability or intelligence. Again, there were no differences by religious affiliation.

Muslim and Christian respondents also reported similar rationales for sending children to school. This was an open-ended question where

---

[26] This survey was part of a larger project on banking to which I was able to add a module on beliefs about schooling. See Dupas et al. (2018), which used the data for which the study was designed. Pascaline Dupas generously offered to include a module on education to the baseline survey in Masaka in 2013. I am grateful for her generosity and to the research team who worked to add the module on short notice.

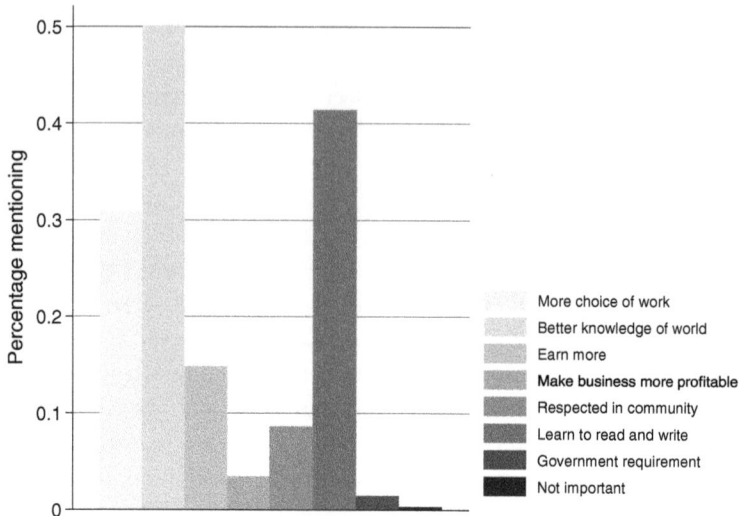

FIGURE 6.14 Reasons why it is important to send children to school. *Source*: Uganda Household Survey, 2013.

respondents were simply asked, "In your opinion, why is it important to send children to school?" and their responses were coded and grouped by theme. The most commonly mentioned response was having better knowledge of the world, followed by learning skills such as reading and writing.

Relatively few respondents mentioned earning more, which lends support to the idea that it is not simply or even primarily economic considerations that are driving schooling – at least these are not top of mind for respondents. A little less than 10 percent also mentioned being respected in the community. Among other responses were having a "bright" or "better" future, helping the family, and socialization and social skills. Figure 6.14 shows the frequency with which respondents mentioned a set of reasons as to why they thought school attendance was important. There were no differences in the distribution of these responses between Christian and Muslim respondents.

While unable to document respondents' second-order beliefs, this survey demonstrates two things. First, there is both high demand for, and considerable importance placed on, schooling in this district. Second, there are no differences between Christians and Muslims on any measure of beliefs about schooling. This provides at least suggestive evidence of a strong schooling norm among both Christians and Muslims. This survey also highlights considerable differences between Ugandan Muslims and Nigerian Muslims, particularly concerning gender. In central Uganda, there is no evidence that Muslims prioritize boys' schooling over that of girls or generally have different expectations of what is considered appropriate for boys and girls with respect to schooling.

These three cases, Malawi, Nigeria, and Uganda, all suggest the presence of strong schooling norms in Christian communities, and significant variation in the strength and content of schooling norms among Muslims. Variation in Muslims' beliefs and expectations across countries and subnational regions suggests these beliefs are not "Islamic" beliefs, but rather a product of the context in which Muslims find themselves.

7

Generalizing the Argument

If one were to select a child at random who lives in Nigeria, Malawi, or Uganda today, how would their odds of attending primary school compare? Throughout this book, I have shown that the answer depends critically on whether the child is Christian or Muslim, and whether most of their neighbors are Muslim or Christian. If the child is Christian, the likelihood that they are attending school is high, and roughly the same across all three countries. If the child is Muslim, however, the odds that they are in school are much higher in Uganda and Malawi, and especially so if they live in areas where Muslims are a minority. Figure 7.1 shows the average rates of school attendance among children between the ages of 8 and 12 as measured in recent Demographic and Health Surveys in the three countries. Rates of school attendance among Muslim children in Nigeria are 30–45 percentage points lower than that of Christians, while in Uganda they are essentially at par. In Malawi, rates of schooling are at a similar level to those in Uganda, but Christians are slightly more likely to be in school.

These patterns are surprising given what we know about precolonial and colonial legacies, as well as the relationship between income per capita and educational attainment. While scholars have long noted differences in educational attainment across colonizers,[1] with British colonies experiencing higher levels of education, all three of the cases in this book experienced British colonialism, and were sometimes governed by the same British administrators. Precolonial statehood is also associated

---

[1] White (1996), Bolt and Bezemer (2009)

7 Generalizing the Argument

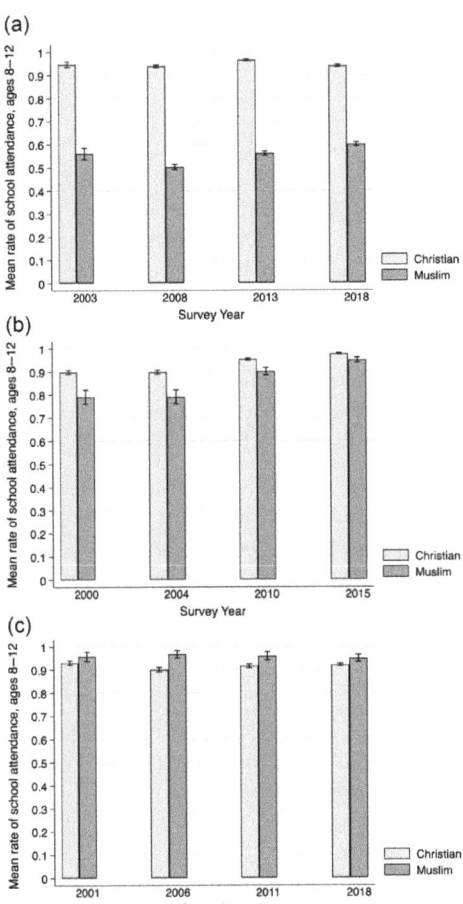

FIGURE 7.1 School attendance rates in (a) Nigeria, (b) Malawi, and (c) Uganda by religion.
Source: DHS, various years.

with higher levels of economic development,[2] but northern Nigeria and central Uganda, which had two of the strongest precolonial states in Africa, could hardly look more different in their educational outcomes today. Moreover, Nigeria's income per capita is more than double that of Uganda, and more than three times that of Malawi, but the likelihood of school attendance for Muslim children – who make up about half of the population – is much lower than in countries that are significantly poorer.

---

[2] Bandyopadhyay and Green (2016), Michalopoulos and Papaioannou (2013), Wilfahrt (2018)

In this book I have shown that even within empire, Muslim populations experienced different educational outcomes depending on the extent of Islamization at the time of colonization. In those places with larger Muslim populations, and especially those with Islamic political institutions, there were fewer investments in schools by colonizers and especially missionaries, and low demand for this new form of education. Where Muslims were a minority, however, they faced competition with Christian missionaries, and viewed the provision and attendance of mass schooling as imperative to their religious and political survival. Differences in both brick-and-mortar investments, and in ideas about mass schooling, resulted in long-term effects on schooling trends and in the magnitude of the Muslim–Christian schooling gap, and explain why the gap was largest in Muslim areas, and continues to be so.

However, we know that policy differences across colonial powers in Africa were substantial, and especially so in their relationship with Christian missionaries. Further, all three of the cases in this book are those where Muslims are at most 50 percent of the national population. We should therefore ask to what extent the dynamics revealed in the cases of Nigeria, Malawi, and Uganda play out in other parts of Africa, particularly in countries where Muslims are either a large majority or a tiny minority, and in countries outside the British sphere of influence.

In this chapter, I look beyond the three primary cases to provide an overview of the dynamics with respect to colonial-era schooling investments and strategies elsewhere on the continent, and examine in brief two additional cases: Senegal (former French territory, Muslim majority country) and Rwanda (former German and then Belgian territory, Muslim minority country). These additional cases show that colonial-era strategies and investments, and their relation to the size of the local Muslim population, were fairly similar across colonizers and regardless of whether Muslims comprised a majority at the national (or colony/protectorate) level.

The Muslim–Christian Gap beyond British Territories

About three-quarters of African countries were colonized either by Britain or France, and France colonized parts of sub-Saharan Africa with the largest Muslim populations. For these reasons, it is particularly important to understand the extent to which the explanation for the origin of the Muslim–Christian gap I have presented applies to French, and not only British, cases. Indeed, there are reasons to suspect the trajectory of educational outcomes might have been different in French Africa as compared to British Africa. Two policy differences that could have affected educational outcomes in particular are France's emphasis on assimilation and their more restrictive policy toward missionaries, both of which limited the supply of colonial education.

The strategy of assimilation was designed, in broad strokes, to turn Africans (and others) into Frenchmen.[3] This approach differed from that of the British, who tended to govern where possible through existing political institutions and customary law.[4] One aspect of assimilation efforts that is particularly relevant for education was the emphasis placed on French as a language. While many, or even most, schools in British territories taught in local languages, France required most colonial schools, whether government or missionary, to teach in French and use the French curriculum.[5] Language policy mattered in the provision of schooling because restricting instruction to a colonial language limited the number of qualified teachers.

A second major difference between French and British educational policy was that France placed much greater restrictions on missionary work than did the British. As a result, there were many fewer missionary schools in French as compared to British territories, although there was variation in the extent of missionary schooling within French territories. Both of these policies help explain why there were fewer colonial schools (whether missionary or government) in French than British territories.

A restrictive missionary policy, together with the fact that France colonized parts of Africa where Islam had been present for centuries also meant that Christian populations remained small in many French territories, particularly in the interior of West Africa. French West Africa comprised of Mauritania (99.1% Muslim), Niger (98.4% Muslim), Senegal (96.4% Muslim), Mali (92.4% Muslim), Guinea (84.4% Muslim), Burkina Faso (61.6% Muslim), Ivory Coast (37.5% Muslim), and Benin (23.8% Muslim).[6] As shown in Table 7.1, among sub-Saharan

---

[3] Sutton (1965)
[4] For example, in his treatise on colonial rule in Africa, Lugard wrote: "Succession is governed by native law and custom, subject in the case of important chiefs to the approval of the Governor, in order that the most capable claimant be chosen. It is important to ascertain the customary law and to follow it when possible..." Lugard (1922, p. 213). See Crowder (1964) for an elaboration of the differences between British and French approaches to indirect rule.
[5] Cowan, O'Connell, and Scanlon (1965)
[6] There are no reliable estimates of the percentage of Muslims prior to colonization by territory. The figures shown here are 2010 estimates from Pew Research.

TABLE 7.1 *Religious and educational demographics by country in sub-Saharan Africa.*

Country	% Muslim	Muslim pop.	Colonizer	Muslim years of school. Individuals aged 25 and older	Christian years of school. Individuals aged 25 and older	Muslim years of schooling relative to Christian years of schooling
			Muslim super majority (90+ % Muslim)			
Somalia	99.8	9 311 340	Italy	3.5	*	*
Mauritania	99.1	3 428 860	France	*	*	*
Niger	98.4	15 261 840	France	1.1	*	*
Comoros	98.3	717 590	France	4.8	*	*
Djibouti	96.9	862 410	France	*	*	*
Senegal	96.4	11 982 520	France	2.5	5.5	-3.0
Gambia	95.1	1 645 230	Britain	4.6	*	*
Mali	92.4	14 201 880	France	1.5	2.8	-1.3
Sudan	90.7	30 475 200	Britain	*	*	*
			Muslim large majority (60-90% Muslim)			
Guinea	84.4	8 423 120	France	*	*	*
Sierra Leone	78	4 578 600	Britain	1.9	4.9	-3.0
Burkina Faso	61.6	10 145 520	France	1.0	2.7	-1.7
			Mixed (40-60% Muslim)			
Chad	55.3	6 210 190	France	0.7	2.7	-2.0
Nigeria	48.8	77 308 960	Britain	3.0	7.1	-4.1
Guinea-Bissau	45.1	685 520	Portugal	*	*	*

Muslim large minority (10–40% Muslim)						
Cote d'Ivoire	37.5	7 402 500	France	2.1	5.3	-3.2
Eritrea	36.6	1 921 500	Italian	*	*	*
Tanzania	35.2	15 783 680	Britain	5.1	5.3	-0.2
Ethiopia	34.6	28 700 700	Independent	0.9	2.0	-1.1
Benin	23.8	2 106 300	France	1.9	4.1	-2.2
Cameroon	18.3	3 586 800	Britain/France	2.9	6.9	-4.0
Mozambique	18	4 210 200	Portugal	2.9	4.0	-1.1
Mauritius	16.7	217 100	Britain	8.0	7.5	0.5
Ghana	15.8	3 853 620	Britain	3.6	7.6	-4.0
Togo	14	844 200	France	3.7	6.2	-2.5
Malawi	13	1 937 000	Britain	3.3	5.2	-1.9
Liberia	12	478 800	Independent	2.9	4.5	-1.6
Uganda	11.5	3 843 300	Britain	6.4	6.3	0.1
Gabon	11.2	169 120	France	5.0	8.8	-3.8
Muslim small minority (<10% Muslim)						
Kenya	9.7	3 929 470	Britain	4.4	7.8	-3.4
Central African Republic	8.5	374 000	France	*	*	*
South Sudan	6.2	616 900	Britain	*	*	*
Equatorial Guinea	4	28 000	Spain	*	*	*
Madagascar	3	621 300	France	6.0	4.9	1.1
Burundi	2.8	234 640	Germany/Belgium	4.4	2.7	1.7

(continue)

TABLE 7.2 (continued)

Country	% Muslim	Muslim pop.	Colonizer	Muslim years of school. Individuals aged 25 and older	Christian years of school. Individuals aged 25 and older	Muslim years of schooling relative to Christian years of schooling
Muslim small minority (<10% Muslim)						
Rwanda	1.8	191 160	Germany/Belgium	4.4	2.9	1.5
South Africa	1.7	852 210	The Netherlands/Britain	9.4	7.4	2.0
Democratic Republic of the Congo	1.5	989 550	Belgium	7.2	6.9	0.3
Republic of the Congo	1.2	48 480	France	5.2	8.4	-3.2
Seychelles	1.1	990	Britain	*	*	*
Zimbabwe	0.9	113 130	Britain	*	8.6	*
Zambia	0.5	65 450	Britain	7.3	6.7	0.6
Botswana	0.4	8 040	Britain	*	*	*
Namibia	0.3	6 840	Germany/League of Nations	*	7.7	*
Angola	0.2	38 160	Portugal	*	*	*
Swaziland	0.2	2 380	Britain	*	7.3	*
Cape Verde	0.1	500	Portugal	*	6.4	*
Lesotho	0.1	2 170	Britain	*	6.5	*
São Tomé and Príncipe	0.1	170	Portugal	*	*	*

Source: Pew Research Center (2016).

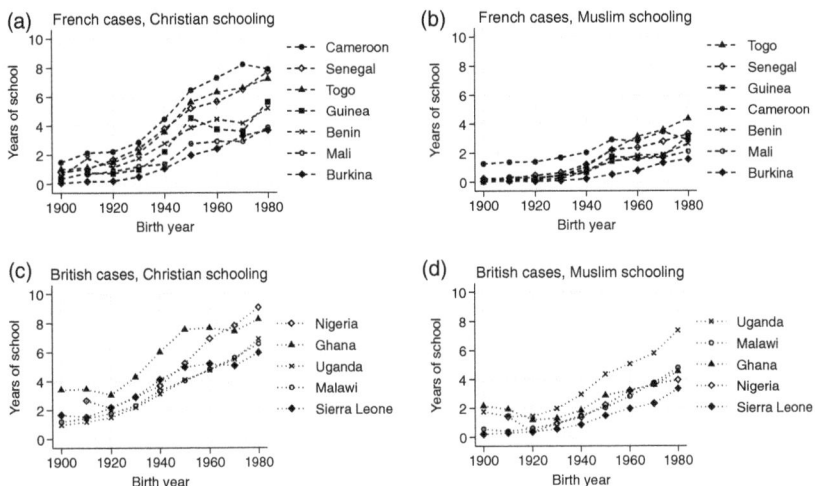

FIGURE 7.2 Average years of schooling by cohort and religion, British and French cases.
Source: IPUMS census data.

African countries today where Muslims are greater than 90 percent of the population, six are former French colonies (Mauritania, Niger, Comoros, Djibouti, Senegal, and Mali), and only two are former British colonies (Gambia and Sudan). Britain had far more territories that were mixed or had Muslim minority populations.

Figure 7.2 uses census data to show schooling trends among birth cohorts between 1900 and 1980 in the set of former French and British territories with substantial Christian and Muslim populations. As shown in Figure 7.2(b, d), Muslim levels of schooling in former French territories are not only much lower than those of Christians (Figure 7.2(a, c)), but also lower than those of Muslims living in former British territories. By 1980, Muslims in former British territories had at least four years of school on average, with the exception of Sierra Leone, while among French territories, in only a single country, Cameroon, did Muslims have at least four years of school on average. Cameroon is also a somewhat unique case as part of it was administered by Britain during the colonial period, and (like Tanzania) it had been a Germany territory up until the end of World War I. Figure 7.2 shows that while there are important differences in the overall levels of Muslim schooling across British and French cases, where Muslim schooling is higher on average in British territories, a significant gap exists in both.

Other colonial powers included the Belgians, Portuguese, Italians, Spanish, and Germans, but these held relatively fewer territories, and Muslim populations therein were, with a few exceptions, quite small.[7] In Belgian, Portuguese, and Spanish territories, Catholics held a monopoly on missionary work. German territories, including German East Africa (Tanzania, Rwanda, and Burundi), Namibia, and parts of Cameroon and Togo came under United Nations mandates following World War I, after which they were administered by other colonial powers, namely the British and French. Although German colonialism in Africa was limited, places under German influence seem to exhibit different patterns with respect to the Muslim–Christian gap from those of other colonial powers. In Tanzania, the Muslim–Christian gap is much smaller and Muslim education higher than countries with a similarly sized Muslim population. The relatively small gap in Tanzania may be due to the comparatively large number of nonmission government schools set up under German rule, and the fact that Germans employed Muslims as administrators in the early colonial period.[8]+

In what follows, I provide short case studies demonstrating that although there were differences in the implementation of colonial rule across colonial powers, religious demographics – namely, the extent of Islamization at the time of colonization – shaped colonial investments in schooling in similar ways across these diverse contexts.

Senegal

Senegal today has a large Muslim majority, comprising over 95 percent of the population. Muslim traders reached the area comprising present-day Senegal shortly after 1000 CE, and it was within the bounds of some of the earliest Islamic states in West Africa, including the Takrur kingdom (tenth to twelfth centuries) and the Mali empire (1230–1450 CE). The fertile soil surrounding the Senegal river attracted many different peoples over time, such that the area is quite ethnically diverse today. Islamic reform movements spread across West Africa and reached the area in the period just prior to colonial occupation, and it was these and their aftermath that French companies and administrators had to consider as they expanded into the interior of the continent in the second half of the nineteenth century.[9]

---

[7] Exceptions include Portuguese-controlled Guinea-Bissau and Mozambique.
[8] Seimu and Komba (2024)
[9] Sluglett and Currie (2015)

7 Generalizing the Argument

French presence in Senegal dates back to the mid 1650s, when trading outposts were set up on two islands that would form the later communes of Saint-Louis and Gorée. French occupation and expansion began in earnest in the mid 1850s, however, with Napoleon's appointment of Louis Faidherbe as governor, under whose leadership the French spread inland from the port cities. Senegal is an important case in and of itself but is particularly important for understanding the role of French colonialism and its interaction with Islam on education because it served as the administrative capital of the Federation of French West Africa (AOF). Because Islam had already spread throughout much of what would become French West Africa by the time of French occupation, French Islamic policy, of which the question of how to organize education was key, was central to the organization of colonial governance.

Despite France's relatively restrictive policy toward missionaries, the Catholic Church had a significant influence on education in Senegal in the second half of the nineteenth century. At that time, France's primary possessions comprised of four communes, Saint-Louis, Gorée, Dakar, and Rufisque, all located on the coast of what is now Senegal. By 1903, nine of the ten primary schools were run by the Catholic Church, and had a total of 1841 boys and 688 girls.[10] As in British territories, a consequence of relying on the Catholic Church was that many Muslims refused to attend these schools, and the fact that there was an early association between this new form of education and Christianity may have discouraged Muslims from attending more generally.[11]

Indeed, throughout the rest of the Protectorate, there were only 21 schools by 1907, and these schools suffered low attendance, underfunding, and a shortage of teachers.[12] Further, the few students that did attend these schools were overwhelmingly male, such that there was nothing resembling universal schooling. Bryant (2015, p. 22) writes: "enrollment at girls' schools never came close to rivaling that at the boys' schools because most families preferred to train girls at home to fulfill their future roles as wives and mothers and because Muslim families opposed such schooling on religious grounds."

The relative scarcity of schools in Senegal mirrored that of the rest of French West Africa, where by 1900 there were 70 schools and

---

[10] Bryant (2015, p. 16–17)
[11] Hailey (1957, p. 1193)
[12] Bryant (2015, p. 16)

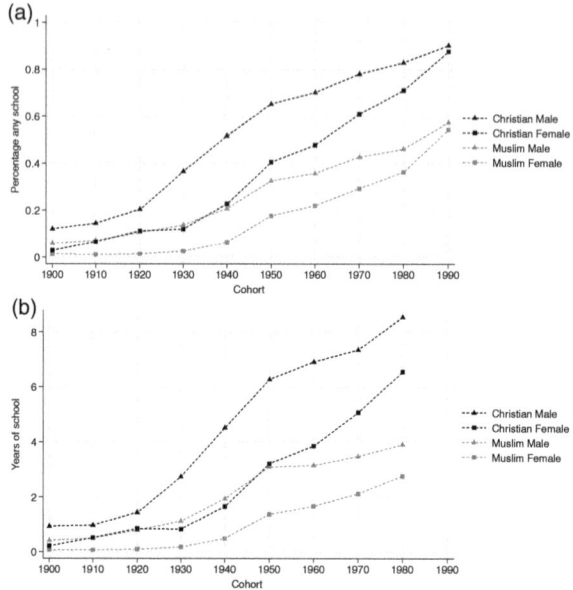

FIGURE 7.3 Schooling rates by religion and gender in Senegal: (a) any school, age 13+; (b) years of school, age 25+.
Source: IPUMS census samples.

approximately 2500 pupils in total – a fraction of the number in Buganda, for example, which itself was a fraction of the size of the French West African territory.[13] Missionary schools remained fewer than state schools, but were not negligible. By 1937–1938 there were around 56,000 pupils in state schools, 12,000 in mission schools, and another 64,000 in Qur'anic schools.[14] Thus, as in Northern Nigeria, Qur'anic school remained an important alternative to the colonial education system. Not only did families often prefer Qur'anic school to French schools, they were also encouraged to attend the former by marabouts, Islamic teachers who relied on these schools both as a source of income and authority.[15]

As shown in Figure 7.3, a gap in rates of school attendance between Muslims and Christians is present from at least 1900, particularly for men. Rates of attendance look similar for Muslim men and Christian

---

[13] Hailey (1957, p. 1194)
[14] Hailey (1957, p. 1197)
[15] Bryant (2015, p. 40)

women up until around 1940, when Christian women surpass Muslim men. The upward trend for Christian women accelerates around this period, such that by the 1990s, attendance of school is at parity between Christian men and women. While total years of school remain higher for Christian men than women, both have higher levels of schooling on average by the 1980s than Muslims.

Given that Senegal is overwhelmingly Muslim, who are the Christians, and how are they distributed spatially and across ethnic groups? Spatially, Christians are concentrated on the coast, the areas historically most exposed to Christian missionaries. This pattern mirrors that in Nigeria, as well as other parts of West Africa, where Islam is most concentrated in the interior. This pattern reflects the nature of the spread of Islam, which came not from the coast but via Islamic trade routes across the Sahara. According to census data, around 35 percent of the Christian population in Senegal today lives in the region of Dakar, with another 16 percent in the neighboring region of Thies. Twenty percent live in the coastal region of Ziguinchor, and another 15 percent live in the regions on the northern border of the Gambia, which also had several Catholic missions. Less than 5 percent live in the regions further to the interior. The majority of Senegal's ethnic groups have large Muslim majorities, at close to 99 percent of group members.[16] However, there are a few smaller groups with Christian majorities, and groups like the Diola have sizeable Christian minorities (around 20 percent).

In Senegal today, Muslims are significantly less likely to have any schooling than Christians, even after taking into account region and ethnicity. This gap is substantively quite large – about a 30 percentage point difference. Within ethnic groups, the Muslim–Christian gap exists in groups where Muslims are a majority (such as the Serer or Diola), but there is no gap among the Manjango, where Christians are a majority. While there are no survey data that allow me to examine first- or second-order beliefs about schooling, the pattern of schooling trends in Senegal, as well as the relationship between minority status and Muslim schooling outcomes, mirrors those documented in the cases of Malawi, Uganda, and Nigeria, despite being under a different colonizer and despite being an overwhelmingly Muslim country. We might be concerned that in a case like Malawi, Uganda, or even Nigeria, with large Christian

---

[16] Senegal has over two dozen ethnic groups, with the largest being the Wolof (40%), Pulaar (17%), Serer (15%), Peul (6%) and Diola (4%).

populations and where many or most positions of political power are held by Christians, religious favoritism might explain the relatively lower levels of schooling among Muslims, as has been documented in some African countries with respect to ethnicity.[17] However, this explanation seems unlikely in a case like Senegal, and the fact that the patterns are the same across colonizers and across Muslim majority and minority countries suggests government favoritism towards Christians is probably not the primary explanation in any of these cases.

Rwanda

While Senegal is a case featuring a large Muslim majority, Rwanda is one at the opposite end of the spectrum, with a Muslim population estimated at around 2 percent in the 2022 census; just over a quarter of a million people. Over 90 percent of Rwanda's population is Christian, the largest denomination being Catholic, at 40 percent of the population, followed by 21 percent Pentecostal, 15 percent mainline Protestant, and 12 percent Adventist. The Muslim population has remained fairly constant in relative size over time, while the Catholic population has declined substantially, falling by about 20 percentage points between 1991 and 2022. This decline may be due in part to the complicity of the Catholic Church[18] during the 1994 genocide.[19] The Muslim population is not concentrated in any particular part of Rwanda, but they are more likely to live in urban than rural areas.[20] Because Rwanda has not collected data on ethnicity since the genocide, we cannot know the distribution of religious affiliation across ethnic groups, but the vast majority are native Rwandans.

There has been relatively little written about the history of Islam in Rwanda, perhaps because the Muslim population is so small and Islam is relatively new to the region. In the precolonial period, nearly the whole of present-day Rwanda was part of a kingdom. Although Muslim traders were successful in seeking the audience of the Kabaka in Buganda,

---

[17] Franck and Rainer (2012)
[18] See Longman (2009)
[19] Kubai (2007a)
[20] 2022 Census. Although the census data are not released at a level that allows us to determine respondents' location below the district, DHS data show that only a few survey clusters have a majority of respondents that are Muslim: one cluster out of 492 in 2014, two out of 462 in 2005, and and two out of 197 in 1992. Around three-quarters of all survey clusters have no Muslim respondents, while the rest are relatively evenly distributed between 1 percent and 50 percent Muslim.

the King of Rwanda is reported to have resisted their penetration into the kingdom.[21] During a short period of German colonial rule, however, Muslim clerks and administrators from German-administered Tanganyika were recruited to work in Rwanda, and thereafter some Rwandans converted to Islam as well. As was the case elsewhere in Africa, these initial conversions seem to have taken place in urban and commercial centers where Muslim administrators were based. Linden and Linden (1977, p. 110) note that under the Richard Kandt, the first Resident of Rwanda as part of German colonial rule, "Government service and towns proved to be the milieux most favorable to Islam," and that Kandt "opened the floodgates to large numbers of Muslim traders."

Some accounts suggest that Muslim traders played an important role in the process of conversion, with Islam associated with both commerce and "civilized" living – particularly the emphasis on cleanliness, as well as dress and food influenced by coastal or Swahili Muslims. Interviews with members of the Muslim leadership in Rwanda today suggest that there was a close relationship with the Rwandan monarchy during colonial rule, and the former Mufti of Rwanda reports that under German rule, "Muslims enjoyed an elevated place in Rwandan society. As such, they eventually began to marry into the Rwandan elite, even into the family of the monarchy. You might even say they were a type of 'super-class' in those days."[22]

Other prominent members of the Muslim community in Rwanda reported that under Belgian rule the Muslim community was associated with the monarchy, and by proxy, the Tutsi.[23] When the King was seen as a threat to colonial rule, so too was the Muslim community. Habimana (2009) reports that under Belgian rule Muslims were denied access to jobs, ownership of land, and education. As in British colonial Africa, education under Belgian rule was primarily provided by Christian – mostly Catholic – missionaries. Government-aided Catholic schools, *écoles libres subsidiées*, were the schools through which, as King (2013, p. 49) notes, "the colonial administration acquitted itself of almost all moral obligations to educate Rwandans, and that missionaries largely made schools instruments in the pursuit of religious conversion." Despite the hegemony of Catholicism during the colonial period, the first Muslim

---

[21] See Kasule (1982), although this source also propagates historically inaccurate information about the origins of the Tutsis.
[22] Habimana (2009)
[23] Interviews in Kigali, March 2017.

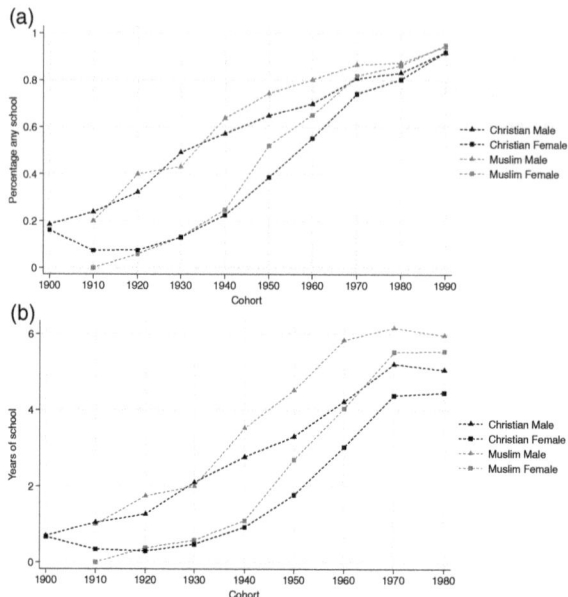

FIGURE 7.4 Schooling rates by religion and gender in Rwanda: (a) any school, age 13+; (b) years of school, age 25+.
Source: IPUMS census samples.

primary school was opened during the period of Belgian rule, receiving a grand inauguration presided over by the King, who subsequently named the school *Intwali*, or "heroes" Primary School, and still exists in Rwanda today.

While during the colonial period and into much of the postindependence period Muslims reported both informal and institutionalized discrimination,[24] census data, shown in Figure 7.4, suggest that levels of education among Rwandan Muslims meet or even surpass those of the Christian majority. These patterns may be due in part to the fact that Muslims were historically more likely to live in urban areas, but also perhaps because they were part of a privileged class in the early part of the colonial period, getting a head start in education, and inspired by foreign Muslims serving administrative positions that required formal education.

Like other countries with very small Muslim minorities, such as the Democratic Republic of Congo, Burundi, and Madagascar, Rwanda has a very small Muslim–Christian schooling gap. In fact, in the absence

[24] Kubai (2007b)

of covariates for wealth and urban residence, the gap is actually positive, with Muslims having higher levels of education, on average, than Christians. With the addition of these covariates, and with fixed effects for subnational regions, a negative gap emerges. While in countries like Nigeria and Cameroon, the inclusion of fixed effects for region and ethnicity reduces the magnitude of the coefficient on Muslim, in those countries with small Muslim populations, like Rwanda and Burundi, it flips the sign from positive to negative. This suggests that while regional effects matter for schooling outcomes, the kinds of regions Muslims live in – relatively poorer or richer than average – varies across countries. In countries like Rwanda and Burundi, it appears that Muslims live in places that are relatively better off, such that Muslims appear to perform better than Christians (in terms of years of schooling) overall. In countries like Nigeria, Muslims are concentrated in less developed regions, on average. Nevertheless, Muslims have lower levels of schooling than Christians within regions, even in countries where the gap is quite small.

The case of Rwanda demonstrates first, that, similar to the British territories this book documents, Christian missionaries played a central role in the provision of education during Belgian colonial rule, which would have discouraged Muslims from attending. However, as in Uganda, Muslims in this case were a minority, and surrounded by large Christian – particularly Catholic – majorities. There were no Islamic political institutions, but Muslims were relatively privileged in the early colonial bureaucracy. These factors led to a much smaller initial gap than in contexts where Muslims were a majority or living in an area governed by Islamic political institutions. Part of the reason why Muslims have relatively high levels of education in Rwanda is that they live in more urban areas with better access to education historically. However, Rwandan Muslims have somewhat lower levels of education than Christians after controlling for place of residence and household assets, underscoring the idea that economic factors alone do not fully explain the gap.

Around one-third of African countries have similarly sized Muslim populations to that in Rwanda, less than 2 or 3 percent of the population. Minority Muslim countries are not all alike, however. In some cases, like Rwanda, the Muslim population is indigenous, while in others, particularly countries in southern Africa, most Muslims are not indigenous but have emigrated relatively recently from South Asia and elsewhere. This book has focused primarily on the Muslim–Christian schooling gap among indigenous Africans, because the educational outcomes among more recent migrants are likely to reflect distinct historical dynamics, and may be confounded with other socioeconomic differences.

The broader take away from these cases is that while African countries exhibit large variation in the size of the Muslim population at the national level, and were exposed to different colonial policies with respect to education, the overall patterns with respect to the Muslim–Christian gap are remarkably uniform. These similarities underscore the idea that Europeans – both colonial administrators and missionaries, regardless of their country of origin – treated Muslim and non-Muslim areas differently, and that Muslims nearly everywhere were at a disadvantage with respect to initial investments in colonial schooling because their provision was so heavily contingent on converting to Christianity.

ISLAMIC STATES AND SCHOOLING IN AFRICA

The primary cases in this book showed that the extent of Islamization – both in the extent to which the population had converted to Islam and the extent to which an area was governed by Islamic political institutions – shaped colonial rule, and particularly investments in mass schooling. In Chapter 1, I showed that the percentage Muslim of a subnational administrative area was predictive of the Muslim–Christian gap, an empirical pattern which prompted the investigation into why Muslims living as a majority tended to have low levels of schooling.

In this section, I expand the empirical analysis to examine the extent to which Islamic political institutions – and not just Muslim majority areas – predicts schooling outcomes and the Muslim–Christian schooling gap beyond the primary cases in the book. To do so, I combine data on the location of Islamic states and areas of Islamic influence from Sluglett and Currie's *Atlas of Islamic History* with data on schooling outcomes from the Demographic and Health Surveys (DHS) from 30 African countries, and data on the availability of schools from the Afrobarometer Surveys.[25]

The *Atlas of Islamic History* includes maps documenting nearly thirty Islamic states from the ninth to twentieth centuries, and around ten major states still in existence by the start of the colonial period. The colonial-era states cover parts of present-day Senegal, Mali, Burkina Faso, Niger, and Nigeria in West Africa, and Sudan, Ethiopia, Eritrea Somalia, Kenya,

---

[25] Sluglett and Currie (2015), the set of Islamic states, which include kingdoms, states, and sultanates is shown in Figure 3.2.

and Tanzania in East and Central Africa. The atlas also codes "areas of Islamic influence" which are areas that surround major trade routes, ports, and hubs, as well as areas surrounding but not in the direct control of Islamic states. It also documents overland trade routes, most of which are concentrated in West and North Africa. I digitized and combined these maps to create a dataset of Islamic states and areas of Islamic influence.[26]

The survey data from the Demographic and Health Surveys, also employed in the analyses in the introductory chapter, include about 1 million individuals born in the first three decades after independence, between 1965 and 1995.[27] About one-third of respondents live in an area that was under an Islamic state that was coded as still in existence at 1900, around the time of colonial rule in most African countries. A little less than 15 percent live in an area of Islamic influence but not under an Islamic state, and about half do not live in either an Islamic state or area of Islamic influence. There are more Muslims than Christians living in former Islamic states or areas of Muslim influence. Seventy-five percent of Muslims in the sample live in an area of a former Islamic state or area of Islamic influence, compared to about one-third of Christians.

In the sample as a whole, close to two-thirds of respondents have ever attended school and a little less than half were able to pass a basic literacy test. Among Christians, over 75 percent have ever attended school and a little less than 60 percent are literate. Among Muslims, just over one-third have ever attended school and less than a quarter are literate, and those who live in an area that was historically under Islamic rule have lower levels of schooling than Muslims elsewhere. Figure 7.5 shows that Muslims living in areas under Islamic political institutions historically are more than ten percentage points less likely to have attended school than those who do not. This figure shows the average rates of schooling

---

[26] This exercise complements that of Bauer, Platas, and Weinstein (2019), in which we compile a dataset of all precolonial kingdoms. That analysis allows us to show that it is specifically Islamic states, rather than any states, that are associated with worse outcomes, particularly in the area of educational attainment.

[27] The survey includes most but not all African countries. The DHS is not available for most or any years in countries with persistent conflict, such as Somalia and Sudan. The sample is also limited to those surveys where information on respondents' location and religious affiliation was collected. For example, the sample excludes Liberia as the survey excludes the question about religious affiliation in this country (usually at the request of the government), and excludes South Africa because the DHS is not conducted in this country. Not all survey rounds, and particular older surveys, include the coordinates of the survey clusters.

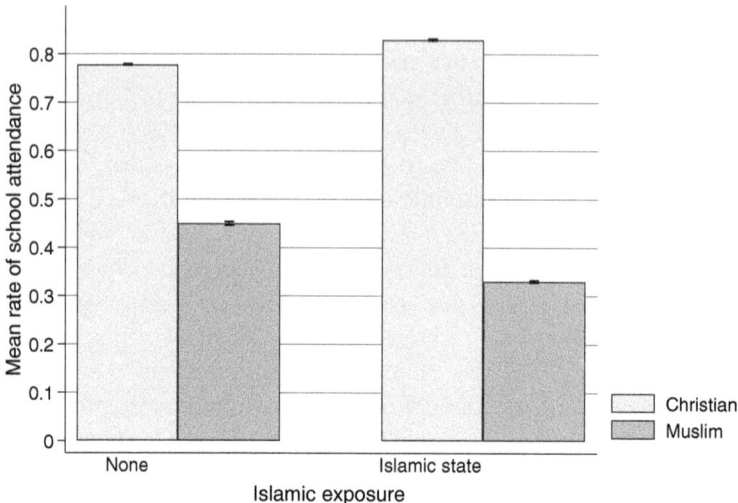

FIGURE 7.5 Mean schooling rate by exposure to Islamic states and religious affiliation.
Source: DHS and Sluglett and Currie (2015).

across religious groups and geographic areas.[28] Clearly, living in an area previously under an Islamic state does not explain the gap in full, as the Muslim–Christian gap remains very large even in places with no history of Islamic statehood. Still, there is a depressive effect on educational attainment of historical Islamic statehood that exists only for Muslims and is not observed among Christians. These findings support those documented in Bauer, Platas, and Weinstein (2019), which finds that Muslims living in Islamic states fare worse in terms of educational attainment than those living within the boundaries in non-Islamic states.

In addition to the categorical measures of historical Islamic rule,[29] I also use the distance to Islamic trade routes, which are another measure

---

[28] A regression analysis, interacting religious affiliation with Islamic state exposure reveals the same pattern. This analysis, shown in Figure A.8, includes controls for individual factors such as respondent's sex and year of birth, and cluster-level measures of urban/rural, annual rainfall, log GDP, malaria incidence (2000), logged nightlight density, logged slope, and logged population density, as well as country fixed effects and standard errors clustered at the level of the survey cluster.

[29] The boundaries of kingdoms and states on the atlas are usually somewhat artificial or at least imprecise, as there were more often zones of influence than policed borders, and these were in flux over time. In Bauer, Platas, and Weinstein (2019) we demonstrate that the effect of Islamic states on development outcomes, and especially educational attainment, however, is not sensitive to moderate shifts in the location of the state's

7 Generalizing the Argument

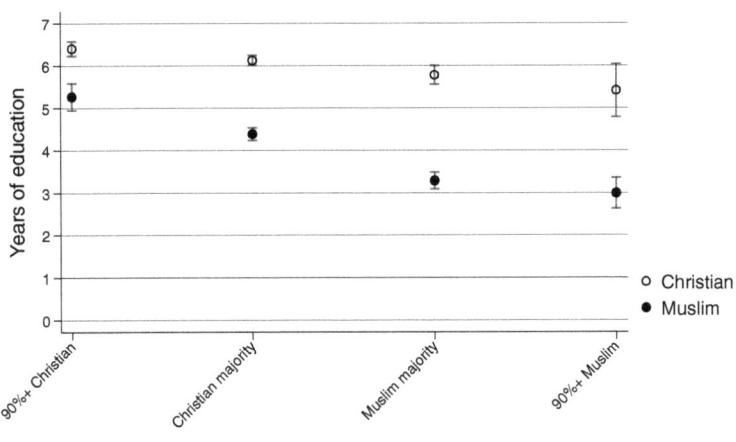

FIGURE 7.6 Predicted years of education by province-level religious demographics.
Source: DHS, World Religions Database, Sluglett and Currie (2015).

of Islamic influence that predates colonial rule. The distance an individual lives from an Islamic trade route, like exposure to historic Islamic rule, is predictive of schooling levels for Christians and Muslims, with schooling levels being lower and the Muslim–Christian gap larger the closer an individual lives to an Islamic trade routes. Closest to the trade route Muslims are nearly half as likely to have any formal schooling as Christians, and the likelihood of having formal education increases substantially as distance from trade routes increases.[30] Together, these data suggest that the patterns identified from the Buganda–Emirates comparison are borne out more broadly. Muslim schooling in the postindependence period is substantially lower in areas of historical Islamic states and areas of Muslim influence than those outside of these areas.

The Muslim–Christian gap exists beyond Islamic states, however, and also exists after controlling for this factor. Figure 7.6 shows the predicted years of education, using DHS data, as the province-level religious demographics vary from Christian majority to Muslim majority. The data on religious demographics at the province-level come from the

borders. Islamic trade routes, while also imprecise to some extent, are probably less error prone than state boundaries.
[30] See Figure A.7.

World Religion Database. This analysis controls for exposure to Islamic states, revealing an independent effect of religious demographics on top of the role of Islamic states in shaping schooling outcomes. In all areas Muslims have fewer years of education than Christians, but the gap widens, driven primarily by decreasing levels of schooling among Muslims, as the percentage Muslim of the province increases.

Together, these additional case studies and cross-national empirical analyses suggest that parts of Africa where Muslims were a local majority at the time of colonization, and areas with Islamic political institutions in particular, experienced distinct long-term schooling trajectories. These patterns are driven specifically by Muslims living in these areas, which I have argued resulted from the association between Christianity and mass schooling, generating differences in schooling norms across religious communities. This also explains why there is a strong correlation between levels of Muslim schooling and the proportion of Muslims at the local level, even after controlling for historical Islamic institutions. In Chapter 8, I discuss the implications of these findings for future research and policy.

8

Matters of Culture

In this book, I have shown that contemporary patterns of schooling in Africa – a region with the fastest growing population, lowest levels of schooling, and where the number of children out of school is increasing – cannot be understood without an examination of what mass schooling has meant socially and politically, from the colonial period to the present. The decision to attend school, and to keep attending school, is not only an economic consideration, although financial constraints are an important barrier to schooling in Africa and elsewhere, it is also a *social* consideration. The goals of mass schooling, the education systems it overrides, and the social status it brings within a community are all important for understanding the extent to which individuals have participated in it historically, and today.

The Muslim–Christian schooling gap in Africa emerged because colonial education – on which the contemporary education system is built – was not designed as the human right it is considered to be today, but as a tool to control and convert. Its supply was not uniform, and was not intended to be. Colonial governments provided very few schools, and their minimal investments were designed to train the elite and staff the civil service. Christian missionaries established many schools, but were constrained by colonial governments and by resistance from communities who did not want to convert to Christianity. The primary objective of missionary schools was to convert Africans to Christianity, but these schools also transformed local politics and economies. Where colonial schooling was abundant, it offered new modes of status-climbing – socially, politically, and economically. Competition for followers and power within the colonial state induced even those who did not convert to Christianity to establish schools in a similar image.

Thus, the initial distribution of and exposure to colonial schools – the majority of which were missionary-founded – affected not only physical access but also *ideas* about this new form of education, which shaped long-term schooling trends. The Muslim–Christian schooling gap that this book has documented arose as a result of these historical processes.

The findings presented here should give pause to those studying or working in the field of education in Africa and beyond. Political scientists and economists have tended to treat education as one item in a bundle of ostensibly universally desired public goods that also includes things like healthcare, water, and infrastructure. Much effort has gone into determining which political institutions and policies deliver public goods most effectively,[1] not only because their provision matters for the wellbeing of individuals but also because they contribute to economic growth, producing even more welfare-enhancing goods and services. Although we expect citizens to vary in their relative prioritization of these goods, for example based on socioeconomic status or ethnicity,[2] and to have different preferences about who should access (and pay for) public goods,[3] we typically assume that in the absence of resource constraints, everyone would prefer more of all of them.

But education is not like other public goods. Unlike a road or clean water, education imparts beliefs about its provider, and about what comprises appropriate behavior in a given society. For these reasons it matters *who* provides education, for what purpose, and with which content. If we conceptualize human capital acquisition as a technical affair, and education as one in a set of universally desired public goods, we will not understand why even today individuals and communities opt out of the schooling systems that governments, scholars, and international institutions consider so essential for economic and human development.

Of course, the quality and content of education is also paramount to understanding and improving educational outcomes. Scholars have been sounding alarm bells for years about the poor quality of education

---

[1] For example, whether democracy leads to higher levels of public goods provision (Lake and Baum 2001); whether transparency improves governance (Kosack and Fung 2014); and how democratic accountability matters for the distribution of goods (Golden and Min 2013).
[2] Lieberman and McClendon (2013)
[3] Kasara and Suryanarayan (2015)

provided by many schools in low income countries,[4] particularly in the aftermath of the rapid expansion of primary schooling that followed the removal of school fees. Poor quality education is a waste of resources, raises concerns about justice, and can depress demand for schooling. In this way it can exacerbate existing inequalities, in that poor quality schooling is likely to have the biggest impact on those with the fewest resources and those whose parents have lower levels of education to begin with. Several decades into universal primary education, it makes a great deal of sense to think beyond expanding access to school (the "spend on school" model),[5] as important as this expansion has been, and focus more on what kind of learning is taking place and how to design education that is of greatest use to its consumers.

In this chapter, by way of conclusion, I discuss some potential next steps for research and policy, and address a few further questions. First, what are the prospects for norm change, and ultimately closing the Muslim–Christian schooling gap or others like it? Second, what are the broader implications of this gap for outcomes beyond educational attainment? Third, what are some goals for research on education, inequality, and culture going forward?

Cultural Change and the Evolution of Norms

Under what conditions will norms change, perhaps supporting higher levels of schooling among groups with the lowest educational attainment historically? Culture is persistent, but it is not static. In fact, it is constantly evolving, particularly when individuals and communities are regularly exposed to new ideas and new ways of doing things. In fact, the case of Malawi shows that there has already been considerable change in the content of schooling norms among Muslims over time. While those who grew up in the colonial period reported fear of conversion and being actively discouraged from attending school, most Muslim parents today do not report concern that their children will be converted, nor do they seem concerned about the religious affiliation of schools or teachers. This change in beliefs about schooling is due at least in part to the decoupling of religion and mass schooling, an important policy change in most African countries. While religious organizations are still involved in the management

---

[4] Pritchett (2013)
[5] Pritchett (2024)

of schools, and maintain private schools, they are not allowed to discriminate on the basis of religion in the way that they did during the colonial period. Children are not forced to convert to Christianity, and public schools often include religious studies curriculum that covers both Christianity and Islam. Thus, policy changes can play an important role in shaping norms by reducing the social costs (e.g. risk of conversion) or increasing the social benefits of school attendance.

For example, free primary education policies may increase school rates not only through reducing financial barriers to schooling, but also by providing a signal about the expectation of school attendance by the state and society. In support of this idea, Hoff and Stiglitz (2016, p. 50) note that girls' school attendance in Uganda following the implementation of universal primary education was much higher than would have been predicted by standard economic models "because it appears to have induced a change in norms: for parents not to take advantage of the free education offered to their daughters came to be viewed as wrong, whereas before, parents were perceived to make reasonable choices in economizing scarce family resources."

Scholars have also demonstrated that policy or legal changes can affect *perceptions* of norms, even if they don't change individuals' personal beliefs. For example, Tankard and Paluck (2017) show that in the United States, a Supreme Court decision in favor of same-sex marriage affected Americans' perceptions of social norms supporting gay marriage even if their own attitudes did not change. However, as Gelfand, Gavrilets, and Nunn (2024) note, policy changes can result in counterintuitive or backfire effects, and do not necessarily bring about norm change in the direction expected or intended. For example, Fouka (2020) finds that policies designed to promote assimilation can inadvertently lead minority communities to reenforce their own identity.

In addition to policy changes, media campaigns and information interventions by governments or nongovernmental organizations can create new ideas and associations with particular behaviors. For example, Frye (2012) documents how nongovernmental organizations (NGOs) and the Malawian government conducted campaigns to present schooling in moral terms in order to promote attendance. The secondary school students she interviewed express school attendance in moral terms – school attendance means not only choosing education, but also the active rejection of alternative uses of time and life choices, particularly sexual relationships. Frye argues that "state policy and NGO programming directly influenced the construction of the cultural models surrounding educational attainment, as well as schoolgirls' imagined futures."[6] Information interventions can also serve to inform the public about others' beliefs. Belief correction can be especially useful if there are widespread misperceptions – that is, that many people hold inaccurate beliefs about what others think or do, which is a common occurrence.[7]

Leaders can also play an important role in norm change or persistence. To do so, they need to be broadly understood as fair, legitimate, and prototypical of the group they represent,[8] as well as be able to communicate clearly what is expected of community members. Leaders can also give permission to deviate from existing behaviors, which may be especially important in cases where deviation by a first mover is socially costly. Of course, the influence of leaders can go in both directions – strengthening or undermining norms about school attendance. For example, Harnischfeger (2008) argues that reservations about mass schooling in Northern Nigeria persist in part "because the highest authorities such as the Sultan of Sokoto warn parents about its corrupting influence: 'Western education destroys our culture.'"[9] Illiteracy persists because many parents "refuse to send their children to school" or prefer that their children attend Qur'anic school.[10]

The study of norm change is a burgeoning field with lots of good ideas to pursue and experiment with if one is interested in designing such policies. For example, changing perceptions of norms is frequently easier than changing personal beliefs, and thus policies to address beliefs about schooling may be more successful if they target perceptions rather than individual attitudes. Strategies to change norm perceptions could include providing information about group member behavior (for example if people underestimate school attendance rates) or exposing individuals to communities or even fictional characters whose behaviors are different from their own.[11]

Bursztyn and Jensen (2017) note several additional strategies to promote norm change, although they have not been extensively tested empirically, particularly in low income settings or regarding schooling specifically. These strategies include using symbolic awards or recognition,[12] which demonstrate social returns to a given behavior,

---

[6] Frye (2012, p. 1609)
[7] Bursztyn and Yang (2022)
[8] Hogg (2010)
[9] Harnischfeger (2008) citing a May 1994 article in the *Guardian*.
[10] Harnischfeger (2008, p. 55)
[11] Tankard and Paluck (2016)
[12] Ashraf, Bandiera, and Lee (2014)

like school attendance or completion; increasing the observability of behavior,[13] for example by publishing lists of students in or out of school; and the implementation of laws which serve not only a legal but expressive function.

Of course, there is always the possibility that well-intentioned efforts based on theory or different contexts fail to change beliefs or behavior, or worse, backfire.[14] Because schooling behavior does not in itself reveal the norms underlying it, a first step to policy design should be to understand what sorts of beliefs children, parents, and communities hold about schooling and the second-order beliefs they hold about others – as well as whose beliefs and opinion they care about.

It is also important to emphasize that new norms do not necessarily displace existing belief repertoires, and it may take time for beliefs to spread and expectations to align. Common knowledge about beliefs and expectations is part of what makes a norm strong. Second-order beliefs are likely to vary more in periods of transition, particularly if people hear competing narratives. Given the widespread nature of free primary schooling policies and rhetoric of basic schooling as a human right, it seems likely that norms about what behaviors are expected of young children will continue to gravitate to school attendance. In Malawi, for example, it now seems to be the norm that children attend for at least some period of time. While existing policies may be already working to strengthen schooling norms, it may nonetheless be worth exploring additional interventions that specifically target communities in which schooling norms are weaker or those that were not exposed to mass schooling until relatively recently.

Broader Implications of the Muslim–Christian Schooling Gap

The main outcome of interest in this book is attendance of mass schooling, which is an important outcome in and of itself, particularly as the skills typically acquired through mass schooling, such as literacy and numeracy, allow individuals greater freedom and autonomy to pursue whatever goals they may have for themselves, or even expand the possible range of goals they might consider.[15] In addition to the intrinsic value of this kind of education, however, we might also care about other outcomes to

---

[13] Perez-Truglia and Troiano (2018)
[14] Acemoglu and Jackson (2017)
[15] Sen (1999)

which education has been linked, including lifetime earnings[16] and political participation. If Muslims have systematically lower levels of schooling than Christians in Africa, are they also disadvantaged economically and politically? The answer is not straightforward.

Throughout this book I have emphasized that the explanation for the Muslim–Christian gap is not simply or even mainly about the relative poverty of Muslims compared to Christians. Perhaps because of the relatively small size of the formal sector in African countries, and because of relatively lower levels of schooling overall, the relationship between education and wealth (often measured as household assets) is not clearcut in this context. There are certainly positive returns to schooling globally, but the patterns over time and across levels of schooling vary. For example, while returns to secondary and tertiary education are relatively high, the returns to primary education have been declining in Africa and elsewhere,[17] a particularly important trend given that the average secondary school completion rate in sub-Saharan Africa is just under 30 percent (2023 estimate), substantially lower than any other world region.[18] Returns are also lower in rural areas of developing countries, which characterize where much of the population live across the region.[19] The rapid expansion of the primary education sector, combined with the relatively poor and even deteriorating quality of primary education in many low income countries,[20] may in part explain why returns to primary education have been declining.

Given the tenuous link between education and earnings at the level of primary schooling, and the fact that in many African countries the majority of the population has at *most* primary-level education, it is not clear how economically disadvantaged Muslims are, relative to Christians, as a result of their lower levels of schooling. A schooling gap of a year or more is substantively large, and rivals or surpasses those measured across ethnic groups in Africa.[21] Nevertheless, it is not obvious that a Christian with, say, six years of education will be substantially better off economically than a Muslim with four years. Moreover, the spread of Islam is negatively correlated with income inequality in Africa, although the mechanisms

---

[16] Psacharopoulos and The World Bank (1994), Psacharopoulos and Patrinos (2018)
[17] Patrinos (2021)
[18] Data from the UNESCO Global Education Monitoring Report 2024/2025, Leadership in Education: Lead for Learning, p. 308.
[19] Peet, Fink, and Fawzi (2015)
[20] Pritchett (2013), Le Nestour, Moscoviz, and Sandefur (2022), Pritchett (2024)
[21] Kramon and Posner (2016), Franck and Rainer (2012)

underlying this relationship are unknown.[22] This negative correlation is somewhat surprising as the relationship between the share of the Muslim population and the Muslim–Christian schooling gap is positive, although nonlinear. Thus, a larger schooling gap does not seem to be correlated with income inequality, at least at the national level. While the distribution of the Muslim population matters for both education and income, there seem to be distinct processes underlying the relationship between each. Unraveling this knot would be a fruitful exercise for future research.

With respect to political participation, there are many reasons to believe that education is of central importance to political participation and to the functioning of political systems, particularly democratic ones.[23] For example, skills such as literacy should better enable one to access information about politics and may increase capacity for critical thinking. Those with higher socioeconomic status generally, of which education is one component, may be more likely to have the time and resources to engage in politics, whether as a voter, participant in community-level organizing, or in holding political office. However, despite the compelling theoretical linkages between education and political participation, empirically the evidence is quite mixed,[24] especially in less consolidated political systems and in lower income settings. It turns out there are many countries in which the poor and those with lower levels of education are *more* likely to vote than the rich and more highly educated. For these reasons, as with income and education, it is not necessarily the case that the Muslim–Christian schooling gap translates into a participation gap.

Why doesn't educational attainment translate into higher voter turnout in contexts like sub-Saharan Africa? First, in authoritarian countries, which comprise a sizable percentage of countries in Africa, the educated may actively opt out of politics, perhaps because they view participation as legitimating the regime or simply see it as a waste of time.[25] Second, the wealthy (and, usually, more educated) are more likely to turnout when they have skin in the game – namely, when their policy preferences, particularly concerning redistribution, diverge from those of the poor and when the state is capable of collecting taxes effectively.[26] In many African

---

[22] Chancel et al. (2023). In this work the spread of Islam is operationalized as the percentage of Muslims nationally.
[23] Almond and Verba (1963)
[24] Willeck and Mendelberg (2022)
[25] Croke et al. (2016)
[26] Kasara and Suryanarayan (2015)

countries, the ability of the state to collect taxes is quite low and the wealthy may not believe that voting that will lead to the implementation of their preferred policies. Third, the poorer and less educated may be more likely to turn out than the richer and more educated because they are more efficient targets of clientelism.[27] For these and other reasons, empirical work from sub-Saharan Africa in particular has found that education is not necessarily a strong predictor of political behavior; higher levels of education are not always associated with greater levels of political participation.[28]

Thus, we should not assume that the fact that Muslims have lower levels of schooling on average than Christians means that they are disadvantaged politically. As shown in Figure 8.1, which draws on Afrobarometer surveys from 32 African countries, while Muslims have slightly lower rates of (self-reported) voter turnout on average, turnout rates are similar to those reported by Christians at each level of education. In fact, voting rates are higher among those with less education, which is the category where Muslims are overrepresented. Indeed, after taking into

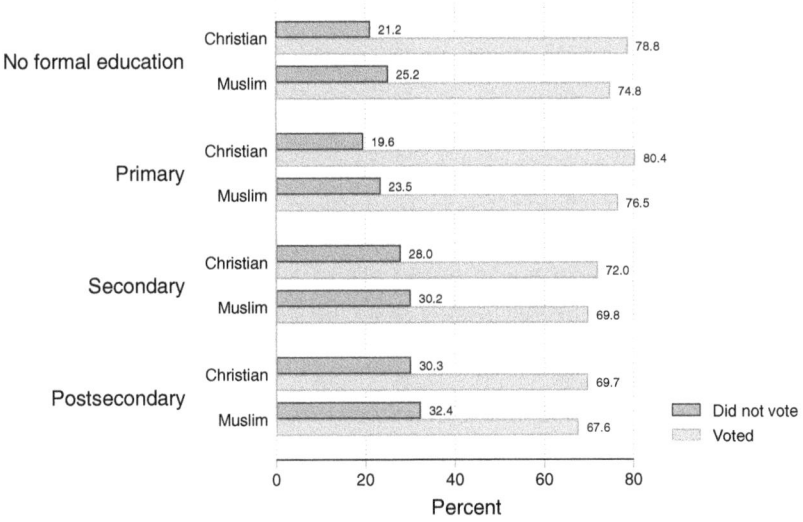

N=35,371. Afrobarometer Round 7.

FIGURE 8.1 Voter turnout by religion and highest level of education completed.
Source: Afrobarometer Round 7.

---

[27] Blaydes (2011), Stokes (2005), Calvo and Murillo (2004)
[28] Mattes and Mughogho (2009), Isaksson, Kotsadam, and Nerman (2014)

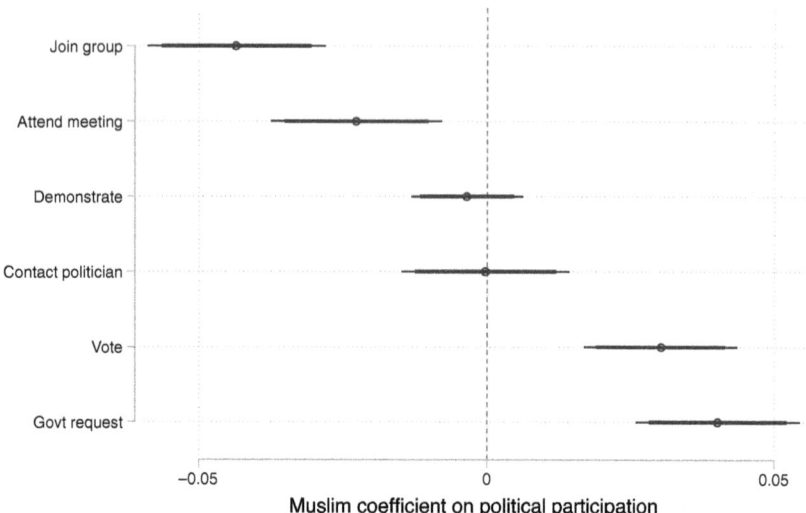

FIGURE 8.2 Differences in political participation between Christians and Muslims.
Source: Afrobarometer Round 7.

account gender, birth cohort, urban residence, and country-level differences, Muslims are about 3 percentage points more likely to turn out than Christians. For other measures of political participation the results are mixed, as shown in Figure 8.2, which plots the estimates of the coefficient on Muslim (omitted category is Christian) for six different types of political participation. Muslims are more likely than Christians to report voting in the last election and to organize with others to make a request from government, are equally likely to attend a demonstration or contact government officials, and are less likely to attend a meeting or join a group.

It is possible that more fine-grained measures of political participation would reveal greater differences between those who have attended school and those who have not. For example, Bleck (2013; 2015) finds that in Mali, education does not predict voting or party affiliation, but those with higher levels of education are more likely to correctly answer factual questions about politics. She also finds that even those with only informal education knew more about politics than those with no education. These findings suggest that Muslims' lower rates of schooling could mean that they have lower levels of political knowledge, even if levels of electoral participation are the same as those who have attended school.

It is also possible that relatively lower levels of education negatively affect political representation. Ricart-Huguet (2021) finds that subnational regions with higher levels of colonial investments in education (proxied by missionaries in British colonies) tend to be over-represented in postcolonial cabinets, relative to the size of the region's population. This may mean that those coming from Muslim majority areas are likely to be underrepresented in postcolonial governments.

Another channel through which education could affect political representation is educational requirements for office. If there are educational requirements in order to run for office, those with lower levels of education or no education will obviously be disadvantaged. For example, Kenya's Election Act requires a university degree for all those contesting to be a senator, governor, or president; Uganda's constitution requires completion of Advanced Level (upper secondary) to contest for member of parliament; in Senegal, the constitution does not specify a level of education to contest for the presidency, but candidates must be able to read and write. For these reasons, the Muslim–Christian schooling gap is likely to introduce a gap in the extent to which individuals have the opportunity to hold political office.

As this discussion makes clear, there are several potential avenues for future research to examine the ways in which the Muslim–Christian schooling gap matters for outcomes such as income and political participation. At the very least, the relationship between the Muslim–Christian schooling gap and inequality in income or political participation is complex – an education gap does not necessarily imply an income or participation gap. Rather, there are likely a set of factors that produce heterogeneous effects of education on income and political participation (or vice versa) that would be worth exploring further in this context.

Reflections on the Study of Education, Inequality, and Culture

This brings me to some closing reflections on the study of education, inequality, and culture. I see several goals going forward. The first is to lean into engagement with culture as an explanatory variable. As noted in the opening pages of this book, the study of culture and inequality has a complicated history, and it is easy to weaponize cultural arguments against historically marginalized groups. As Valentino and Vaisey (2022) note, there has been a "general distrust of cultural explanations among inequality scholars," due in large part to the "specter of victim-blaming," particularly concerning the Black–white poverty gap in the United States. Anyone who engages with culture as an explanation for inequality of educational outcomes or anything else should be aware of this history, and neither repeat mistakes nor flog "long dead and buried horses" like the culture of poverty thesis.[29]

But we needn't throw out culture as a concept just because others have poorly defined or misused it. Rather, we should identify its constituent components, and continue to examine when and how these operate on behavior. Part of the challenge of studying culture is that the definition itself is a moving target, and culture is often packaged under a variety of different labels. For example, norms (which themselves have multiple definitions and labels) often feature centrally in the definition of culture,[30] but some work on norms hardly mentions culture at all.[31] Similarly, there is a burgeoning literature on aspirations, and mounting evidence to suggest that aspirations can affect outcomes such as educational attainment and perpetuate inequality.[32] These aspirations are shaped by social contexts and influenced by peers, neighbors, and role models, operating in ways that could be conceived as part of culture. But although a seminal work in this field defined aspirations as a "cultural capacity," much subsequent work has not developed the idea of aspirations as being part of culture.[33]

Differences in terminology are challenging primarily because they make it difficult to find and build on existing work, especially work beyond one's own field. At present there is no consensus either within or across fields as to what exactly culture is, which requires any scholar employing the concept to state their own definition and how it relates to that of others. This absence of consensus speaks to the need, I believe, for more interdisciplinary work – or at least conversation – to guard against inadvertently reinventing the wheel and calling it by another name. Work that explicitly tries to synthesize findings about culture and its components across fields, such as the excellent interdisciplinary review article on norm behavior by Gelfand, Gavrilets, and Nunn (2024), would be helpful in consensus-building and expanding the frontier of knowledge about the role of culture in the political, economic, and social world.

---

[29] Patterson (2014, p. 2)
[30] For example Nunn (2012, S109), Bisin and Verdier (2011, p. 340), Cavapozzi, Francesconi, and Nicoletti (2021, p. 113), Lehman, Chiu, and Schaller (2004, p. 690).
[31] For example Krupka and Weber (2013), Bursztyn and Jensen (2017), Bašić and Verrina (2024).
[32] Fruttero, Muller, and Calvo-González (2024), Genicot and Ray (2020)
[33] Appadurai (2004)

A second goal pertains to the measurement of norms, which are an important component of culture in many recent empirical accounts. While mine is certainly not the first work suggesting norms can affect schooling behavior,[34] schooling norms are not presently top of mind among those who study education, particularly in the field of political science, but even in the field of education itself. Perhaps for this reason, there have been few efforts to measure norms about schooling systematically. To my knowledge, beyond the present study there are no survey data that measure second-order beliefs about schooling, in Africa or elsewhere. Existing data collection efforts (such as the Demographic and Health Surveys and censuses, two commonly used sources to study educational attainment) collect information about the school attendance of children, educational attainment of adults, and in a few cases first-order beliefs about education, but they do not collect second-order beliefs that would allow us to assess community-level schooling expectations.

In fact, second-order beliefs are rarely measured about any subject, despite the fact that we believe them to matter for many behaviors that are consequential to human well-being and overcoming collective action problems. A number of researchers have argued that norms and culture are key mechanisms in explaining the persistence of historical events,[35] and that culture interacts with institutions,[36] but our measures of the beliefs that comprise this mechanism are still not very good. Cultural beliefs and norms in empirical work are frequently measured using only first-order beliefs and preferences, such as measures of trust.

The dearth of convincing measures of culture and norms may be due in part to the fact that the beliefs underlying them can be difficult to elicit – these beliefs may not be top of mind for respondents and will not be evident unless drawn out intentionally. As Bicchieri (2016, p. 128) notes, "People might not be actively aware of the normative and empirical expectations that they hold until those expectations are challenged or explicitly elicited, as in when we measure them." And even when they are top of mind, respondents may have incentives to misrepresent their beliefs. They may do so if they believe their community is being "judged" by enumerators or the organizations that send them, particularly because it will be clear that enumerators are literate and have fairly high levels

---

[34] See, for example, Prentice (2012), Hoff and Stiglitz (2016), and Bursztyn and Jensen (2017).
[35] Nunn (2012)
[36] Alesina and Giuliano (2015)

of education. They may also believe providing a particular answer may be more likely to get them resources in the future, even if this is not the case. It was for this reason that in Malawi I provided monetary incentives for respondents to accurately estimate others' beliefs, as recommended by Bicchieri (2016). Still, respondents could very well have believed that everyone thought I wanted to hear a particular answer, and that everyone would report this belief instead of the one they thought others truly held. Thus, while monetary incentives may increase the accuracy of reported beliefs, they do not fully address the challenge of social desirability bias. Laboratory experiments are another tool that can be useful in both measuring beliefs and also in manipulating them to test for causal effects. These experiments are costly, however, and not easy to execute over many communities.

Yet another measurement challenge is that it may be easier to explain why something *isn't* done compared to why something *is* done. For example, Hoff and Stiglitz (2016, p. 43) discuss findings from a survey in India where girls' schooling was high in some communities and low in others. When parents in the low schooling communities were asked to explain why, their explanations were along the lines of "girls don't go to school in our community." In the high schooling communities, by contrast, parents often didn't know how to explain why girls were in school as it was just the obvious thing to do, from their perspective.[37]

Despite these challenges, if we believe that others' beliefs and expectations matter for our behavior, it is worthwhile to try to measure them. This may require a diversity of methods, as each has its own benefits and drawbacks. At a minimum, it would be useful to add questions about second-order beliefs to existing surveys. For example, female genital cutting (FGC) has long been thought to be perpetuated (at least in some places) through pluralistic ignorance or because it has the features of a classic coordination problem – both of which concern second-order beliefs.[38] However, although surveys like the DHS already include modules about FGC in countries where it is practiced, they only ask about respondents' own beliefs, not their empirical and normative expectations regarding *others'* beliefs, even though these are thought to be key to the perpetuation of the practice. Collecting systematic data on second-order beliefs about FGC would help us establish the conditions under

---

[37] This example and quote cited are taken from De (1999).
[38] Mackie (1996).

which FGC is perpetuated as a result of a coordination problem or not, which has implications for the design of appropriate policy responses.[39] Similarly, existing surveys that measure educational outcomes could also include questions to measure second-order beliefs about schooling.

A third goal going forward is to better understand the impact of schooling beliefs on behavior relative to other factors, including resource constraints and structural inequalities, and how the relative importance of norms in explaining schooling behavior varies across contexts. It is not clear how feasible or useful it would be to do a "horse race" between economic costs and schooling norms, but it may be possible to focus more on norm change in cases where removing resource constraints to schooling is insufficient to close schooling gaps or where children remain out of school.

We might also take more seriously what people themselves say, while acknowledging risks of social desirability bias. The 2021–2022 UNESCO Global Monitoring Report cited "dispositional barriers," which they describe as personal attitudes, as a significant factor in explaining why many children remain out of school. They use survey evidence from several countries, including Malawi and Nigeria, to show that the most common reason given for not attending secondary school is disposition, namely that parents and children are "not interested." These findings resonate with my own in Malawi, where many parents with children out of school said children didn't want to go. The report notes that few policies to increase attendance are designed to address dispositional barriers and that the prevalence of dispositional barriers "demonstrates that supplying affordable education of good quality is not enough."[40]

Existing education policies that address resource constraints, such as the removal of school fees, are very expensive. It seems likely that policies targeting beliefs, or dispositional barriers, would be much cheaper. Why have these policies been uncommon to date? There are at least two possible reasons. The first is that these policies may be harder to design than policies addressing structural or financial barriers. If there is no school building present, the obvious thing to do is to construct one. If you want to reduce the amount of money households spend on schooling, remove school fees. But to address dispositional factors, you need to understand

---

[39] Efferson et al. (2015) use a clever design to measure FGC in Sudan, and having done so, demonstrated that patterns of FGC across communities deviate from what we would expect to see if the practice of FGC was really about coordination.
[40] UNESCO (2021)

what kind of beliefs about schooling you are dealing with. And these beliefs, as already noted, are going to vary even among those who say they are "not interested" or even opposed to school. Policies addressing schooling beliefs do not lend themselves to universality – they require contextual and historical knowledge. Policy design of this kind also requires a reckoning about what kinds of tools, ideas, and knowledge parents and communities want their children to be learning.

The second possible reason policies to address dispositional factors have been rare is that policymakers and donors, and scholars for that matter, may be hesitant to be perceived as placing blame on families for low school attendance, particularly in cases where there are clearly economic or structural barriers as well. Recognizing the hazards of arguments that blame the victim for the condition she finds herself in, we may be also doing a disservice to that same individual by not taking seriously her own explanation, or explaining them away with ignorance. If school is actually unattractive, why is this the case? We can agree that contaminated water and potholed roads are a bad thing no matter where or who you are, but a universal understanding of what constitutes an appropriate collection of skills and knowledge may not now or ever exist. Therefore, to lack a particular type of education may not be considered a normatively bad thing. Schooling, where not compulsory or not enforced, is a choice. If parents and families are making choices to do something else with children's time, we should endeavor to understand why.

This brings me to a final consideration, which is about the content and structure of education going forward. How might we tailor and strengthen the content and teaching of education to make it better suited to the contexts in which children are growing up, the economies in which they are likely to participate, and the local and global challenges they are likely to face? Content which better matches the needs of the communities in which it is being provided is likely to inspire greater demand, and provide students with the tools and knowledge that will be most useful to them. To be clear, there are some basic competencies which everyone should have the opportunity to acquire. But beyond these, the knowledge and skills that will be useful and valued within a community may vary quite a bit.

The past two centuries have brought economic and political change that fundamentally altered life as we know it. As noted at the outset of this book, these changes have allowed much of humanity to avoid living lives that are nasty, brutish, and short. But with tremendous growth has come soaring inequality, the destruction of the natural environment, and technological change whose impact on society is hard to predict. We face a rapidly evolving global economy, constantly shifting political landscapes, and a changing climate that is already affecting how and where we can live. Millions of people are migrating to urban areas, and crossing oceans and deserts – sometimes at the cost of their lives – to seek better opportunities. Yet for all of this fast-paced change, education systems and curricula are slow moving and lag behind economic and political trends. Moreover, educational reforms are political, and not always designed to improve educational outcomes in the aggregate but rather the outcomes of those who are more powerful to begin with.

In the face of economic and political change, as well as demographic change – by 2100, for example, it is expected that 40 percent of the global population will live in Africa – governments, civil society, international institutions, and citizens themselves will need to consider what kind of skills and knowledge will allow individuals to pursue lives that are meaningful and allow the collective to thrive. Although there is a tendency to copy curricula, mirror institutions,[41] and standardize tests, it is likely that beyond a set of basic skills, the content that best serves those growing up in a given community will be context specific, and constantly evolving. This makes policy-making more difficult, but may be the only way to keep pace with a rapidly changing economic environment that varies across and within countries. Ideally, individuals should be able to thrive in their own communities, and have the freedom to explore beyond them, if they so choose. How to achieve flexible, context-specific mass schooling is a challenge I leave to future work, but one that I hope we take seriously going forward. I suspect our ability to support the substantial swath of humanity that has not yet escaped a life of insecurity depends on it.

---

[41] DiMaggio et al. (1983)

Appendix

A.1 RELIGIOUS AFFILIATION AND SCHOOLING OUTCOMES

This section provides additional results demonstrating the relationship between religious affiliation and schooling outcomes using data from the Demographic and Health Surveys.

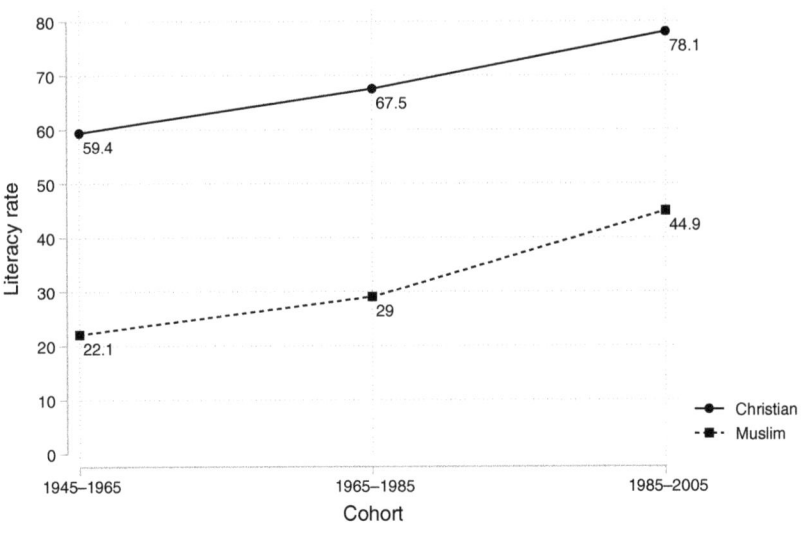

FIGURE A.1 Literacy rate (age 14+) by religion and cohort.
Source: DHS, various years.

TABLE A.1 *Religious Affiliation and schooling outcomes.*

	(1) Any school	(2) Any school	(3) Literate	(4) Literate	(5) Years school	(6) Years school
Muslim	−0.297***	−0.148***	−0.261***	−0.143***	−2.916***	−1.664***
	(0.018)	(0.010)	(0.015)	(0.009)	(0.199)	(0.099)
Female	−0.130***	−0.142***	−0.172***	−0.191***	−1.773***	−1.878***
	(0.005)	(0.006)	(0.006)	(0.006)	(0.067)	(0.062)
Urban		0.085***		0.091***		0.973***
		(0.005)		(0.005)		(0.052)
Wealth		0.067***		0.088***		1.073***
		(0.003)		(0.002)		(0.033)
Constant	0.604***	0.226***	0.608***	0.199***	4.219***	0.219
	(0.029)	(0.019)	(0.019)	(0.023)	(0.157)	(0.162)
Country FE	Yes	Yes	Yes	Yes	Yes	Yes
Region FE	No	Yes	No	Yes	No	Yes
Ethnic FE	No	Yes	No	Yes	No	Yes
N	1580555	1200243	1545315	1188424	1104516	837693
R^2	0.317	0.458	0.252	0.400	0.287	0.506

Notes: *** indicates 99% confidence level; ** indicates 95% confidence level; * indicates 90% confidence level. All models are specified as ordinary least squares regression. Data come from the Demographic and Health Surveys. *Literate* takes a value of 1 if the respondent can read fluently or with difficulty, and 0 if unable to read. *Any school* takes a value of 1 if the respondent has at least one year of school, and 0 if less than one year. *Years school* is the total number of years of school the respondent attended. wealth is an indicator of the household's wealth quintile, based on assets. All models include covariates for 10-year birth cohorts. Standard errors are clustered by survey-region.

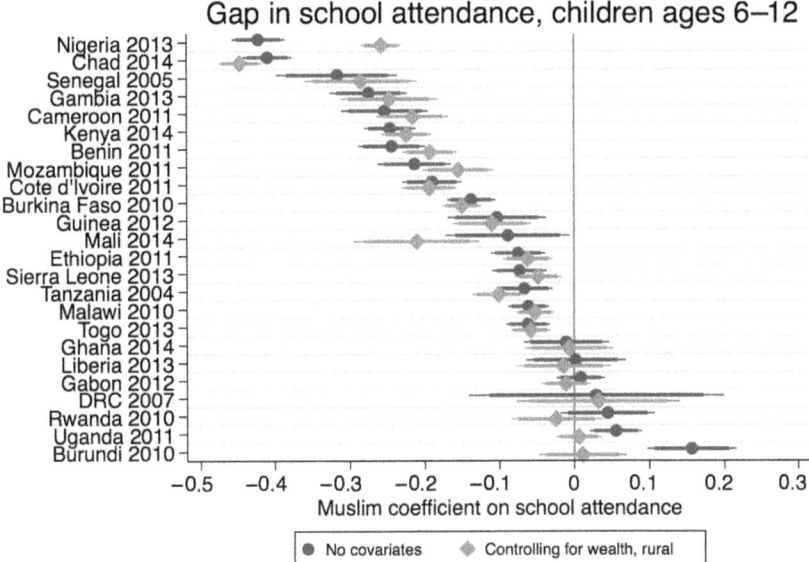

FIGURE A.2 Gap in school attendance for Muslims compared to Christians, ages 6–12.
Source: DHS.

A.2 MUSLIM MAJORITY STATUS AND EDUCATIONAL ATTAINMENT

Table A.2 shows the results from the set of regressions where the outcomes are adult literacy and school attendance, and the main independent variables are Muslim affiliation, percentage of Muslims of the administrative area where the respondent lives, and the interaction between these two. The data for this analysis come from census data from eleven African countries. Standard errors are clustered by administrative unit. This table shows there is some variation in country-level trends, with several countries showing a sharp divergence in educational attainment as percentage Muslim increases, such as Malawi, Ethiopia, and Burkina Faso, but some showing parallel trends, where both Muslim and Christian educational attainment decline as percentage Muslim increases, such as Cameroon, Ghana, and Mozambique.

TABLE A.2 *Educational attainment and Muslim majority status, by country.*

Adult literacy, ages 18 and above

	Burkina	Cameroon	Ethiopia	Ghana	Malawi	Mali	Mozam.	Nigeria	Senegal	Sierra Leone	Uganda
Muslim	0.403	−1.653***	0.344**	−1.072***	−0.057	0.321	−0.110	−0.943***	−0.507	0.552	0.837***
	(0.505)	(0.257)	(0.149)	(0.103)	(0.182)	(0.696)	(0.194)	(0.340)	(0.591)	(1.171)	(0.212)
% Muslim	0.013***	−0.036***	0.014***	−0.021***	−0.002	0.017***	−0.012**	−0.007**	0.000	−0.012	0.025*
	(0.005)	(0.012)	(0.003)	(0.008)	(0.003)	(0.006)	(0.005)	(0.003)	(0.003)	(0.029)	(0.014)
Muslim x	−0.026***	0.022*	−0.026***	0.003	−0.017***	−0.012	−0.002	0.006	0.004	−0.019	−0.044***
% Muslim	(0.009)	(0.011)	(0.004)	(0.006)	(0.004)	(0.008)	(0.006)	(0.006)	(0.007)	(0.016)	(0.010)
Constant	−1.280***	1.799***	−0.982***	1.309***	0.917***	−1.770***	0.225	1.221***	−0.382	0.871	0.188*
	(0.239)	(0.290)	(0.203)	(0.151)	(0.130)	(0.434)	(0.138)	(0.113)	(0.243)	(2.353)	(0.108)
N	836484	777489	2886906	2032203	1044984	587454	700406	38474	817696	252989	1793017

School attendance, ages 6 to 17

	Burkina	Cameroon	Ethiopia	Ghana	Malawi	Mali	Mozam.	Nigeria	Senegal	Sierra Leone	Uganda
Muslim	0.038	−0.416***	0.367**	−0.583***	0.064	−0.411	−0.207	−0.535	5.916***	0.056	0.554***
	(0.429)	(0.128)	(0.158)	(0.085)	(0.132)	(0.844)	(0.150)	(0.489)	(2.253)	(0.851)	(0.121)
% Muslim	0.007*	−0.004**	0.011***	−0.024***	−0.001	0.002	−0.015***	−0.015***	−0.014***	−0.018	0.022**
	(0.004)	(0.002)	(0.002)	(0.004)	(0.002)	(0.003)	(0.004)	(0.004)	(0.004)	(0.019)	(0.008)
Muslim x	−0.015*	0.001	−0.025***	0.010***	−0.012***	−0.003	0.002	−0.005	−0.073***	−0.007	−0.022***
% Muslim	(0.008)	(0.004)	(0.003)	(0.003)	(0.003)	(0.009)	(0.004)	(0.008)	(0.024)	(0.012)	(0.007)
Constant	−0.156	1.797***	−1.314***	1.950***	0.910***	0.338	1.086***	2.776***	1.996***	2.554*	0.807***
	(0.161)	(0.037)	(0.181)	(0.066)	(0.084)	(0.280)	(0.108)	(0.213)	(0.361)	(1.449)	(0.116)
N	350425	389798	1911444	1048690	627107	414171	428469	20252	489901	136665	1192620

Notes: *** indicates 99% confidence level; ** indicates 95% confidence level; * indicates 90% confidence level. All models are specified as logistic regression with clustered standard errors by administrative unit.

A.3 BIVARIATE RELATIONSHIPS BETWEEN DEMOCRACY, INCOME PER CAPITA, AND THE COUNTRY-LEVEL MUSLIM–CHRISTIAN GAP

Figure A.3 shows the bivariate relationship between the average polity score from 1960 to 2010 and the Muslim–Christian gap in years of schooling for cohorts born between 1965 and 1995. If anything, countries with a higher average polity score have a slightly larger schooling gap, though in general the relationship is weak. A similar result obtains if we consider the percent of years under democracy. Figure A.4 shows the bivariate relationship between log GDP per capita in 1990 and the Muslim–Christian gap in years of education, and suggests there is no obvious relationship between income per capita and the Muslim–Christian schooling gap.

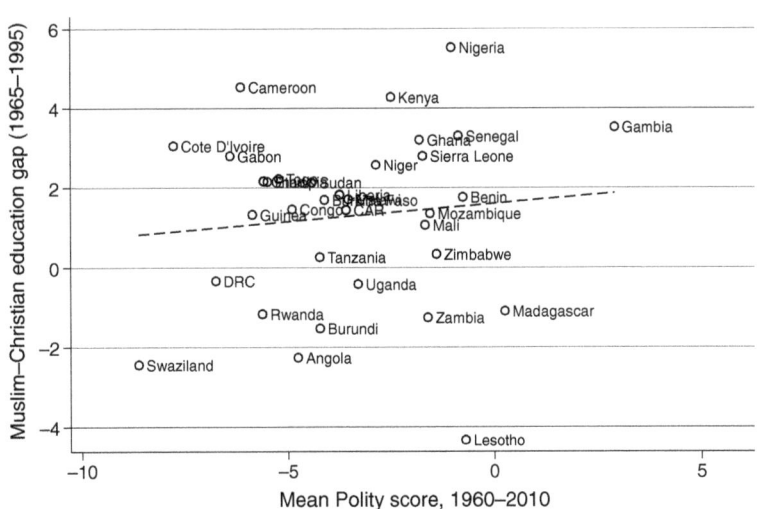

FIGURE A.3 Bivariate relationship between regime type and the Muslim–Christian education gap.
Source: DHS and Polity IV project.

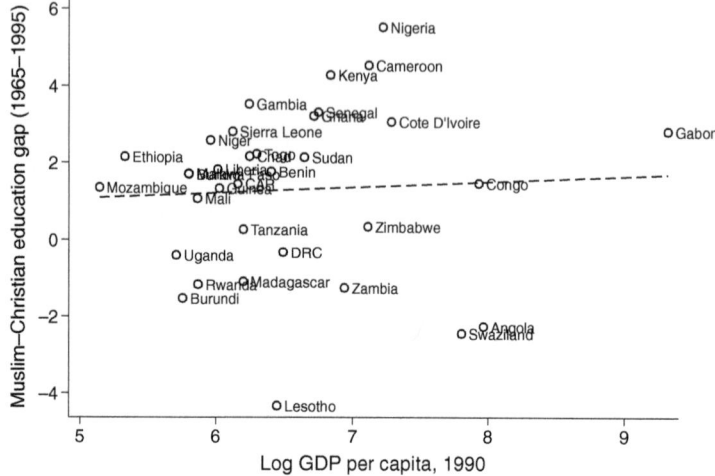

FIGURE A.4 Bivariate relationship between logged GDP per capita in 1990 and the Muslim–Christian education gap.
Source: DHS and World Bank DataBank.

A.4 EDUCATIONAL ATTAINMENT IN COLONIAL BUGANDA

Figure A.5 shows a map of Uganda with the number of schools, both primary and secondary, from the Blue Book data by county, where darker shades of gray indicate a greater number of schools.[1]

Table A.3 shows the relationship between county-level missionary school density and Muslim educational attainment as measured by any schooling, literacy, and years of school from the 2002 census.[2] The table shows that the number of missionary schools in a county is a strong predictor of Muslim educational attainment. The predicted probability that a Muslim would have attended school at all is 0.52 if there are no missionary schools in the county and 0.85 if there are 11 (the maximum number in any county). Similarly, the predicted probability that a Muslim is literate is 0.45 if there are no missionary schools in the county and 0.82

---

[1] The data on schools comes from annually produced reports, Blue Books, that include the name and location of schools, and a map from the 1931 education report. The quality and detail of the data varies from year to year, such that the location of schools can be confidently traced to the county, but not the precise geographic coordinates of the school. It is also not possible to determine which schools on the 1931 map are duplicates of the Blue Book data, and which are unique. For this reason, the most conservative estimate of school density is the Blue Book data.

[2] From the census, I focus on the cohort of individuals born between 1940 and 1955. These individuals would have been of primary-school age at the end of the colonial period.

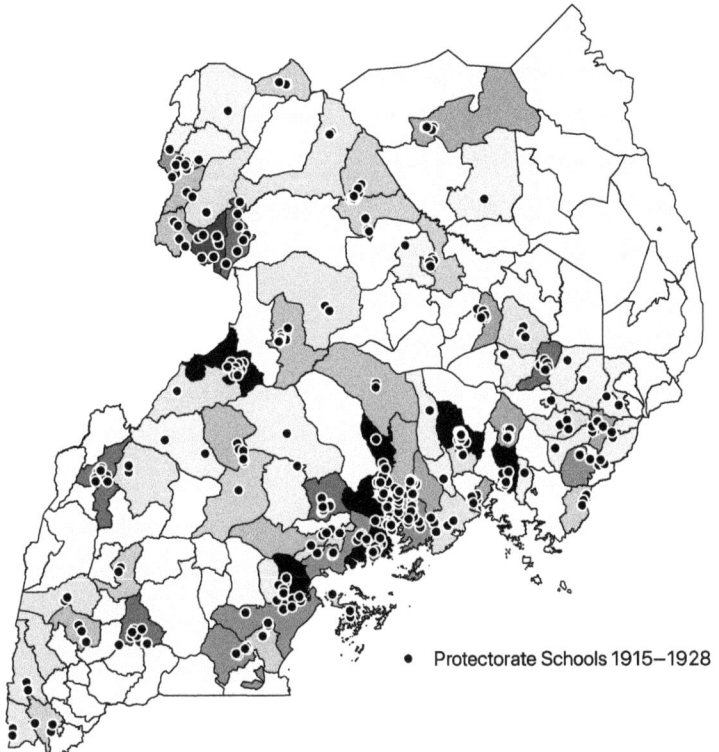

FIGURE A.5 Missionary schools by county in the Uganda Protectorate, 1915–1928.
Source: Uganda Protectorate Blue Books 1915–1928.

if there are 11. Finally, the predicted years of school for a Muslim living in a county with no missionary schools is 3.1 years, and 7.5 for a Muslim living in a county with 11 missionary schools.

This analysis provides suggestive evidence that exposure to and competition with Christians produced higher demand for education, and subsequently higher educational attainment, among Muslims.

A.5 RELIGIOUS DEMOGRAPHICS AND WEALTH

Figure A.6 shows the results of a regression analysis where religious affiliation is interacted with region percent Muslim and the outcome is the wealth quintile of the household. This figure suggests there is not a Muslim–Christian gap in wealth that corresponds with the education gap.

Appendix

TABLE A.3 *Missionary schools by county and Muslim educational attainment.*

	(1) Any school	(2) Any school	(3) Literate	(4) Literate	(5) Years of school	(6) Years of school
Number of schools	0.154** (0.0482)	0.0757** (0.0269)	0.156** (0.0473)	0.0805** (0.0291)	0.438** (0.126)	0.255** (0.0912)
Female		−1.760** (0.0425)		−1.914** (0.0461)		−3.311** (0.119)
Birth year		0.0796** (0.00243)		0.0806** (0.00217)		0.163** (0.00905)
Ethnic group FE		Yes		Yes		Yes Yes
N	128225	128224	128225	128224	128225	128225
r^2					0.0611	0.270

Notes: ** indicates 99% confidence level; * indicates 95% confidence level; + indicates 90% confidence level. Standard errors in parentheses, clustered by county. *Any school*, a dichotomous variable indicating whether an individual has ever attended school; *Literate*, a dichotomous variable indicating whether or not the individual is literate in any language; and *Years of school* a continuous variable indicating the total number of years the individual attended school. Models 1–4 employ logistic regression and models 5–6 employ OLS. Models 2, 4, and 6 include a dichotomous variable indicating whether the respondent is female, birth year, and ethnic group fixed effects.

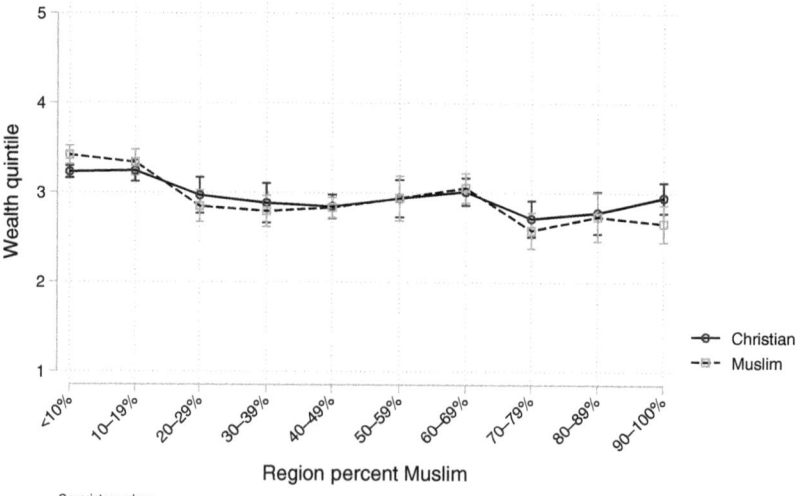

Covariates: urban.
Country fixed effects; SE clustered by survey-region.
Each observation is weighted by the inverse of the total number of observations in a country.
N= 862,490, across 28 countries.

FIGURE A.6 Household wealth quintile and region percent Muslim.
Source: DHS.

A.6 HISTORIC ISLAMIC RULE

Figure A.7 shows the predicted values for the attendance of any school as a function of the interaction between distance to Islamic trade routes and respondent religion. This suggests that the gap is largest closest to the trade routes, which were areas that were most likely to be exposed to Islam in the precolonial period.

Figure A.8 shows the predicted values for having any schooling. The model includes an interaction term between respondent religion and the type of area in which they live – no exposure to Islamic influence or states, an area of Islamic influence (near but outside of states), and an area that was previously part of an Islamic state. The Muslim–Christian gap is largest in areas that were part of Islamic states though it exists everywhere.

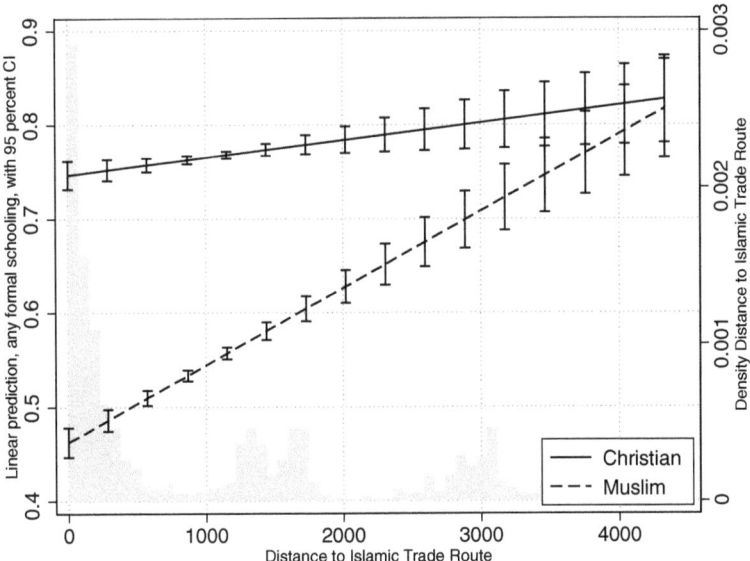

FIGURE A.7 Predicted margins for educational attainment by exposure to Islamic trade routes and religious affiliation.
Source: DHS and Sluglett and Currie (2015).

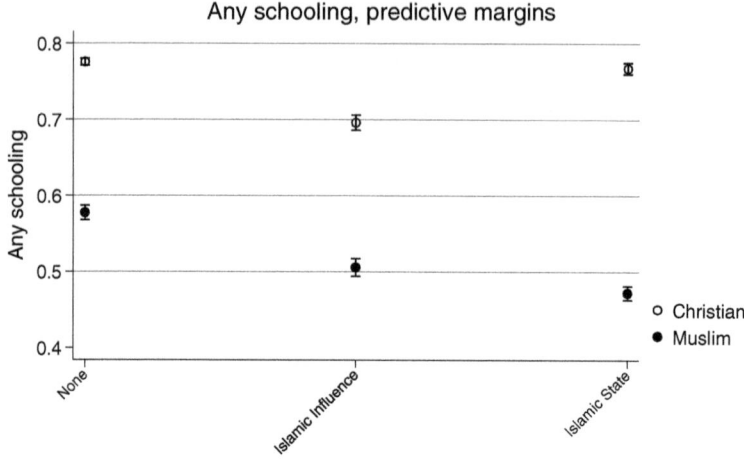

FIGURE A.8 Predicted margins for educational attainment by exposure to Islamic influence and religious affiliation.
Source: DHS and Sluglett and Currie (2015).

TABLE A.4 *Balance across cluster-level covariates by exposure to Islam.*

	None Mean/(SD)	Islamic Influence Mean/(SD)	Islamic State Mean/(SD)	Total Mean/(SD)
Cluster % Muslim	0.16	0.46	0.55	0.33
	(0.29)	(0.42)	(0.45)	(0.41)
Urban	0.39	0.27	0.33	0.36
	(0.49)	(0.44)	(0.47)	(0.48)
Annual Precipitation (2000)	111.35	94.45	72.31	95.27
	(51.57)	(38.07)	(28.09)	(46.37)
Gross Cell Production	1721.06	920.61	1205.45	1434.08
	(3200.45)	(395.37)	(560.14)	(2353.30)
Malaria Incidence (2000)	0.38	0.45	0.39	0.39
	(0.18)	(0.20)	(0.16)	(0.18)
Nightlights Composite	2.83	1.03	2.20	2.37
	(7.01)	(3.06)	(5.85)	(6.25)
UN Population Density (2000)	1043.45	318.67	1058.96	950.95
	(2933.22)	(1173.20)	(2811.60)	(2729.55)
Enhanced Vegetation Index (2015)	2710.80	2823.26	2568.39	2677.43
	(2691.22)	(1569.88)	(1437.54)	(2203.39)

A.7 MALAWI SURVEYS AND COORDINATION GAMES

Figure A.9 is a plot showing the percentage of Christians and Muslims, respectively, in each enumeration area in Malawi; it shows that as the percentage of Muslims of the enumeration area increases, the Muslim–Christian gap in school attendance grows and Muslim attendance declines.

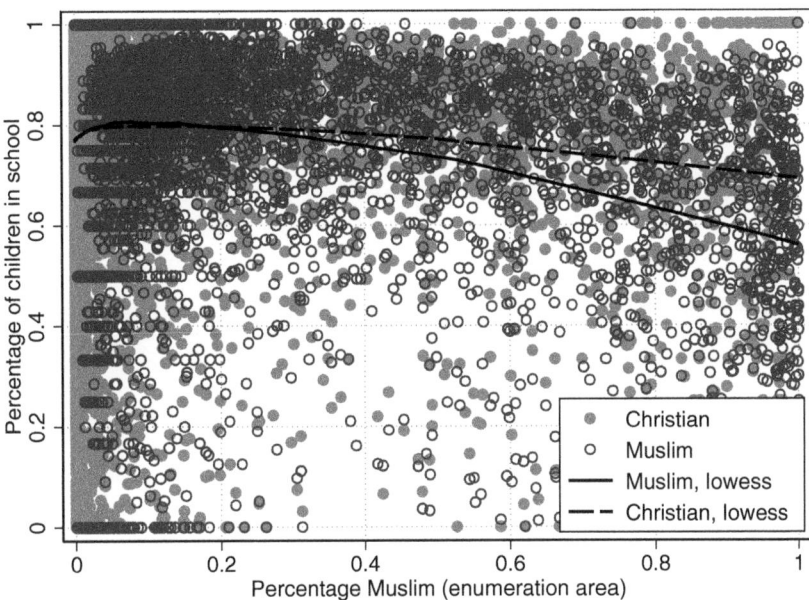

FIGURE A.9 The Muslim–Christian schooling gap by enumeration area in Malawi.
Source: Malawi 2008 Census.

Interviews

TABLE A.5 *Interviews in Malawi.*

ID	Description	Location	Date
1	Officer	USAID Lilongwe	6-Nov-13
2	Sheikh	Islamic Information Bureau, Zomba	9-Nov-13
3	Director, Center for Education Research	Zomba	11-Nov-13
4	Primary Education Advisor	Domasi, Zomba	12-Nov-13
5	Professor	Chancellor College, Zomba	13-Nov-13
6	District Education Manager	Mangochi	14-Nov-13
7	Teacher	Mangochi Town	14-Nov-13
8	Brother to TA Chowe	Islamic Information Bureau, Mangochi	14-Nov-13

TABLE A.5 *(continued)*

ID	Description	Location	Date
9	Primary Education Advisor	Chilipa Zone, Mangochi	14-Nov-13
10	Traditional Authority Chimwala	Chimwala, Mangochi	14-Nov-13
11	Traditional Authority Chowe	Mangochi	29-Jul-14
12	Sheikh	Islamic Information Bureau, Blantyre	1-Aug-14
13	Diplomat	Blantyre	4-Aug-14
14	Secretary General	Muslim Association of Malawi, Blantyre	4-Aug-14
15	District Education Manager	Mangochi	29-Aug-14
16	Village Head	TA Chowe, M1 village	21-Nov-16
17	Parent 1	TA Chowe, M1 village	21-Nov-16
18	Parent 2	TA Chowe, M1 village	21-Nov-16
19	Parent 3	TA Chowe, M1 village	21-Nov-16
20	Teacher 1	TA Chowe, M1 village	21-Nov-16
21	Village Head	TA Mponda, K1 village	22-Nov-16
22	Parent 1	TA Mponda, K1 village	22-Nov-16
23	Parent 2	TA Mponda, K1 village	22-Nov-16
24	Parent 3	TA Mponda, K1 village	22-Nov-16
25	Parent 4	TA Mponda, K1 village	22-Nov-16
26	Parent 5	TA Mponda, K1 village	22-Nov-16
27	Head teacher	TA Mponda, K1 village	22-Nov-16
28	Teacher 1	TA Mponda, K1 village	22-Nov-16
29	Village Head	TA Katuli, L1 village	23-Nov-16
30	Parent 1	TA Katuli, L1 village	23-Nov-16
31	Parent 2	TA Katuli, L1 village	23-Nov-16
32	Parent 3	TA Katuli, L1 village	23-Nov-16
33	Parent 4	TA Katuli, L1 village	23-Nov-16
34	Head teacher	TA Katuli, L1 village	23-Nov-16
35	Teacher 1	TA Katuli, L1 village	23-Nov-16
36	Village Head	TA Jalasi, K1 village	24-Nov-16
37	Parent 1	TA Jalasi, K1 village	24-Nov-16
38	Parent 2	TA Jalasi, K1 village	24-Nov-16
39	Parent 3	TA Jalasi, K1 village	24-Nov-16
40	Parent 4	TA Jalasi, K1 village	24-Nov-16
41	Head teacher	TA Jalasi, K1 village	24-Nov-16
42	Teacher 1	TA Jalasi, K1 village	24-Nov-16
43	Village Head	TA Chimwala, L1 village	25-Nov-16
44	Parent 1	TA Chimwala, L1 village	25-Nov-16
45	Parent 2	TA Chimwala, L1 village	25-Nov-16
46	Parent 3	TA Chimwala, L1 village	25-Nov-16
47	Parent 4	TA Chimwala, L1 village	25-Nov-16
48	Head teacher	TA Chimwala, L1 village	25-Nov-16
49	Teacher 1	TA Chimwala, L1 village	25-Nov-16
50	District Education Manager	Mangochi	9-Dec-16
51	Village Head	TA Nkalo, M1 village	30-Jan-17
52	Parent 1	TA Nkalo, M1 village	30-Jan-17
53	Parent 2	TA Nkalo, M1 village	30-Jan-17

(continued)

TABLE A.5 *(continued)*

ID	Description	Location	Date
54	Parent 3	TA Nkalo, M1 village	30-Jan-17
55	Parent 4	TA Nkalo, M1 village	30-Jan-17
56	Parent 5	TA Nkalo, M1 village	30-Jan-17
57	Head teacher	TA Nkalo, M1 village	30-Jan-17
58	Teacher 1	TA Nkalo, M1 village	30-Jan-17
59	Religious Leader 1	TA Nkalo, M1 village	30-Jan-17
60	Village Head	TA Kadewere, M1 village	2-Feb-17
61	Parent 1	TA Kadewere, M1 village	2-Feb-17
62	Parent 2	TA Kadewere, M1 village	2-Feb-17
63	Parent 3	TA Kadewere, M1 village	2-Feb-17
64	Parent 4	TA Kadewere, M1 village	2-Feb-17
65	Head teacher	TA Kadewere, M1 village	2-Feb-17
66	Teacher 1	TA Kadewere, M1 village	2-Feb-17
67	Religious Leader 1	TA Kadewere, M1 village	2-Feb-17
68	Religious Leader 2	TA Kadewere, M1 village	2-Feb-17
69	Village Head	TA Likoswe, K1 village	3-Feb-17
70	Parent 1	TA Likoswe, K1 village	3-Feb-17
71	Parent 2	TA Likoswe, K1 village	3-Feb-17
72	Parent 3	TA Likoswe, K1 village	3-Feb-17
73	Parent 4	TA Likoswe, K1 village	3-Feb-17
74	Head teacher	TA Likoswe, K1 village	3-Feb-17
75	Teacher 1	TA Likoswe, K1 village	3-Feb-17
76	Religious Leader 1	TA Likoswe, K1 village	3-Feb-17
77	Religious Leader 2	TA Likoswe, K1 village	3-Feb-17
78	Village Head	TA Likoswe, N1 village	5-Feb-17
79	Parent 1	TA Likoswe, N1 village	5-Feb-17
80	Parent 2	TA Likoswe, N1 village	5-Feb-17
81	Parent 3	TA Likoswe, N1 village	5-Feb-17
82	Parent 4	TA Likoswe, N1 village	5-Feb-17
83	Parent 5	TA Likoswe, N1 village	5-Feb-17
84	Head teacher	TA Likoswe, N1 village	5-Feb-17
85	Teacher 1	TA Likoswe, N1 village	5-Feb-17
86	Religious Leader 1	TA Likoswe, N1 village	5-Feb-17
87	Religious Leader 2	TA Likoswe, N1 village	5-Feb-17
88	Village Head	TA Mtchema, C1 village	8-Feb-17
89	Parent 1	TA Mtchema, C1 village	8-Feb-17
90	Parent 2	TA Mtchema, C1 village	8-Feb-17
91	Parent 3	TA Mtchema, C1 village	8-Feb-17
92	Parent 4	TA Mtchema, C1 village	8-Feb-17
93	Parent 5	TA Mtchema, C1 village	8-Feb-17
94	Head teacher	TA Mtchema, C1 village	8-Feb-17
95	Teacher 1	TA Mtchema, C1 village	8-Feb-17
96	Religious Leader 1	TA Mtchema, C1 village	8-Feb-17
97	Religious Leader 2	TA Mtchema, C1 village	8-Feb-17
98	Teacher 1	Machinga, N2 village	1-Mar-18
99	Teacher 2	Machinga, N2 village	1-Mar-18
100	Head teacher	Machinga, N2 village	1-Mar-18
101	Traditional Authority Kawinga	Machinga, N2 village	1-Mar-18

TABLE A.5 *(continued)*

ID	Description	Location	Date
102	Village Head	TA Kadewere, C1 village	11-Mar-18
103	Community Member 1	Machinga, S1 village	12-Mar-18
104	Focus Group Member 1	Machinga, S1 village	12-Mar-18
105	Focus Group Member 2	Machinga, S1 village	12-Mar-18
106	Focus Group Member 3	Machinga, S1 village	12-Mar-18
107	Focus Group Member 4	Machinga, S1 village	12-Mar-18
108	Community Member 2	Machinga, S1 village	12-Mar-18
109	Community Member 1	Balaka, M1 village	13-Mar-18
110	Community Member 2	Balaka, M1 village	13-Mar-18
111	Focus Group Member 1	Balaka, M2 village	13-Mar-18
112	Focus Group Member 2	Balaka, M2 village	13-Mar-18
113	Focus Group Member 3	Balaka, M2 village	13-Mar-18
114	Community Member 1	Balaka, M2 village	13-Mar-18
115	Community Member 1	TA Mpama, L1 village	14-Mar-18
116	Community Member 2	TA Mpama, L1 village	14-Mar-18
117	Community Member 1	TA Kadewere, M2 village	14-Mar-18
118	Focus Group Member 1	Machinga, N1 village	14-Mar-18
119	Focus Group Member 2	Machinga, N1 village	14-Mar-18
120	Focus Group Member 1	Machinga, N1 village	14-Mar-18
121	Focus Group Member 2	Machinga, N1 village	14-Mar-18
122	Focus Group Member 3	Machinga, N1 village	14-Mar-18
123	Community Member 1	TA Jalasi, N1 village	15-Mar-18
124	Focus Group Member 1	Mangochi, N1 village	16-Mar-18
125	Focus Group Member 2	Mangochi, N1 village	16-Mar-18
126	Focus Group Member 3	Mangochi, N1 village	16-Mar-18
127	Focus Group Member 4	Mangochi, N1 village	16-Mar-18
128	Focus Group Member 5	Mangochi, N1 village	16-Mar-18
129	Focus Group Member 6	Mangochi, N1 village	16-Mar-18
130	Focus Group Member 7	Mangochi, N1 village	16-Mar-18
131	Focus Group 2 Member 8	Mangochi, N1 village	16-Mar-18
132	Focus Group 2 Member 1	Mangochi, N1 village	16-Mar-18
133	Focus Group 2 Member 2	Mangochi, N1 village	16-Mar-18
134	Focus Group 2 Member 3	Mangochi, N1 village	16-Mar-18
135	Focus Group 2 Member 4	Mangochi, N1 village	16-Mar-18
136	Focus Group 2 Member 5	Mangochi, N1 village	16-Mar-18
137	Focus Group 2 Member 6	Mangochi, N1 village	16-Mar-18
138	Focus Group 2 Member 7	Mangochi, N1 village	16-Mar-18
139	Traditional Authority Mponda	TA Mponda	16-Mar-18
140	Focus Group Elder 1	TA Mpama, K1 village	27-Apr-18
141	Focus Group Elder 2	TA Mpama, K1 village	27-Apr-18
142	Focus Group Elder 3	TA Mpama, K1 village	27-Apr-18
143	Focus Group Elder 4	TA Mpama, K1 village	27-Apr-18
144	Focus Group Elder 5	TA Mpama, K1 village	27-Apr-18
145	Focus Group Elder 6	TA Mpama, K1 village	27-Apr-18
146	Focus Group Elder 7	TA Mpama, K1 village	27-Apr-18

(continued)

TABLE A.5 *(continued)*

ID	Description	Location	Date
147	Focus Group Elder 1	TA Mpama, K2 village	27-Apr-18
148	Focus Group Elder 2	TA Mpama, K2 village	27-Apr-18
149	Focus Group Elder 3	TA Mpama, K2 village	27-Apr-18
150	Focus Group Elder 4	TA Mpama, K2 village	27-Apr-18
151	Focus Group Elder 5	TA Mpama, K2 village	27-Apr-18
152	Focus Group Elder 6	TA Mpama, K2 village	27-Apr-18
153	Focus Group Elder 7	TA Mpama, K2 village	27-Apr-18
154	Focus Group Elder 1	TA Sitola, M1 village	28-Apr-18
155	Focus Group Elder 2	TA Sitola, M1 village	28-Apr-18
156	Focus Group Elder 3	TA Sitola, M1 village	28-Apr-18
157	Focus Group Elder 4	TA Sitola, M1 village	28-Apr-18
158	Focus Group Elder 5	TA Sitola, M1 village	28-Apr-18
159	Focus Group Elder 1	TA Sitola, N1 village	28-Apr-18
160	Focus Group Elder 2	TA Sitola, N1 village	28-Apr-18
161	Focus Group Elder 3	TA Sitola, N1 village	28-Apr-18
162	Focus Group Elder 4	TA Sitola, N1 village	28-Apr-18
163	Focus Group Elder 5	TA Sitola, N1 village	28-Apr-18
164	Focus Group Elder 6	TA Sitola, N1 village	28-Apr-18
165	Focus Group Elder 7	TA Sitola, N1 village	28-Apr-18

TABLE A.6 *Mfano education committee members.*

Parent–Teacher Association					
Position	Age	Religion	Gender	Education	Village position
Chairman	67	Muslim	M	STD8	Chief counselor
Vice chairmain	70	Muslim	M	None	None
Secretary	52	Muslim	M	Form 4	Head teacher
Vice secretary	38	Christian	M	Form 4	Teacher
Treasurer	35	Christian	F	Form 4	Teacher
Member	38	Muslim	F	None	Parent
Member	42	Muslim	F	None	Parent
School Management Committee					
Position	Age	Religion	Gender	Education	Village position
Chairman	56	Muslim	M	STD5	Chief counselor
Vice chairmain	57	Muslim	M	STD3	None
Secretary	70	Muslim	M	STD4	None
Treasurer	52	Muslim	M	Form 4	None
Member	65	Muslim	M	None	None
Member	70	Muslim	F	None	None
Member	68	Muslim	F	None	None
Member	54	Muslim	F	None	None

MALAWI SURVEYS AND EXPERIMENT

2014 Malawi Parents' Survey

The districts, enumeration areas, and respondents for the 2014 survey were selected in order to explicitly examine possible mechanisms linking Muslim concentration to Muslims' schooling, and the survey was designed to control for physical access to schools as a mechanism by including Christians and Muslims inhabiting the same village, where distance to school is effectively held constant. In the analysis of the survey data, I compare outcomes across the two religious groups and districts.

The survey was conducted in 50 enumeration areas, 25 in each of the two districts. The districts are divided into Traditional Authority (TA) areas, each of which have a number of enumeration areas (EA). Within each district, I constructed a variable that is the quintile of the percentage Muslim of the EA within each district. That is, after calculating the percentage of Muslims of the EA, for each district, the enumeration areas were assigned to a quintile of the percentage of Muslims. Then, five TAs were selected in each district, and five EAs were randomly selected in each TA, one from each quintile. The one exception is that TA Nkalo in Chiradzulu included six EAs and TA Nchema included four EAs, as there were only four TAs in Chiradzulu that included EAs for every quintile.

Within each EA, twelve respondents were randomly selected: three Christian men, three Christian women, three Muslim men, and three Muslim women. On the advice of the research firm implementing the survey, I excluded enumeration areas that had less than 60 individuals of the minority religion, according to the 2008 census. This was done primarily for logistical purposes, so that all four types of respondents could be included in each EA.

Enumerators used a random-walk approach to identify households, each conducting one interview of each respondent type in each EA. Thus, the sample targeted a total of 600 respondents, 75 of each of the four respondent types in each district. The final sample size was 596, with 148 Christian men, 150 Christian women, 147 Muslim men, and 151 Muslim women. Because an equal number of Christians and Muslims were selected in each EA, physical access, in terms of distance to a school, is ruled out as a potential mechanism. The EAs are geographic units that are small enough that those living within an EA have equal access to schools.

Two additional variables were considered in household selection. First, since a central goal of the study is to compare behavior across religious groups, respondents were required to self-identify as either Christian or Muslim in order to participate in the survey. A very small minority of Malawians state "other" or "no religion" in Malawi. Thus, this selection criterion excluded only a fraction of the population in any given EA. Second, because the survey primary sought to explain schooling behavior, respondents were only included in the sample if there was a child between the ages of 5 and 13 living in the household. The survey includes the schooling history of 1282 children between the ages of 5 and 18 living in the households of the respondents.

Discrimination Experiment

To evaluate this potential explanation, I designed a survey experiment where respondents were randomly assigned to receive a cue (or not) about the religious affiliation of two hypothetical job candidates for a primary school teacher – half saw two candidates with no religious cue, and half saw two candidates, one of whom was Muslim and the other Christian. All respondents were then asked to assess the likelihood that the candidate would be hired, as well as which candidate they would prefer for their own children. I found that if anything, in the presence of a religious cue about the identity of the job candidate, Muslims are more likely to say the *Muslim* candidate will get the job. Both Christians and Muslims also had a preference for a teacher who shared their own religion.

The experiment involved presenting respondents with images of two job candidates they were told were applying for the position of primary school teacher in their district. They were also presented with information about the candidates' age and quality, which were held constant.[3] Half of the respondents were provided with cues about the candidates' religion, signaling that Candidate 1 was Muslim and Candidate 2 was Christian. These cues, in the form of names and dress (a cross and prayer cap, for Christians and Muslims, respectively), comprised the treatment in the experiment. The image respondents were shown, with and without religious cues, as shown in Figure A.10.

---

[3] The measure of quality was the candidates' score on the Malawi School Certificate of Education (MSCE), a national exam students take upon completion of secondary school. The exam score is comprised of the sum of scores for six subjects, where the best score for each subject is 1 and the worst score is 9. Therefore, scores for the full exam range from 6 (best score) to 56 (worst score). A score of 15, therefore, would be considered a very good, though not suspiciously perfect score. The pass rate for the 2014 MSCE was 54.8 percent.

(a) (b)

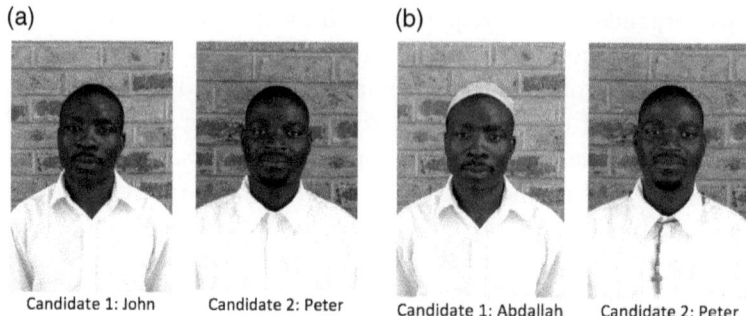

Candidate 1: John   Candidate 2: Peter   Candidate 1: Abdallah   Candidate 2: Peter

FIGURE A.10 Images shown in discrimination experiment. (a) Treatment A: no religious cue. (b) Treatment B: religious cue.

Then, respondents were asked which candidate they thought would be more likely to get a job as a primary school teacher at a government school in their district, as well as which candidate they preferred to teach their own children. If it is the case that Muslims in Muslim majority areas perceive greater discrimination against Muslims than Muslims in Muslim minority areas or than Christians in Muslim majority areas, we should expect to see that, when provided the religion cue of the respondent (treatment B), Muslim respondents in the majority Muslim district are more likely to say that the Christian candidate will be hired – that is, less likely to believe the Muslim candidate will be hired.

Do Muslims living as a majority perceive greater discrimination against Muslims in the formal labor market? The discrimination experiment suggests that this is not the case. When assessing the likelihood that a job candidate for primary school teacher will be hired, we would expect that in the presence of a cue indicating the religious affiliation of the candidate, Muslims in the majority area would be more likely to say the Christian candidate is likely to get the job if they perceive discrimination against Muslims. In fact, if anything, in the presence of a religious cue about the identity of the job candidate, Muslims are more likely to say the *Muslim* candidate will get the job.

Estimating Returns to Schooling

To estimate expected returns, survey respondents were asked to estimate monthly income for a given level of schooling. The question is asked iteratively over several levels of schooling, including no schooling, some primary, complete primary, and complete secondary. The survey included two versions of the question, one asking for monthly income estimates for the average Malawian man at age twenty-five, and one for a boy from the respondent's household when he reached twenty-five years of age. Formal sector is defined from the answer choices, where teacher, civil servant, policeman, and military are included as formal sector job.

Data presented on perceived returns to schooling have been cleaned to exclude estimated income at the 99th percentile of the distribution. This is because estimates at the 99th percentile are likely the result of enumerator error, for example, adding an extra zero. Results are similar for the 95th percentile. The average estimated monthly income for no school was around US$25, and for completion of secondary school around US$85. At the time of the survey the exchange rate was approximately 390 Kwacha to the dollar. Collecting accurate income data is notoriously difficult, and in the household survey was estimated using an asset-based wealth index, so it is not possible to know how closely respondents' estimates reflected their own earnings. However, given that the income per capita of Malawi is around US$230, approximately US$19, per month, the estimates provided by respondents seem higher than could be realistically attained. See Figure A.11.

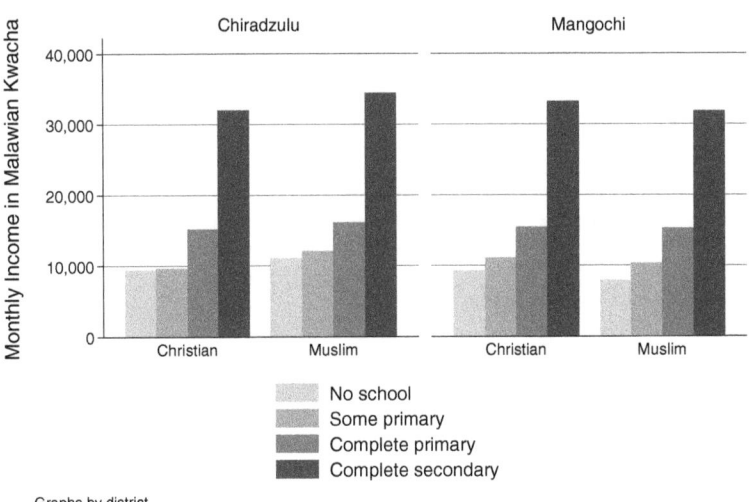

FIGURE A.11 Mean expected income across levels of schooling, by religion and Christian and Muslim majority areas.
Source: Malawi 2014 Survey.

Beliefs, Trust, and Religious Practice

TABLE A.7 *Ethnic and religious cultural explanations.*

	Muslim majority	Christian majority	N	p-value
Beliefs about marriage and childbearing				
Girls should get married after menstrual period (1–4)	1.32	1.16	298	0.063*
Age man should get married	23.65	23.63	298	0.957
Age woman should get married	21.64	21.28	298	0.405
Age man should have first child	24.52	24.70	298	0.694
Age woman should have first child	21.55	21.75	298	0.613
Religious practice				
Attend mosque (1–3)	2.41	2.38	298	0.616
Do you fast during Ramadan (No = 0, Yes = 1)	0.97	0.83	298	0.000***
Give Zakat	0.93	0.94	298	0.601
How often pray (0–6)	4.71	5.08	298	0.053*
Attended madrasa (men)	0.37	0.55	147	0.025**
Attended madrasa (women)	0.28	0.68	151	0.000***
Total years in madrasa (given attendance)	5.02	6.12	141	0.308
In-group preferences				
Trust your religious leader (0–3)	2.71	2.49	296	0.021**
Trust your TA (0–3)	2.52	2.27	298	0.033**
Trust people from own religion (0–3)	2.54	2.44	298	0.295
Trust people from own ethnic group (0–3)	2.39	2.25	298	0.175
Allow daughter marry different religion (No = 0, Yes = 1)	0.65	0.84	297	0.000***
Allow son marry different religion (No = 0, Yes = 1)	0.73	0.87	298	0.004***
Allow daughter marry different tribe (No = 0, Yes = 1)	0.79	0.90	297	0.007***
Allow son marry different tribe (No = 0, Yes = 1)	0.80	0.91	298	0.006***
Observations	147	149		

Note: *** indicates 99% confidence level; ** indicates 95% confidence level; * indicates 90% confidence level.

2018 Malawi Surveys and Coordination Games

The village selection procedure for the 2018 Malawi survey and coordination games are as follows.

1. Regress percentage of Muslim children out of school, percentage Muslim by enumeration area (EA) in Mangochi district, and generate predicted values for the percentage of Muslim children out of school.
2. Create a new variable that is quintiles of the differences between the actual and predicted value of the percentage of Muslim children out of school from step 1.
3. Create strata for bins of percentage Muslim (5–25 percent and 75–95 percent) and traditional authority area, restricting to EAs with a school within 2.5 kilometers.[4]
4. Randomly select EAs that are in the lowest quintile of the difference between actual and predicted value (on-the-line) for each strata, maximizing coverage across traditional authority areas.

After completing the above, I made a few EA replacements. Replacements were made for the following reasons:

- EAs were neighboring, and thus likely included overlapping villages (not independent observations),
- EA was a government outpost (in this case, a marine observation center),
- EA was at the border of Mangochi town, and thus effectively an urban area,
- EA was so far from any other selected EA (3–4 hours by road) that it would be impossible to include for logistical reasons.

In only one case did I select an EA that did not meet the criteria listed in the sampling strategy: There is one EA that is greater than 2.5 kilometers from the nearest school.

Communities were to be mobilized one day in advance of the field visit. In each village, a mobilization team of four enumerators introduced themselves to the village headman and asks about the layout of the village (where Muslim and Christian families live). Then, the team conducted a random-walk procedure to select Muslims and Christians (eighteen of each), striving to attain balance across gender and age. Mobilizers entered respondent names into a mobilization sheet where respondent ID numbers (corresponding to group type) had been randomly assigned.

---

[4] I also restricted sample to exclude a TA that was greater than 4 hours by road from Mangochi town, for logistical reasons.

The fieldwork teams consisted of one team of four mobilizers, and one team of thirteen enumerators plus one supervisor and one team leader. In each village, respondents were given nametags and respondent ID cards and were divided into the three sessions. Following the games, the enumerators administrated a survey on tablets to each participant. Participants received payment for the games after they completed the survey. The questions randomly selected for payment were randomized/selected prior to fieldwork. Participants never learned which questions were selected or whether their responses matched the modal response. Maximum payout was 2300 Kwacha.

Summary Statistics

TABLE A.8 *Summary statistics of villages.*

	Majority Christian	Majority Muslim	p-value
How good at problem solving (1–5)	4.20	4.50	0.38
Contribute money to projects (1–5)	1.90	3.20	0.09+
Contribute labor to projects (1–5)	3.80	4.40	0.28
Contribute in kind to projects (1–5)	0.90	0.40	0.29
Contribute to school infrastructure	0.60	0.50	0.67
School cited as problem area	0.50	0.30	0.39
Religious segregation (1–3)	2.60	2.20	0.14
Working electricity grid	0.10	0.40	0.13
Road quality (1–6)	3.80	3.90	0.84
Nursery in village	0.50	0.60	0.67
Government primary school	0.90	1.00	0.33
Government secondary school	0.20	0.10	0.56
Private secondary school	0.10	0.10	1.00
Vocational training	0.00	0.00	1.00
Government health center	0.10	0.30	0.29
Private health center	0.10	0.10	1.00
Community center	0.00	0.10	0.33
Market in village	0.60	0.80	0.36
# of functional water points	3.00	5.40	0.19
# of functional latrines/toilets	0.10	0.30	0.54
# of savings groups	4.90	3.90	0.59
# of farmers groups	1.10	0.50	0.49
# of churches in village	4.90	2.00	0.02*
# of mosques	0.70	2.90	0.02*
Madrasa in village	0.40	1.00	0.00**
N	10	10	

Note: + $p < 0.10$, * $p < 0.05$, ** $p < 0.01$, *** $p < 0.001$.

TABLE A.9 *Summary statistics of Traditional Authorities.*

	Muslim TAs	Christian TAs	N	p-value
Individual TA characteristics				
TA has any schooling	0.76	1.00	62	0.013**
TA speaks English	0.22	0.43	62	0.089*
TA population characteristics				
TA % Muslim (actual)	58.19	11.15	62	0.000***
TA % Muslim (perceived)	69.50	30.00	61	0.000***
TA % literate (actual)	55.54	67.01	62	0.000***
TA % literate (perceived)	43.50	52.86	61	0.093*
TA % literate, Muslims (actual)	50.02	62.39	61	0.000***
TA % literate, Christians (actual)	67.51	69.49	62	0.357
Individual TA beliefs and behavior				
TA proposed education project	0.28	0.24	61	0.760
TA says education is main problem	0.22	0.33	62	0.340
Population values education (1–4)	3.17	3.57	61	0.027**
Appropriate schooling level, Christian girl (0–12)	11.40	11.81	61	0.308
Appropriate schooling level, Muslim girl (0–12)	10.50	10.48	61	0.967
Appropriate schooling level, Christian boy (0–12)	11.45	11.81	61	0.352
Appropriate schooling level, Muslim girl (0–12)	11.00	10.48	61	0.304
Observations	41	21		

Note: *** indicates 99% confidence level; ** indicates 95% confidence level; * indicates 90% confidence level.

TABLE A.10 *Characteristics of Traditional Authorities by project type.*

	Education project	Other project	N	p-value
TA is Muslim	0.69	0.64	61	0.760
TA has any schooling	1.00	0.78	61	0.040**
TA population values education (1–4)	3.12	3.38	61	0.199
Rate of primary school completion (perceived)	62.50	60.89	61	0.766
Education main problem	0.31	0.24	61	0.602
TA % Muslim	47.94	39.06	61	0.327
Ta % Literate	58.31	60.29	61	0.565
TA % Literate, Muslim	50.95	55.79	60	0.164
TA % Literate, Christian	69.19	67.54	61	0.474
Muslim–Christian literacy gap	17.90	11.75	60	0.062*
Observations	16	45		

Note: *** indicates 99% confidence level; ** indicates 95% confidence level; * indicates 90% confidence level.

Additional Results

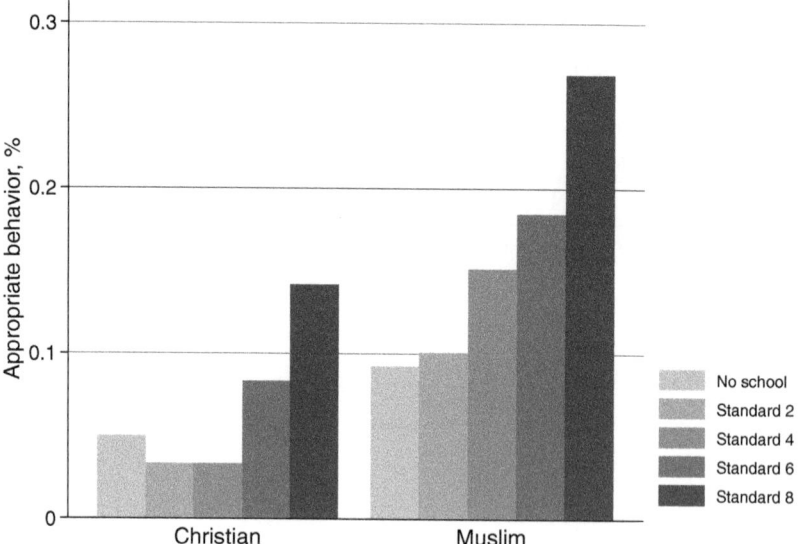

FIGURE A.12 Percentage of respondents who believe others think it is appropriate to leave school (Muslim majority villages), by religion. *Source*: Malawi 2018 Survey.

TABLE A.11 *Predictors of Traditional Authority education project proposals.*

	Proposed education project
Any school	0.393**
	(0.100)
Literacy gap	0.009**
	(0.003)
Primary school completion (perceived)	0.005**
	(0.002)
Muslim	−0.004
	(0.167)
TA % Muslim	0.002
	(0.002)
Constant	−0.607***
	(0.111)
N	60
R^2	0.185

Notes: *** indicates 99% confidence level; ** indicates 95% confidence level; * indicates 90% confidence level. Model estimated using OLS. Standard errors clustered by district.

A.8 COLONIAL ADMINISTRATORS IN UGANDA AND NORTHERN NIGERIA

Table A.12 lists the set of colonial administrators in the Uganda Protectorate and Northern Nigeria, highlighting in bold those that served in both places and demonstrating the overlap in administrators across the two.

TABLE A.12 *Colonial administrators in Uganda and Northern Nigeria.*

Territory	Title	Name	Dates
Uganda	Military Administrator	**Frederick Lugard**	1890–1892
Uganda	Commissioner	Gerald Herbert Portal	1893
Uganda	Commissioner	James MacDonald (acting)	1893
Uganda	Commissioner	Henry Edward Colville	1893–1894
Uganda	Commissioner	Frederick Jackson (acting)	1894
Uganda	Commissioner	Ernest James Berkeley	1894–1899
Uganda	Commissioner	Harry Hamilton Johnston	1899–1901
Uganda	Commissioner	James Hayes Sadler	1902–1907
Uganda	Commissioner	**Henry Hesketh Bell**	1907–1910
Uganda	Commissioner	Harry Cordeaux	1910
Uganda	Governor	Harry Cordeaux	1910–1911
Uganda	Governor	Frederick Jackson	1911–1918
Uganda	Governor	Robert Coryndon	1918–1922
Uganda	Governor	Geoffrey Archer	1922–1925
Uganda	Governor	**William Gowers**	1925–1932
Uganda	Governor	Bernard Henry Bourdillon	1932–1935
Uganda	Governor	Philip Mitchell	1935–1940
Uganda	Governor	Charles Dundas	1940–1945
Uganda	Governor	John Hathorn Hall	1945–1952
Uganda	Governor	Andrew Cohen	1952–1957
Uganda	Governor	Frederick Crawford	1957–1961
Uganda	Governor	Walter Coutts	1961–1962
N. Nigeria	High Commissioner	**Frederick Lugard**	1900–1906
N. Nigeria	High Commissioner	Percy Girouard	1907–1909
N. Nigeria	High Commissioner	**Henry Hesketh Bell**	1909–1911
N. Nigeria	High Commissioner	Charles Lindsay	1911–1912
N. Nigeria	Lieutenant Governor	**Frederick Lugard**	1912–1914
N. Nigeria	Lieutenant Governor	Charles Lindsay	1914–1917
N. Nigeria	Lieutenant Governor	Herbert Symonds Goldsmith	1917–1921
N. Nigeria	Lieutenant Governor	**William Gowers**	1921–1925
N. Nigeria	Lieutenant Governor	Herbert Richmond Palmer	1925–1930
N. Nigeria	Chief Commissioner	Cyril Wilson Alexander	1930–1932
N. Nigeria	Chief Commissioner	George Sinclaire Browne	1932–1936
N. Nigeria	Chief Commissioner	Theodore Samuel Adams	1936–1943
N. Nigeria	Chief Commissioner	John Robert Patterson	1943–1947
N. Nigeria	Chief Commissioner	Eric Westbury Thompstone	1947–1951
N. Nigeria	Lieutenant Governor	Eric Westbury Thompstone	1951–1952
N. Nigeria	Governor General	Eric Westbury Thompstone	1952–1953
N. Nigeria	Governor General	Bryan Sharwood-Smith	1954–1957
N. Nigeria	Governor General	Gawain Westray Bell	1957–1962

References

Abu, Aiah (1974). "Islam Versus Christianity in Sierra Leone". In: *African Reactions to Missionary Education*. Ed. by Edward H. Berman. Teachers College Press, pp. 92–115.

Acemoglu, Daron and Matthew O. Jackson (2017). "Social Norms and the Enforcement of Laws". *Journal of the European Economic Association* 15.2, pp. 245–295.

Acemoglu, Daron and James A. Robinson (2021). *Culture, Institutions and Social Equilibria: A Framework*. Tech. rep. National Bureau of Economic Research.

Adida, Claire L., David D. Laitin, and Marie-Anne Valfort (2016). *Why Muslim Integration Fails in Christian-Heritage Societies*. Harvard University Press.

Adjei, Ako (1944). "Imperialism and Spiritual Freedom: An African View". *American Journal of Sociology* 50.3, pp. 189–198.

Al-Samarrai, Samer and Hassan Zaman (2007). "Abolishing School Fees in Malawi: The Impact on Education Access and Equity". *Education Economics* 15.3, pp. 359–375.

Alesina, Alberto and Paola Giuliano (2015). "Culture and Institutions". *Journal of Economic Literature* 53.4, pp. 898–944.

Alesina, Alberto, Stelios Michalopoulos, and Elias Papaioannou (2016). "Ethnic Inequality". *Journal of Political Economy* 124.2, pp. 428–488.

Alesina, Alberto et al. (2023). "Religion and Educational Mobility in Africa". *Nature* 618, pp. 134–143.

Allcott, Hunt (2011). "Social Norms and Energy Conservation". *Journal of Public Economics* 95.9-10, pp. 1082–1095.

Almond, Gabriel A. and Sidney Verba (1963). *The Civic Culture: Political Attitudes and Democracy in Five Nations*. Princeton University Press.

Amasyali, Emre (2022). "Indigenous Responses to Protestant Missionaries: Educational Competition and Economic Development in Ottoman Turkey". *European Journal of Sociology/Archives Européennes de Sociologie* 63.1, pp. 39–86.

Anderson-Levitt, Kathryn M. (2003). "A World Culture of Schooling?" In: *Local Meanings, Global Schooling*. Springer, pp. 1–26.

Angrist, Joshua D. (2014). "The Perils of Peer Effects". *Labour Economics* 30, pp. 98–108.

Ansell, Ben W. (2010). *From the Ballot to the Blackboard: The Redistributive Political Economy of Education*. Cambridge University Press.

Ansell, Ben W. and Johannes Lindvall (2013). "The Political Origins of Primary Education Systems: Ideology, Institutions, and Interdenominational Conflict in an Era of Nation-Building". *American Political Science Review* 107.3, pp. 505–522.

Appadurai, Arjun (2004). "The Capacity to Aspire: Culture and the Terms of Recognition". In: *Cultural Politics in a Global Age: Uncertainty, Solidarity and Innovation*. Ed. by Vijayendra Rao, and Michael Walton. Stanford University Press, pp. 59–84.

Ashraf, Nava, Oriana Bandiera, and Scott S. Lee (2014). "Awards Unbundled: Evidence from a Natural Field Experiment". *Journal of Economic Behavior & Organization* 100, pp. 44–63.

Austen, Ralph A. (2010). *Trans-Saharan Africa in World History*. Oxford University Press.

Bandyopadhyay, Sanghamitra and Elliott Green (2016). "Precolonial Political Centralization and Contemporary Development in Uganda". *Economic Development and Cultural Change* 64.3, pp. 471–508.

Bartholomew, John George (1911). *World Atlas of Christian Missions: Containing a Directory of Missionary Societies, a Classified Summary of Statistics, an Index of Mission Stations, and Maps Showing the Location of Mission Stations Throughout the World*. Student Volunteer Movement for Foreign Missions.

Bašić, Zvonimir and Eugenio Verrina (2024). "Personal Norms – and Not Only Social Norms – Shape Economic Behavior". *Journal of Public Economics* 239, p. 105255.

Basu, Kaushik (1999). "Child Labor: Cause, Consequence, and Cure, with Remarks on International Labor Standards". *Journal of Economic Literature* 37.3, pp. 1083–1119.

Baten, Joerg et al. (2021). "Educational Gender Inequality in Sub-Saharan Africa: A Long-Term Perspective". *Population and Development Review* 47.3, pp. 813–849.

Bauer, Vincent, Melina R. Platas, and Jeremy M. Weinstein (2019). "The Historical Legacies of Islamic Rule in Africa". Working paper.

Beaman, Lori, Niall Keleher, and Jeremy Magruder (2016). "Do Job Networks Disadvantage Women? Evidence from a Recruitment Experiment in Malawi". Working paper.

Becker, Bastian and Carina Schmitt (2023). "License to Educate: The Role of National Networks in Colonial Empires". *World Development* 169, p. 106286.

Becker, Sascha O. and Ludger Woessmann (2008). "Luther and the Girls: Religious Denomination and the Female Education Gap in Nineteenth-Century Prussia". *The Scandinavian Journal of Economics* 110.4, pp. 777–805.

Benavot, Aaron et al. (1991). "Knowledge for the Masses: World Models and National Curricula, 1920–1986". *American Sociological Review*, pp. 85–100.
Berkman, Michael and Eric Plutzer (2010). *Evolution, Creationism, and the Battle to Control America's Classrooms*. Cambridge University Press.
Berman, Edward H. (1974). "African Responses to Christian Mission Education". *African Studies Review* 17.3, pp. 527–540.
Berman, Eli (2000). "Sect, Subsidy, and Sacrifice: An Economist's View of Ultra-Orthodox Jews". *The Quarterly Journal of Economics* 115.3, pp. 905–953.
Bicchieri, Cristina (2016). *Norms in the Wild: How to Diagnose, Measure, and Change Social Norms*. Oxford University Press.
Bisin, Alberto and Thierry Verdier (2011). "The Economics of Cultural Transmission and Socialization". In: *Handbook of Social Economics*. Vol. 1. Elsevier, pp. 339–416.
Blaydes, Lisa (2011). *Elections and Distributive Politics in Mubarak's Egypt*. Cambridge University Press.
— (2014). "How Does Islamist Local Governance Affect the Lives of Women?" *Governance* 27.3, 489–509.
Bleck, Jaimie (2013). "Do Francophone and Islamic Schooling Communities Participate Differently? Disaggregating Parents' Political Behaviour in Mali". *The Journal of Modern African Studies* 51.03, pp. 377–408.
— (2015). *Education and Empowered Citizenship in Mali*. John Hopkins University Press.
Boateng, F. Yao (1974). "The Catechism and the Rod: Presbyterian Education in Ghana". In: *African Reactions to Missionary Education*. Ed. by Edward H. Berman. Teachers College Press, pp. 75–91.
Bobonis, Gustavo J. and Frederico Finan (2009). "Neighborhood Peer Effects in Secondary School Enrollment Decisions". *Review of Economics and Statistics* 91.4, pp. 695–716.
Bolt, Jutta and Dirk Bezemer (2009). "Understanding Long-Run African Growth: Colonial Institutions or Colonial Education?" *The Journal of Development Studies* 45.1, pp. 24–54.
Bone, David S. (1982). "Islam in Malawi". *Journal of Religion in Africa* 13.2, pp. 126–138.
Bourdieu, Pierre (1977). *Outline of a Theory of Practice*. Cambridge University Press.
Boustan, Leah Platt and Robert A. Margo (2015). "Racial Differences in Health in the United States: A Long-Run Perspective". *The Oxford Handbook of Economics and Human Biology*, pp. 730–750.
Boyer, Christopher et al. (2022). "Religious Leaders Can Motivate Men to Cede Power and Reduce Intimate Partner Violence: Experimental Evidence from Uganda". *Proceedings of the National Academy of Sciences* 119.31, e2200262119.
Bramoullé, Yann, Habiba Djebbari, and Bernard Fortin (2020). "Peer Effects in Networks: A Survey". *Annual Review of Economics* 12.1, pp. 603–629.
Briggs, Ryan C. (2017). "Explaining Case Selection in African Politics Research". *Journal of Contemporary African Studies* 35.4, pp. 565–572.

Bryant, Kelly M. Duke (2015). *Education as Politics: Colonial Schooling and Political Debate in Senegal, 1850s–1914*. University of Wisconsin Press.
Buchanan, Keith M., and John C. Pugh (1955). *Land and People in Nigeria: The Human Geography of Nigeria and its Environmental Background*. University of London Press.
Buell, Raymond Leslie (1928). *Native Problem in Africa. Vol. I*. Macmillan and Company Limited.
Burde, Dana and Leigh L. Linden (2013). "Bringing Education to Afghan Girls: A Randomized Controlled Trial of Village-Based Schools". *American Economic Journal: Applied Economics* 5.3, pp. 27–40.
Bursztyn, Leonardo and Robert Jensen (2015). "How Does Peer Pressure Affect Educational Investments?" *The Quarterly Journal of Economics* 130.3, pp. 1329–1367.
Bursztyn, Leonardo and Robert Jensen (2017). "Social Image and Economic Behavior in the Field: Identifying, Understanding, and Shaping Social Pressure". *Annual Review of Economics* 9, pp. 131–153.
Bursztyn, Leonardo and David Y. Yang (2022). "Misperceptions about Others". *Annual Review of Economics* 14.1, pp. 425–452.
Cagé, Julia and Valeria Rueda (2013). "The Long Term Effects of the Printing Press in Sub Saharan Africa". Working paper.
— (2020). "Sex and the Mission: the Conflicting Effects of Early Christian Missions on HIV in Sub-Saharan Africa". *Journal of Demographic Economics* 86.3, pp. 213–257.
Calvi, Rossella, Lauren Hoehn-Velasco, and Federico G. Mantovanelli (2022). "The Protestant Legacy: Missions, Gender, and Human Capital in India". *Journal of Human Resources* 57.6, pp. 1946–1980.
Calvi, Rossella and Federico G. Mantovanelli (2018). "Long-Term Effects of Access to Health Care: Medical Missions in Colonial India". *Journal of Development Economics* 135, pp. 285–303.
Calvo, Ernesto and Maria Victoria Murillo (2004). "Who Delivers? Partisan Clients in the Argentine Electoral Market". *American Journal of Political Science* 48.4, pp. 742–757.
Calvó-Armengol, Antoni and Matthew O. Jackson (2004). "The Effects of Social Networks on Employment and Inequality". *American Economic Review* 94.3, pp. 426–454.
Cammett, Melani and Sukriti Issar (2010). "Bricks and Mortar Clientelism: Sectarianism and the Logistics of Welfare Allocation in Lebanon". *World Politics* 62.3, pp. 381–421.
Capoccia, Giovanni (2016). "Critical Junctures". *The Oxford Handbook of Historical Institutionalism*, pp. 89–106.
Carey, John et al. (2023). "Partisanship Unmasked? The Role of Politics and Social Norms in COVID-19 Mask-Wearing Behavior". *Journal of Experimental Political Science* 10.3, pp. 377–390.
Carland, John M. (1985). *The Colonial Office and Nigeria, 1898–1914*. Hoover Press.

Cavapozzi, Danilo, Marco Francesconi, and Cheti Nicoletti (2021). "The Impact of Gender Role Norms in Mothers' Labor Supply". *Journal of Economic Behavior & Organization* 186, pp. 113–134.
Chancel, Lucas et al. (2023). "Income Inequality in Africa, 1990–2019: Measurement, Patterns, Determinants". *World Development* 163, p. 106162.
Chetty, Raj and Nathaniel Hendren (2018). "The Impacts of Neighborhoods on Intergenerational Mobility I: Childhood Exposure Effects". *The Quarterly Journal of Economics* 133.3, pp. 1107–1162.
Chetty, Raj, Nathaniel Hendren, and Lawrence F. Katz (2016). "The Effects of Exposure to Better Neighborhoods on Children: New Evidence from the Moving to Opportunity Experiment". *American Economic Review* 106.4, pp. 855–902.
Chetty, Raj et al. (2014). "Where is the Land of Opportunity? The Geography of Intergenerational Mobility in the United States". *The Quarterly Journal of Economics* 129.4, pp. 1553–1623.
Chetty, Raj et al. (2020). "Race and Economic Opportunity in the United States: An Intergenerational Perspective". *The Quarterly Journal of Economics* 135.2, pp. 711–783.
Chwe, Michael Suk-Young (2001). *Rational Ritual: Culture, Coordination, and Common Knowledge*. Princeton University Press.
Chyn, Eric and Lawrence F. Katz (2021). "Neighborhoods Matter: Assessing the Evidence for Place Effects". *Journal of Economic Perspectives* 35.4, pp. 197–222.
Cialdini, Robert B. (2007). "Descriptive Social Norms as Underappreciated Sources of Social Control". *Psychometrika* 72, pp. 263–268.
Cialdini, Robert B. and Noah J. Goldstein (2004). "Social Influence: Compliance and Conformity". *Annual Review of Psychology* 55.1, pp. 591–621.
Cogneau, Denis and Alexander Moradi (2014). "Borders that Divide: Education and Religion in Ghana and Togo since Colonial Times". *The Journal of Economic History* 74.3, pp. 694–729.
Coleman, James S. (1958). *Nigeria: Background to Nationalism*. University of California Press.
Coleman, James S. et al. (1966). *Equality of Educational Opportunity Study*. Tech. rep. Washington: U.S. Department of Health, Education, and Welfare.
Collins, William J. and Robert A. Margo (2006). "Historical Perspectives on Racial Differences in Schooling in the United States". *Handbook of the Economics of Education* 1, pp. 107–154.
Cowan, L. Gray, James O'Connell, and David G. Scanlon, eds. (1965). *Education and Nation-Building in Africa*. F. A. Praeger.
Croke, Kevin et al. (2016). "Deliberate Disengagement: How Education Can Decrease Political Participation in Electoral Authoritarian Regimes". *American Political Science Review* 110.3, pp. 579–600.
Cross, Michael (1987). "The Political Economy of Colonial Education: Mozambique, 1930–1975". *Comparative Education Review* 31.4, pp. 550–569.
Crowder, Michael (1964). "Indirect Rule – French and British Style". *Africa* 34.3, pp. 197–205.

Dancygier, Rafaela M. (2018). *Dilemmas of Inclusion: Muslims in European Politics*. Princeton University Press.
Darwin, John (2012). *Unfinished Empire: The Global Expansion of Britain*. Bloomsbury Publishing USA.
Das, Jishnu et al. (2013). "US and Them: The Georgraphy of Academic Research". *Journal of Development Economics* 105, pp. 112–130.
Daughton, James Patrick (2006). *An Empire Divided: Religion, Republicanism, and the Making of French Colonialism, 1880–1914*. Oxford University Press.
De, Anuradha (1999). *Public Report on Basic Education in India*. Oxford University Press, USA.
De Haas, Michiel and Ewout Frankema (2018). "Gender, Ethnicity, and Unequal Opportunity in Colonial Uganda: European Influences, African Realities, and the Pitfalls of Parish Register Data". *The Economic History Review* 71.3, pp. 965–994.
Deaton, Angus (2013). *The Great Escape: Health, Wealth, and the Origins of Inequality*. Princeton University Press.
DiMaggio, Paul J. et al. (1983). "The Iron Cage Revisited: Institutional Isomorphism and Collective Rationality in Organizational Fields". *American Sociological Review* 48.2, pp. 147–160.
Dupas, Pascaline (2011). "Health Behavior in Developing Countries". *Annual Review of Economics* 3, pp. 425–449.
Dupas, Pascaline et al. (2018). "Banking the Unbanked? Evidence from Three Countries". *American Economic Journal: Applied Economics* 10.2, pp. 257–297.
Durlauf, Steven N. (2004). "Neighborhood Effects". *Handbook of Regional and Urban Economics* 4, pp. 2173–2242.
Easterly, William and Ross Levine (1997). "Africa's Growth Tragedy: Policies and Ethnic Divisions". *The Quarterly Journal of Economics* 112.4, pp. 1203–1250.
Efferson, Charles et al. (2015). "Female Genital Cutting Is Not a Social Coordination Norm". *Science* 349.6255, pp. 1446–1447.
Etherington, Norman (2005). "Education and Medicine". In: *Missions and Empire*. Ed. by Norman Etherington. Oxford University Press. Chapter 7, pp. 261–284.
— (2012). "Afterword: The Missionary Experience in British and French Empires". In: *In Gods Empire: French Missionaries and the Modern World*. Ed. by Owen White and J. P. Daughton. Oxford University Press, pp. 279–302.
Farrow, Katherine, Gilles Grolleau, and Lisette Ibanez (2017). "Social Norms and Pro-Environmental Behavior: A Review of the Evidence". *Ecological Economics* 140, pp. 1–13.
Fernández, Raquel and Alessandra Fogli (2009). "Culture: An Empirical Investigation of Beliefs, Work, and Fertility". *American Economic Journal: Macroeconomics* 1.1, pp. 146–177.
Fisher, Humphrey (1977). "The West and Central Sudan and East Africa". In: *The Cambridge History of Islam*. Ed. by P.M. Hold, Ann K.S. Lambton, and Bernard Lewis. Cambridge University Press.

Fisman, Raymond and Edward Miguel (2007). "Corruption, Norms, and Legal Enforcement: Evidence from Diplomatic Parking Tickets". *Journal of Political Economy* 115.6, pp. 1020–1048.

Fouka, Vasiliki (2020). "Backlash: The Unintended Effects of Language Prohibition in US Schools after World War I". *The Review of Economic Studies* 87.1, pp. 204–239.

Franck, Raphael and Ilia Rainer (2012). "Does the Leader's Ethnicity Matter? Ethnic Favoritism, Education, and Health in sub-Saharan Africa". *American Political Science Review* 106.2, pp. 294–325.

Frankema, Ewout H. P. (2012). "The Origins of Formal Education in Sub-Saharan Africa: Was British Rule More Benign?" *European Review of Economic History* 16.4, pp. 335–355.

Fruttero, Anna, Noël Muller, and Óscar Calvo-González (2024). "The Power and Roots of Aspiration". *The World Bank Research Observer*, lkae004.

Frye, Margaret (2012). "Bright Futures in Malawi's New Dawn: Educational Aspirations as Assertions of Identity". *American Journal of Sociology* 117.6, pp. 1565–1624.

Gallego, Francisco A. (2010). "Historical Origins of Schooling: The Role of Democracy and Political Decentralization". *Review of Economics and Statistics* 92.2, pp. 228–243.

Gamoran, Adam (2001). "American Schooling and Educational Inequality: A Forecast for the 21st Century". *Sociology of Education*, pp. 135–153.

Garnier, Maurice and Mark Schafer (2006). "Educational Model and Expansion of Enrollments in Sub-Saharan Africa". *Sociology of Education* 79.2, pp. 153–176.

Gelfand, Michele J., Sergey Gavrilets, and Nathan Nunn (2024). "Norm Dynamics: Interdisciplinary Perspectives on Social Norm Emergence, Persistence, and Change". *Annual Review of Psychology* 75, pp. 341–378.

Genicot, Garance and Debraj Ray (2020). "Aspirations and Economic Behavior". *Annual Review of Economics* 12.1, pp. 715–746.

Gerber, Alan S., Donald P. Green, and Christopher W. Larimer (2008). "Social Pressure and Voter Turnout: Evidence from a Large-Scale Field Experiment". *American Political Science Review* 102.1, pp. 33–48.

Gerber, Alan S. and Todd Rogers (2009). "Descriptive Social Norms and Motivation to Vote: Everybody's Voting and so Should You". *The Journal of Politics* 71.1, pp. 178–191.

Gerring, John et al. (2011). "An Institutional Theory of Direct and Indirect Rule". *World Politics* 63.03, pp. 377–433.

Gift, Thomas and Erik Wibbels (2014). "Reading, Writing, and the Regrettable Status of Education Research in Comparative Politics". *Annual Review of Political Science* 17.1, pp. 291–312.

Glewwe, Paul and Karthik Muralidharan (2016). "Improving Education Outcomes in developing Countries: Evidence, Knowledge Gaps and Policy Implications". In: *Handbook of the Economics of Education*. Vol. 5. Elsevier, pp. 653–743.

Golden, Miriam and Brian Min (2013). "Distributive Politics around the World". *Annual Review of Political Science* 16.1, pp. 73–99.

Granovetter, Mark S. (1973). "The Strength of Weak Ties". *The American Journal of Sociology* 78.6, pp. 1360–1380.
Grant, Monica J. and Jere R. Behrman (2010). "Gender Gaps in Educational Attainment in Less Developed Countries". *Population and Development Review* 36.1, pp. 71–89.
Greif, Avner (1994). "Cultural Beliefs and the Organization of Society: A Historical and Theoretical Reflection on Collectivist and Individualist Societies". *Journal of Political Economy* 102.5, pp. 912–950.
Grossman, Guy et al. (2015). "Deliberate Disengagement: How Education Decreases Political Participation in Electoral Authoritarian Regimes". *American Political Science Review*, pp. 1–52.
Grzymala-Busse, Anna (2012). "Why Comparative Politics Should Take Religion (More) Seriously". *Annual Review of Political Science* 15.1, pp. 421–442.
— (2015). *Nations under God: How Churches Use Moral Authority to Influence Policy*. Princeton University Press.
Gust, Sarah, Eric A. Hanushek, and Ludger Woessmann (2024). "Global Universal Basic Skills: Current Deficits and Implications for World Development". *Journal of Development Economics* 166, p. 103205.
Habimana, Saleh (2009). *A Discussion with Sheikh Saleh Habimana, Head Mufti of the Islamic Community in Rwanda*. https://berkleycenter.georgetown.edu/interviews/a-discussion-with-sheikh-saleh-habimana-head-mufti-of-the-islamic-community-of-rwanda
Hailey, William Malcolm (1951). *Native Administration in the British African Territories. Part III: West Africa: Nigeria, Gold Coast, Sierra Leone, Gambia*. London: His Majesty's Stationery Office.
— (1957). *An African Survey Revised 1956: A Study of Problems Arising in Africa South of the Sahara*. London: Oxford University Press.
Hansen, Eric R. and Andrew Tyner (2021). "Educational Attainment and Social Norms of Voting". *Political Behavior* 43, pp. 711–735.
Hanushek, Eric A. and Steven G. Rivkin (2009). "Harming the Best: How Schools Affect the Black–White Achievement Gap". *Journal of Policy Analysis and Management* 28.3, pp. 366–393.
Harnischfeger, Johannes (2008). *Democratization and Islamic Law: The Sharia Conflict in Nigeria*. Campus Verlag.
Hastings, Adrian (1994). *The Church in Africa, 1450–1950*. Oxford: Clarendon Press.
Henrich, Joseph (2016). *The Secret of Our Success: How Culture Is Driving Human Evolution, Domesticating Our Species, and Making Us Smarter*. Princeton University Press.
Hoff, Karla and Joseph E. Stiglitz (2016). "Striving for Balance in Economics: Towards a Theory of the Social Determination of Behavior". *Journal of Economic Behavior & Organization* 126, pp. 25–57.
Hogg, Michael A. (2010). "Influence and Leadership". In: *Handbook of Social Psychology*. Ed. by S. T. Fiske, D. T. Gilbert, and G. Lindzey (5th ed.). John Wiley & Sons Inc., pp. 1166–1207.
Hoxby, Caroline M. (2000). *Peer Effects in the Classroom: Learning from Gender and Race Variation*. NBER working paper.

Huntington, Samuel P. (1993). "The Clash of Civilizations?" *Foreign Affairs* 72.3, pp. 22–49.

Imberman, Scott A., Adriana D. Kugler, and Bruce I. Sacerdote (2012). "Katrina's Children: Evidence on the Structure of Peer Effects from Hurricane Evacuees". *American Economic Review* 102.5, pp. 2048–2082.

Isaksson, Ann-Sofie, Andreas Kotsadam, and Måns Nerman (2014). "The Gender Gap in African Political Participation: Testing Theories of Individual and Contextual Determinants". *Journal of Development Studies* 50.2, pp. 302–318.

Izeogu, Vine Chukudi (1974). "Adventism in Eboland". In: *African Reactions to Missionary Education*. Ed. by Edward H. Berman. Teachers College Press, pp. 163–181.

Jedwab, Remi, Felix Meier zu Selhausen, and Alexander Moradi (2021). "Christianization without Economic Development: Evidence from Missions in Ghana". *Journal of Economic Behavior & Organization* 190, pp. 573–596.

— (2022). "The Economics of Missionary Expansion: Evidence from Africa and Implications for Development". *Journal of Economic Growth* 27.2, pp. 149–192.

Jencks, Christopher et al. (1990). "The Social Consequences of Growing up in a Poor Neighborhood". *Inner-City Poverty in the United States* 111, p. 186.

Jensen, Robert (2010). "The (Perceived) Returns to Education and the Demand for Schooling". *Quarterly Journal of Economics* 125.2, pp. 515–548.

Kadzamira, Esme and Pauline Rose (2003). "Can Free Primary Education Meet the Needs of the Poor?: Evidence from Malawi". *International Journal of Educational Development* 23.5, pp. 501–516.

Kan, Sophia and Stephan Klasen (2021). "Evaluating Universal Primary Education in Uganda: School Fee Abolition and Educational Outcomes". *Review of Development Economics* 25.1, pp. 116–147.

Kasara, Kimuli and Pavithra Suryanarayan (2015). "When Do the Rich Vote Less Than the Poor and Why? Explaining Turnout Inequality across the World". *American Journal of Political Science* 59.3, pp. 613–627.

Kasozi, Abdu B. (1986). *The Spread of Islam in Uganda*. Oxford University Press.

— (1996). *The Life of Prince Badru Kakungulu Wasajja: The Development of a Forward Looking Muslim Community in Buganda, 1907–1991*. Progressive Publishing House, Ltd.

Kasule, Omar Hassan (1982). "Muslims in Rwanda: A Status Report". *Institute of Muslim Minority Affairs Journal* 4, pp. 133–144.

King, Elisabeth (2013). *From Classrooms to Conflict in Rwanda*. Cambridge University Press.

Kosack, Stephen and Archon Fung (2014). "Does Transparency Improve Governance?" *Annual Review of Political Science* 17.1, pp. 65–87.

Kramon, Eric and Daniel N. Posner (2016). "Ethnic Favoritism in Education in Kenya". *Quarterly Journal of Political Science* 11, pp. 1–58.

Kremer, Michael and Alaka Holla (2009). "Improving Education in the Developing World: What Have We Learned from Randomized Evaluations?" *Annual Review of Economics* 1.1, pp. 513–542.

Kremer, Michael and Dan Levy (2008). "Peer Effects and Alcohol Use among College Students". *Journal of Economic Perspectives* 22.3, pp. 189–206.

Krupka, Erin L. and Roberto A. Weber (2013). "Identifying Social Norms Using Coordination Games: Why Does Dictator Game Sharing Vary?" *Journal of the European Economic Association* 11.3, pp. 495–524.

Kubai, Anne (2007a). "Post-Genocide Rwanda: The Changing Religious Landscape". *Exchange* 36.2, pp. 198–214.

— (2007b). "Walking a Tightrope: Christians and Muslims in Post-Genocide Rwanda". *Islam–Christian Muslim Relations* 18.2, pp. 219–235.

Kuran, Timur (2011). *The Long Divergence: How Islamic Law Held Back the Middle East*. Princeton University Press.

Laitin, David D. (1986). *Hegemony and Culture: Politics and Change among the Yoruba*. University of Chicago Press.

Laitin, David D. and Barry Weingast (2006). "An Equilibrium Alternative to the Study of Culture". *The Good Society* 15.1, pp. 15–20.

Lake, David A. and Matthew A. Baum (2001). "The Invisible Hand of Democracy: Political Control and the Provision of Public Services". *Comparative Political Studies* 34.6, pp. 587–621.

Lalive, Rafael and M. Alejandra Cattaneo (2009). "Social Interactions and Schooling Decisions". *Review of Economics and Statistics* 91.3, pp. 457–477.

Lamba, Isaac Chikwekwere (1984). "The History of Post-War Western Education in Colonial Malawi 1945–61: A Study of the Formulation and Application of Policy". PhD Thesis. University of Edinburgh.

Launay, Robert (2016). *Islamic Education in Africa: Writing Boards and Blackboards*. Bloomington: Indiana University Press.

Launay, Robert and Rudolph T. Ware (2016). "How (Not) to Read the Qur'an? Logics of Islamic Education in Senegal and Cote d'Ivoire". Chapter 13 in: *Islamic Education in Africa: Writing Boards and Blackboards*, pp. 255–267.

Le Nestour, Alexis, Laura Moscoviz, and Justin Sandefur (2022). *The Long-Run Decline of Education Quality in the Developing World*. Tech. rep. Center for Global Development.

Lehman, Darrin R., Chi-yue Chiu, and Mark Schaller (2004). "Psychology and Culture". *Annual Review of Psychology* 55, pp. 689–714.

Levtzion, Nehemia and Randall L. Pouwels (2000). *The History of Islam in Africa*. Athens: Ohio University Press.

Lewis, Oscar (1966). "The Culture of Poverty". *Scientific American* 215.4, pp. 19–25.

Lieberman, Evan S. (2005). "Nested Analysis as a Mixed-Method Strategy for Comparative Research". *American Political Science Review* 99.3, pp. 435–452.

Lieberman, Evan S. and Gwyneth H. McClendon (2013). "The Ethnicity–Policy Preference Link in Sub-Saharan Africa". *Comparative Political Studies* 46.5, pp. 574–602.

Linden, Ian and Jane Linden (1977). *Church and Revolution in Rwanda*. Manchester University Press.

Logan, Carolyn (2009). "Selected Chiefs, Elected Councillors and Hybrid Democrats: Popular Perspectives on the Co-Existence of Democracy and Traditional Authority". *The Journal of Modern African Studies* 47.1, pp. 101–128.
Loimeier, Roman (2013). *Muslim Societies in Africa: A Historical Anthropology*. Bloomington: Indiana University Press.
Longman, Timothy (2009). *Christianity and Genocide in Rwanda*. Vol. 112. Cambridge University Press.
Low, D. A. and D. C. Pratt (1960). *Buganda and British Overrule, 1900–1955*. Oxford University Press.
Lubeck, Paul (1986). *Islam and Urban Labor in Northern Nigeria*. Cambridge University Press.
Lucas, Adrienne M. and Isaac M. Mbiti (2012). "Access, Sorting, and Achievement: The Short-Run Effects of Free Primary Education in Kenya". *American Economic Journal: Applied Economics* 4.4, pp. 226–253.
Lugard, Frederick (1922). *The Dual Mandate in British Tropical Africa*. Routledge.
Lust, Ellen (2011). "Missing the Third Wave: Islam, Institutions, and Democracy in the Middle East". *Studies in Comparative International Development* 46, pp. 163–190.
Mackenzie, Clayton G. (1993). "Demythologising the Missionaries: A Reassessment of the Functions and Relationships of Christian Missionary Education under Colonialism". *Comparative Education* 29.1, pp. 45–66.
Mackie, Gerry (1996). "Ending Footbinding and Infibulation: A Convention Account". *American Sociological Review*, pp. 999–1017.
Mahoney, James (2000). "Path Dependence in Historical Sociology". *Theory and Society* 29.4, pp. 507–548.
Maiden, Emily (2021). "Recite the Last Bylaw: Chiefs and Child Marriage Reform in Malawi". *The Journal of Modern African Studies* 59.1, pp. 81–102.
Mair, Lucy (1934). *An African People in the Twentieth Century*. George Routledge & Sons, Ltd.
Makubuya, Apollo (2018). *Protection, Patronage, or Plunder? British Machinations and (B)ugandas Struggle for Independence*. Cambridge Scholars Publishing.
Manski, Charles F. (2000). "Economic Analysis of Social Interactions". *Journal of Economic Perspectives* 14.3, pp. 115–136.
Marshall, Monty G. and Ted R. Gurr (2020). *Polity V Project, Political Regime Characteristics and Transitions, 1800–2018*. Center for Systemic Peace.
Mattes, Robert and Dangalira Mughogho (2009). *The Limited Impacts of Formal Education on Democratic Citizenship in Africa*. Centre for Social Science Research.
McCauley, John F. (2017). *The Logic of Ethnic and Religious Conflict in Africa*. New York: Cambridge University Press.
McClendon, Gwyneth and Rachel Beatty Riedl (2019). *From Pews to Politics: Religious Sermons and Political Participation in Africa*. Cambridge University Press.

Michalopoulos, Stelios, Alireza Naghavi, and Giovanni Prarolo (2018). "Trade and Geography in the Spread of Islam". *The Economic Journal* 128.616, pp. 3210–3241.
Michalopoulos, Stelios and Elias Papaioannou (2013). "Pre-colonial Ethnic Institutions and Contemporary African Development". *Econometrica* 81.1, pp. 113–152.
Miguel, Edward (2004). "Tribe or Nation?: Nation Building and Public Goods in Kenya versus Tanzania". *World Politics* 56.3, pp. 327–362.
Miller, Walter R. S. (1936). *Reflections of a Pioneer*. Church Missionary Society.
Mokyr, Joel (2016). *A Culture of Growth*. Princeton University Press.
Mubangizi, Michael (2012). "They Stand Tall in a New Found Faith". *The Observer (Kampala)*, January 11.
Müller-Crepon, Carl (2020). "Continuity or Change? (In)direct Rule in British and French Colonial Africa". *International Organization* 74.4, pp. 707–741.
Mungeam, Gordon H. (1970). "Masai and Kikuyu Responses to the Establishment of British Administration in the East Africa Protectorate". *The Journal of African History* 11.1, pp. 127–143.
Murdock, George Peter (1967). "Ethnographic Atlas: A Summary". *Ethnology* 6.2, pp. 109–236.
Murray, Victor A. (1929). *The School in the Bush. A Critical Study of the Theory and Practice of Native Education in Africa*. London: Longmans, Green & Co.
— (1935). "Education under Indirect Rule". *Journal of the Royal African Society* 34.136, pp. 227–268.
Nakajima, Ryo (2007). "Measuring Peer Effects on Youth Smoking Behaviour". *The Review of Economic Studies* 74.3, pp. 897–935.
Narayan, Ambar et al. (2018). *Fair Progress? Economic Mobility Across Generations Around the World*. Tech. rep. Washington, DC: World Bank.
Nasiru, Wahab Oladejo Adigun (1977). "Islamic Learning among the Yoruba, 1896–1963". PhD thesis. University of Ibadan.
NCTR (2015). *Residential Schools Overview*. Tech. rep.
Nielsen, Richard A. (2017). *Deadly Clerics: Blocked Ambition and the Paths to Jihad*. Cambridge University Press.
North, Douglass C. and Robert Paul Thomas (1973). *The Rise of the Western World: A New Economic History*. Cambridge University Press.
Nunn, Nathan (2012). "Culture and the Historical Process". *Economic History of Developing Regions* 27.S1, S108–S126.
— (2014). "Gender and Missionary Influence in Colonial Africa". In: *Africa's Development in Historical Perspective*. February, pp. 489–512.
Nunn, Nathan and Leonard Wantchekon (2011). "The Slave Trade and the Origins of Mistrust in Africa". *American Economic Review* 101.7, pp. 3221–3252.
Ostrom, Elinor (2000). "Collective Action and the Evolution of Social Norms". *Journal of Economic Perspectives* 14.3, pp. 137–158.
Ozigi, Albert and Lawrence Ocho (1981). *Education in Northern Nigeria*. Allen & Unwin Pty, Limited.

Paglayan, Agustina S. (2022). Education or Indoctrination? The Violent Origins of Public School Systems in an Era of State-Building. *American Political Science Review* 116(4): 1242–1257.

— *Raised to Obey: The Rise and Spread of Mass Education*. Princeton University Press.

Patrinos, Harry Anthony (2021). "The Changing Pattern of Returns to Education: What Impact Will This Have on Earnings Inequality?" Chapter 2 in: *Reforming Education and Challenging Inequalities in Southern Contexts: Research and Policy in International Development*. Ed. by Pauline Rose et al. Routledge, pp. 19–36.

Patterson, Orlando (2014). "Making Sense of Culture". *Annual Review of Sociology* 40, pp. 1–30.

Peet, Evan D., Günther Fink, and Wafaie Fawzi (2015). "Returns to Education in Developing Countries: Evidence from the Living Standards and Measurement Study Surveys". *Economics of Education Review* 49, pp. 69–90.

Pepinsky, Thomas B., R. William Liddle, and Saiful Mujani (2012). "Testing Islam's Political Advantage: Evidence from Indonesia". *American Journal of Political Science* 56.3, pp. 584–600.

Perez-Truglia, Ricardo and Ugo Troiano (2018). "Shaming Tax Delinquents". *Journal of Public Economics* 167, pp. 120–137.

Perham, Margery (1968). *Lugard: The Years of Authority, 1898–1945*. Collins.

Peterson, Richard A. (1979). "Revitalizing the Culture Concept". *Annual Review of Sociology* 5, pp. 137–166.

Pew Research Center (2010). *Tolerance and Tension: Islam and Christianity in Sub-Saharan Africa*. Tech. rep. Pew Forum on Religion and Public Life.

— (2015). *The Future of World Religions: Population Growth Projections, 2010–2050*. Tech. rep. Pew Research Center.

— (2016). *Educational Differences by Religion around the World*. Tech. rep. Pew Research Center.

Posner, Daniel N. (2005). *Institutions and Ethnic Politics in Africa*. Cambridge University Press.

Prentice, Deborah A. (2012). "Al-Qaeda, Oil Dependence, and U.S. Foreign Policy". In: *Understanding Social Action, Promoting Human Rights*. Ed. by Ryan Goodman, Derek Jinks, and Andrew K. Woods. Oxford University Press, pp. 23–46.

Pritchett, Lant (2013). *The Rebirth of Education: Schooling Ain't Learning*. CGD Books.

— (2024). "Investing in Human Capital in Africa: A Framework for Research". *International Journal of Educational Development* 107, p. 103048.

Psacharopoulos, George and The World Bank (1994). "1994 – Returns to Investment in Education – A Global Update". *World Development* 22.9, pp. 1325–1343.

Psacharopoulos, George and Harry Anthony Patrinos (2018). "Returns to Investment in Education: A Decennial Review of the Global Literature". *Education Economics* 26.5, pp. 445–458.

Putnam, Robert D., Robert Leonardi, and Raffaella Nanetti (1993). *Making Democracy Work: Civic Traditions in Modern Italy*. Princeton University Press.
Quinn, Charlotte A. and Frederick Quinn (2003). *Pride, Faith, and Fear: Islam in Sub-Saharan Africa*. Oxford University Press.
Reichmuth, Stefan (2000). "Islamic Education in Sub-Saharan Africa". Chapter 19 in: *The History of Islam in Africa*. Ohio University Press.
Ricart-Huguet, Joan (2021). "Colonial Education, Political Elites, and Regional Political Inequality in Africa". *Comparative Political Studies* 54.14, pp. 2546–2580.
Richards, Audrey I. (1960). "The Ganda". In: *East African Chiefs: A Study of Political Development in Some Uganda and Tanganyika Tribes*. Ed. by Audrey I. Richards. Frederick A. Praeger.
Robinson, James A. and Daron Acemoglu (2012). *Why Nations Fail: The Origins of Power, Prosperity and Poverty*. Profile London.
Rosenzweig, Leah R. (2019). *Social Voting in Semi-Authoritarian Systems*. Tech. rep. Working paper.
Rubin, Jared (2017). *Rulers, Religion, and Riches: Why the West Got Rich and the Middle East Did Not*. Cambridge University Press.
Rueda, Valeria (2023). "Evaluating the Long-Term Development Impact of Christian Missions". *The Economics of Religion*, pp. 97–110.
Sacerdote, Bruce (2011). "Peer Effects in Education: How Might They Work, How Big Are They, and How Much Do We Know Thus Far?" In: *Handbook of the Economics of Education*. Vol. 3. Elsevier, pp. 249–277.
— (2014). "Experimental and Quasi-Experimental Analysis of Peer Effects: Two Steps Forward?" *Annual Review of Economics* 6.1, pp. 253–272.
Salvy, Sarah-Jeanne et al. (2012). "Influence of Peers and Friends on Children's and Adolescents' Eating and Activity Behaviors". *Physiology & Behavior* 106.3, pp. 369–378.
Sampson, Robert J., Jeffrey D. Morenoff, and Thomas Gannon-Rowley (2002). "Assessing "Neighborhood Effects": Social Processes and New Directions in Research". *Annual Review of Sociology* 28.1, pp. 443–478.
Seimu, Somo M. L. and Yustina Samwel Komba (2024). "The Role of the Colonial State in the Spread and Strengthening of Christianity in Colonial Tanganyika, Circa 1890–1961". *Journal of Religion in Africa* 1.aop, pp. 1–30.
Selhausen, Felix Meier zu (2019). "Missions, Education and Conversion in Colonial Africa". In: *Globalization and the Rise of Mass Education*. Ed. by D. Mitch and G. Cappelli. Cham: Palgrave Macmillan, pp. 25–59.
Sen, Amartya (1999). *Development as Freedom*. Oxford University Press.
Sharkey, Patrick and Jacob W. Faber (2014). "Where, When, Why, and for Whom Do Residential Contexts Matter? Moving away from the Dichotomous Understanding of Neighborhood Effects". *Annual Review of Sociology* 40, pp. 559–579.
Sherif, Muzafer (1936). *The Psychology of Social Norms*. Harper.
Sluglett, Peter and Andrew Currie (2015). *Atlas of Islamic History*. Routledge.

Small, Mario Luis, David J. Harding, and Mich'ele Lamont (2010). "Reconsidering Culture and Poverty". *The Annals of the American Academy of Political and Social Science* 629.1, pp. 6–27.

Sperber, Elizabeth and Erin Hern (2018). "Pentecostal Identity and Citizen Engagement in sub-Saharan Africa: New Evidence from Zambia". *Politics and Religion* 11.4, pp. 830–862.

Stasavage, David (2005). "Democracy and Education Spending in Africa". *American Journal of Political Science* 49.2, pp. 343–358.

Stevens, Peter A. J. and Anthony Gary Dworkin (2019). *The Palgrave Handbook of Race and Ethnic Inequalities in Education*. Springer.

Stokes, Susan C. (2005). "Perverse Accountability: A Formal Model of Machine Politics with Evidence from Argentina". *American Political Science Review* 99.3, pp. 315–325.

Sutton, Francis X. (1965). "Education and the Making of Modern Nations". *Education and Political Development*, pp. 51–74.

Tabellini, Guido (2010). "Culture and Institutions: Economic Development in the Regions of Europe". *Journal of the European Economic Association* 8.4, pp. 677–716.

Tankard, Margaret E. and Elizabeth Levy Paluck (2016). "Norm Perception as a Vehicle for Social Change". *Social Issues and Policy Review* 10.1, pp. 181–211.

— (2017). "The Effect of a Supreme Court Decision regarding Gay Marriage on Social Norms and Personal Attitudes". *Psychological Science* 28.9, pp. 1334–1344.

Temple, C. L. (1918). *Native Races and Their Rulers*. Argus Printing and Publishing Company, Ltd.

Thompson, Virginia and Richard Adloff (1957). *French West Africa*. Stanford University Press.

Tibenderana, Peter K. (1983). "The Emirs and the Spread of Western Education in Northern Nigeria, 1910–1946". *The Journal of African History* 24.4, pp. 517–534.

Triaud, Jean-Louis (2000). "Islam in Africa under French Colonial Rule". Chapter 8 in: *The History of Islam in Africa*. Ohio University Press.

Tyler, J.W. (1969). *Education and National Identity*. University of California Press.

UNESCO (2019a). *Migration, Displacement & Education: Building Bridges, Not Walls*. Tech. rep. UNESCO Institute for Statistics, Global Education Monitoring Report 2019.

— (2019b). *UIS Fact Sheet no. 56*. Tech. rep. UNESCO Institute for Statistics, Global Education Monitoring Report 2019.

— (2021). *Global Education Monitoring Report 2021/2: Non-State Actors in Education: Who Chooses? Who Loses?* Tech. rep. UNESCO Institute for Statistics.

— (2022). *New Estimation Confirms Out-of-School Population is Growing in Sub-Saharan Africa*. Tech. rep. UNESCO Institute for Statistics, Global Education Monitoring Report Team.

UNGA (1948). "Universal Declaration of Human Rights". *UN General Assembly* 302.2, pp. 14–25.

UNICEF (2024). Malawi 2024/2025 Education Budget Brief. September 2024.
Valencia Caicedo, Felipe (2019). "Missionaries in Latin America and Asia: A First Global Mass Education Wave". *Globalization and the Rise of Mass Education*. Ed. by D. Mitch and G. Cappelli. Cham: Palgrave Macmillan, pp. 61–97.
Valentino, Lauren and Stephen Vaisey (2022). "Culture and Durable Inequality". *Annual Review of Sociology* 48, pp. 109–129.
Villalón, Leonardo Alfonso (1995). *Islamic Society and State Power in Senegal: Disciples and Citizens in Fatick*. Cambridge University Press.
Waldinger, Maria (2017). "The Long-Run Effects of Missionary Orders in Mexico". *Journal of Development Economics* 127, pp. 355–378.
Walsh, Aisling et al. (2018). "The Role of the Traditional Leader in Implementing Maternal, Newborn and Child Health Policy in Malawi". *Health Policy and Planning* 33.8, pp. 879–887.
Wantchekon, Leonard, Marko Klasnja, and Natalija Novta (2015). "Education and Human Capital Externalities: Evidence from Colonial Benin". *The Quarterly Journal of Economics* 130.2, p. 52.
Weber, Max (1958). *The Protestant Ethic and the Spirit of Capitalism*. Translated by Talcott Parsons. New York: Free Press.
Wedeen, Lisa (2002). "Conceptualizing Culture: Possibilities for Political Science". *American Political Science Review* 96.4, pp. 713–728.
West, Martin R. and Ludger Woessmann (2010). "'Every Catholic Child in a Catholic School': Historical Resistance to State Schooling, Contemporary Private Competition and Student Achievement across Countries". *The Economic Journal* 120.546, F229–F255.
White, Bob W. (1996). "Talk about School: Education and the Colonial Project in French and British Africa, 1860–1960". *Comparative Education* 32.1, pp. 9–25.
Wietzke, Frank Borge (2015). "Long-Term Consequences of Colonial Institutions and Human Capital Investments: Sub-National Evidence from Madagascar". *World Development* 66, pp. 293–307.
— (2023). *Power and Conviction: The Political Economy of Missionary Work in Colonial-Era Africa*. Cambridge University Press.
Wilfahrt, Martha (2018). "Precolonial Legacies and Institutional Congruence in Public Goods Delivery: Evidence from Decentralized West Africa". *World Politics* 70.2, pp. 239–274.
Willeck, Claire and Tali Mendelberg (2022). "Education and Political Participation". *Annual Review of Political Science* 25.1, pp. 89–110.
Wilson, William Julius (2012). *The Truly Disadvantaged: The Inner City, the Underclass, and Public Policy*. University of Chicago Press.
Wolske, Kimberly S., Kenneth T. Gillingham, and P. Wesley Schultz (2020). "Peer Influence on Household Energy Behaviours". *Nature Energy* 5.3, pp. 202–212.
Woodberry, Robert D. (2012). "The Missionary Roots of Liberal Democracy". *American Political Science Review* 106.02, pp. 244–274.
Zizzo, Daniel John (2010). "Experimenter Demand Effects in Economic Experiments". *Experimental Economics* 13, pp. 75–98.

Index

Achebe, Chinua, 49
Adjei, Ako, 46
Afghanistan, 39
Anglicans, *see also* Protestants, 49, 72, 75
Arabic, 14, 51, 66, 76, 101
aspirations, 28, 32, 48, 109, 110, 114
associations, parent–teacher, 28, 90, 91, 121–125, 159
attendance, church, 45, 48, 87
authorities, native, 67, 67–70, 78, 86

Banda, Hastings Kamuzu, 89
beliefs, second-order, 10, 11, 130–132, 140, 142, 147, 154, 155, 158, 190, 197, 199
Benin, 43, 47, 167, 169
Berlin Conference, 60
Bicchieri, Cristina, 11, 130, 132, 197, 198
Blue Books, 55, 65, 72–74, 85, 86, 101, 206, 207, 208
Buganda, 25–27, 54, 58, 64–76, 78, 79, 89, 120, 154, 174, 177, 206

Cameroon, 16, 19, 43, 56, 169, 171, 172, 179, 204
capital, social, 34, 38, 137
Catholic, 14, 41, 42, 44–46, 72, 75, 119, 124, 172, 173, 175
Chetty, Raj, 34
chiefs, local, *see* chiefs, village
chiefs, village, 50, 57, 75, 91, 112, 118, 121–124, 133, 136, 137, 167
Chiradzulu district, 92, 117, 217

civil service, colonial, 53, 62, 71, 74, 75, 94, 185
"Clash of Civilizations?", *see* Huntington, Samuel
clergy, 44, 59
CMS, 73
Coleman Report, 31, 32
colonialism
  Belgian, 17, 28, 42, 44, 166, 169, 172, 177, 178
  British, 17, 25–28, 42–44, 54, 57, 64–74, 77, 78, 80–83, 85, 164, 166, 167, 171, 171–173
  French, 17, 27, 28, 42–44, 50, 61, 166, 167, 168, 171–174
  Portuguese, 42, 44, 168, 172
  Spanish, 44, 169, 172
committee, school management, 90, 91, 121–126, 216
conversion, 40, 46, 72
  to Christianity, 4, 5, 11, 14, 28, 44, 46, 47, 50, 52, 53, 62, 63, 75, 76, 80, 81, 87, 88, 108, 127, 185–187
  to Islam, 58–60, 64, 66, 83, 87, 177

data
  administrative, 38, 83, 90, 92, 99, 98
  census, 19, 20, 83–84, 92, 98–106, 134, 155, 171, 178, 204
democracy, *see also* regime type, 19, 74, 82, 89, 186, 192, 206
Democratic Republic of Congo, 16, 17, 178

245

Demographic and Health Surveys (DHS), 2, 3, 16, 16, 26, 94, 95, 155, 176, 198, 202, 203, 204, 210
dropping out, 9, 14, 104, 107, 112, 113, 117, 122–124, 139, 143, 147

education
 free primary, 2, 6, 15, 38, 82, 89, 105, 106, 115, 188, 190
 tertiary, 38, 78, 191, 195
effects
 neighborhood, 31, 33, 34, 40
 peer, 9, 31–35, 40, 48
ethnicity, 1, 2, 4, 16, 17, 18, 25, 32, 40, 47, 82, 83, 92, 103, 131, 157, 158, 175, 176, 179, 203, 209, 221
exams, primary school leaving, 115, 124
expectations
 empirical, 4, 9, 10, 36–38, 129, 141, 147, 152
  definition, 10, 130
  measurement of, 130, 138, 141, 147, 150–153, 197
 normative, 4, 9–11, 13, 37, 38, 127, 129, 130, 137, 140, 141, 143, 147, 150–153, 197, 198
explanations, alternative, 92
 economic, 93
 family structure, 101, 104
 religious, 100, 102
 structural, 97

Faidherbe, Louis, 61, 173
Fodio, Usman dan, 65
French West Africa, 27, 42, 43, 50, 61, 167, 173

games, coordination, 28, 106, 129, 132, 133, 142, 147, 151, 222
gaps, gender, 45, 72, 94, 102, 175, 188
German East Africa, 55, 166, 169–172, 177
Ghana, *see also* Gold Coast, 46, 169, 204
Gold Coast, *see also* Ghana, 48
goods, public, 19, 33, 133, 136, 137, 186
Greif, Avner, 11

habitus, 52, 53
Hausa, 65
Horn of Africa, 60
Huntington, Samuel, 12, 21

independence, 2, 6, 15, 19, 55, 82, 83, 86–89, 156, 178
infrastructure, 5, 42, 43, 58, 62, 91, 97, 98, 99, 134, 136, 137, 153, 223
institutions, Islamic political, 27, 55, 57, 58, 61, 65–67, 70, 79, 166
Islamization, 56, 58, 65, 67, 79, 81, 166, 172

Judaism, ultra-orthodox, 41

Kabaka, 66, 68, 69, 71, 72, 176
Kakungulu, Badru, 75, 76
Kano, 59, 65, 69
Kasozi, Abdu, 50, 64, 66, 75, 76
Kenya, 15, 43, 49, 55, 169
kingdoms, precolonial, 56, 58, 64–66, 70, 72, 79, 80, 165, 176, 177

Laitin, David, 10, 21–22
leaders, religious, 28, 40, 54, 87, 104, 107, 117, 214, 221
Lewis, Oscar, *see also* culture of poverty, 12
literacy, 2, 7, 15, 20, 45, 47, 51, 53, 58, 59, 59, 62, 67, 69, 92, 111, 115, 134, 135, 150, 153, 154, 156, 189, 190, 192, 197, 202–204, 207, 209, 224–226
Local Education Authority (LEA), 88, 119
Lugard, Frederick, 51, 61, 64, 68, 73, 227
Lukiiko, 75
Luther, Martin, 45

madrasa, *see* Qur'anic schools
Malawi, 13–15, 19, 25–28, 82, 83, 87, 88, 91, 92, 95, 96, 98, 99, 101, 102, 104–106, 114–116, 129, 133, 147–149, 155, 159, 161, 165, 169, 187, 198, 199, 211, 217, 218, 220, 222
Mali, 19, 43, 167, 168, 171, 194
Mangochi, 83, 92, 109, 116, 118, 124, 133, 137, 212
marriage, early, 102, 106, 111, 113, 122, 123, 140, 147, 149, 221
Masai, 54, 55
MDGs, 114
Member of Parliament, 121, 195
Mill Hill Mission, 72
Millennium Development Goals, *see* MDGs
Ministry of Education, Malawi, 88, 89, 126

missionaries, 5, 11, 14, 26, 27, 42–51,
  53–56, 58, 60–67, 71–75, 78, 79, 83,
  88, 167, 173, 175, 185
  Catholic, 44, 45, 172, 175, 177
  competition between, 44, 49, 74, 78, 185
  location of, 62, 85, 89
  Protestant, 40, 44, 45, 51, 72, 82, 82, 90
mobility, intergenerational, 34, 102
mother groups, 91, 122–124
movements, Islamic reform, 65, 172
Mozambique, 19, 42, 126, 169, 172, 204
Muteesa I, Mukabya, 66

Nigeria, 15, 16, 19, 25–28, 48, 50, 52, 56,
  58, 59, 61, 65, 67, 67–71, 73, 74,
  76–79, 82, 83, 89, 101, 102, 104, 154,
  155, 156, 158–160, 163–165, 168,
  174, 175, 179, 189, 199, 226, 227
  Nigerian Emirates, 25, 27, 56, 58, 59,
    64–68, 70–74, 76, 77, 79–82, 85
  Northern Provinces, 65, 68–70, 73, 74,
    77, 78
  Southern Provinces, 68, 74
norms
  change, 29, 187–190, 199
  corruption, 47
  gender, 44, 102, 131, 156, 161, 163
  measurement of, 106, 131–133, 140,
    154–156, 163, 197, 198
  spillover, 54
  top-down enforcement, 38, 39, 188, 189
Nunn, Nathan, 11, 45, 47, 154, 197

Ostrom, Eleanor, 39

participation, political, *see also* voting, 28,
  191–195
policies, colonial
  education, 26, 28, 42, 43, 88, 167
  fiscal, 67, 69
  leadership selection, 62, 67, 74
  regarding missionaries, 5, 26, 42–44, 55,
    71, 73, 166, 167, 173, 185
poverty, 1, 7, 12, 33, 34, 93, 114, 191–193
poverty, culture of, *see also* Lewis, Oscar,
  12
PROGRESA, 35
Protestants, *see also* Anglicans, 40, 41, 44,
  45, 51, 72, 75
psychology, 30, 35, 196
PTA, *see* associations, parent–teacher

Qur'anic schools, 14, 51, 52, 63, 76, 77,
  80, 101, 102, 174
  attendance of, 14, 50, 53, 54, 73,
    100–103, 106, 135, 174, 189, 221
  memorization in, 51
  records of, 72, 74, 101

regime type, *see also* democracy, 17, 19,
  192
religions, indigenous, 46, 57, 60, 61, 79,
  83, 179
repeating grades, 106, 110, 118, 135
returns to education, economic, 6, 93, 96,
  97, 105, 107, 114–116, 127, 190, 191,
  219, 220
Rwanda, 16, 17, 28, 42, 166, 170, 176–179

Sahel, 59
schooling
  girls, 39, 45, 50, 72–74, 77, 85, 89, 102,
    106, 107, 122, 123, 143, 144, 151,
    156, 157, 157, 158, 160, 161, 163,
    173, 188, 198
  informal, 100, 101, 194
schools
  fees, 15, 19, 89, 104, 112, 114, 115, 120,
    126, 199
  missionary, 5, 42, 43, 47, 51, 52, 55, 58,
    62, 63, 71, 74–76, 78, 79, 85, 86, 89,
    127, 167, 174, 185, 186, 207, 208
  residential, 46
  secondary, 28, 38, 39, 43, 75, 88–90, 96,
    107, 108, 112, 113, 115, 116, 124,
    125, 127, 129, 136, 143, 145, 150,
    152, 153, 156, 161, 188, 191, 206,
    218–220, 223
  attendance of, 15, 28, 114–116, 151,
    199
Senegal, 19, 28, 43, 61, 166, 167, 168,
  171–173, 175, 176, 195
Seventh Day Adventist (SDA), 48
Sierra Leone, 19, 49, 101, 104, 168, 171
SMC, *see* committee, school management
sociology, 9, 12, 31, 35, 70
Sokoto, 58, 65, 69, 70, 73, 77, 189
Sokoto Caliphate, 64, 65, 69
succession, hereditary, 54, 62, 67, 69–71,
  79, 81, 148
surveys
  Afrobarometer, 98–101, 149, 154, 193,
    193

EdData II, 155, 156, 157, 159–161
Malawi Parents, 217
Mangochi Household, 92
Masaka, Uganda, 161
    Suuna II, 66

Tanganyika, *see also* Tanzania, 55, 169, 171, 172, 177
teachers, 5, 14, 28, 32, 37, 38, 50, 72, 76, 91, 106–109, 111, 113, 119–122, 124–127, 129, 159, 160, 173, 174, 187
Thiong'o, Ngũgĩ wa, 49
Togo, 42, 169, 172
traders, Arab, 65, 66, 94, 177
Traditional Authorities (Malawi), 106, 108–111, 113, 117, 118, 148–153, 212–216, 217, 221, 222, 224–226
transfers, cash, 35
turnout, *see* voting

Uganda, 16, 25, 26–28, 43, 45, 50, 52, 54, 58, 61, 70, 74, 76, 82, 102, 154, 155, 160, 161, 163, 165, 169, 175, 188, 226, 227

Uganda Agreement (1900), 74
Uganda Muslim Education Association (UMEA), 76
United States of America, 2, 31, 32, 34, 40, 41, 188
Universal Declaration of Human Rights, 8
USA, *see* United States of America

voting, *see also* participation, political, 30, 192–194

Wantchekon, Leonard, 47, 48
wealth, 16, 17, 94, 203, 210, 220
Weber, Max, 11
White Fathers, 72
Woodberry, Robert, 46
workers, medical, 5, 108, 115
World Bank, 8, 20
World Religions Database, 98, 99

Yao, 25, 79, 82, 83, 92
Yoruba, 52, 68, 78, 79

Zanzibar, 71
Zaria, 65, 77, 78

For EU product safety concerns, contact us at Calle de José Abascal, 56–1°,
28003 Madrid, Spain or eugpsr@cambridge.org.

www.ingramcontent.com/pod-product-compliance
Ingram Content Group UK Ltd.
Pitfield, Milton Keynes, MK11 3LW, UK
UKHW041846100426
469783UK00012B/161